Peter Fallon

In memory of
Seamus Heaney and Dennis O'Driscoll,
whose generosity knew no bounds

Peter Fallon

Poet, Publisher, Editor and Translator

EDITOR RICHARD RANKIN RUSSELL

IRISH ACADEMIC PRESS

First published in 2014 by Irish Academic Press
8 Chapel Lane
Sallins
Co. Kildare, Ireland

This edition © 2014 Irish Academic Press
Individual chapters © contributors

British Library Cataloguing in Publication Data
An entry can be found on request

ISBN: 978 0 7165 3159 3 (cloth)
ISBN: 978 0 7165 3225 5 (ebook)

Library of Congress Cataloging-in-Publication Data
An entry can be found on request

Printed and bound by TJ International Ltd, Padstow, Cornwall.

Typeset by www.sinedesign.net

Contents

PART III: FALLON AND THE NATURAL WORLD

PART IV: FALLON AND AMERICA

PART V: POEMS IN HONOUR OF PETER FALLON

Acknowledgements

Many thanks to Peter Fallon's wife Jean and to Conor O'Callaghan for countless helpful suggestions concerning possible contributors to this volume.

Special thanks to Professors Bryan Giemza and Joe Heininger, who along with me, gave papers on the special session dedicated to Peter Fallon's work at the Southern regional meeting of the American Conference for Irish Studies in Chattanooga, Tennessee, in February 2009. Bryan and Joe have both strongly supported my work on this project.

As this book went to press, Seamus Heaney passed away suddenly. He supported this project with his usual enthusiasm and good humor. I am grateful for his encouragement and for two of his final gifts – his essay and his poem that are collected here.

The late Dennis O'Driscoll was an encouragement and a help from early on in this process, despite his own physical suffering. He is sorely missed by his family and friends and the world of poetry is poorer without him.

Maurice Harmon's essay, 'The Sacred and Profane Rituals of Peter Fallon' was originally published in the 2010 issue of *Ríocht na Midhe*. Both Professor Harmon and the Editor of *Ríocht na Midhe*, Séamus MacGabhan, have given permission to reprint this essay here.

Richard Wilbur's 'Horsetail' was originally published in *The New Yorker*, 14 February 2011. His 'Sugar Maples, January' was originally published in *The New Yorker*, 16 January 2012. Mr. Wilbur has given permission to reprint them here.

Wendell Berry and Bob Baris have both given permission to reprint Mr. Berry's introduction to Peter Fallon's 2007 chapbook, *Airs and Angels*, published by Baris's Press on Scroll Road, Carrollton, Ohio.

Nuala Ní Dhomnaill's poem was originally published as a limited edition broadside for the Beall Poetry Festival, 6-8 April 2011, Baylor University, Waco, Texas.

Hearty thanks to my Dean of the College of Arts and Sciences at Baylor University, Lee Nordt, who graciously gave financial support toward the publication of this book.

I am grateful to the joy and love given me by my wife, Hannah, and my sons, Connor and Aidan.

Finally, I hope this collection suggests the great admiration I and many others have for Peter Fallon's work as poet, publisher, editor, and translator. Peter is a paragon of integrity, a man of great virtues, and a friend. In the words of his poem, 'The Lost Field', 'Think of all that lasts'. His work will indeed.

List of Contributors

Wendell Berry lives and farms in Henry County, Kentucky. Author of more than forty well-regarded volumes of poetry, novels, short fiction, and essays, he is also an environmental activist known for his attention to local culture and protests of mountain-top removal in his native Kentucky. He has received the National Humanities Medal and, in 2012, was given the Jefferson Award from the National Endowment for the Humanities. His most recent prose collection, *It All Turns on Affection: The Jefferson Lecture and Other Essays*, appeared in 2012 from Counterpoint Press and his *New Collected Poems*, also from Counterpoint, appeared that year as well. *A Place in Time: Twenty Stories of the Port William Membership* was published in 2012 by Counterpoint.

A native of Belfast, Northern Ireland, **Ciaran Carson** has worked as Literature and Traditional Arts Officer for the Arts Council of Northern Ireland. Author of *Last Night's Fun: In and Out of Time with Irish Music* (1996), a prize-winning translation of Dante's *Inferno* (2002), numerous acclaimed volumes of poetry, including his *Collected Poems* (Wake Forest University Press, 2009), and several works of prose, Carson currently serves as Professor of Poetry and Director of the Seamus Heaney Centre for Poetry at Queen's University, Belfast.

A resident of Carrick-on-Suir, County Tipperary, **Michael Coady** has published prize-winning poetry and fiction. He won the O'Shaughnessy Poetry Award in 2004 and held the Heimbold Chair of Irish Studies at Villanova University in 2005. His recent poetry volumes published by The Gallery Press include *All Souls* (1997), *One Another* (2003), and *Going by Water* (2009).

Bryan Giemza is Associate Professor of English at Randolph-Macon College in Virginia. He co-authored *Poet of the Lost Cause: A Life of Father Ryan* with Donald Beagle (University of Tennessee Press, 2008). His edited collection of essays, *Rethinking the Irish in the American South: Beyond Rounders and Reelers*, appears in 2013 from the University of Mississippi Press, as does his monograph *Irish Catholic Writers and the Invention of the American South* (Louisiana State University Press).

Belfast native **Alan Gillis** lectures in English at Edinburgh University and edits the *Edinburgh Review*. He is the author of three poetry volumes published by The Gallery Press, including *Here Comes the Night* (2010). He also wrote *Irish Poetry of the 1930s* (Oxford University Press, 2005), has edited *Critical Ireland: New Essays on Literature and Culture* (Four Courts Press, 2001) and the *Edinburgh Guide to Studying English Literature* (2010).

Eamon Grennan is Professor of English Emeritus, Vassar College, New York. He has published many collections of poetry. His *Leopardi: Selected Poems* (Princeton University Press, 1997) won the PEN Award for Poetry in Translation, and he has published a collection of critical essays, *Facing the Music: Irish Poetry in the Twentieth Century* (Creighton University Press, 1999). As well as a number of Pushcart Prizes, he has received awards from the National Endowment for the Arts, the National Endowment for the Humanities, and from the John Simon Guggenheim Foundation. His *Out of Sight: New and Selected Poems* was published in 2010 by Graywolf Press.

Vona Groarke lectures in creative writing at Manchester University, England. In 2004, she co-held the Heimbold Chair at Villanova University and she was poet-in-residence at Wake Forest University, North Carolina, from 2005–07. In 2003, she edited a new edition of Oliver Goldsmith's *The Deserted Village*, and in April 2008 her version of the classic eighteenth-century Irish poem *Lament for Art O'Leary* was published, along with an extensive introductory essay. She has published five volumes of poetry with The Gallery Press and Wake Forest University Press and her sixth collection, *X*, is forthcoming in 2014.

Maurice Harmon is Emeritus Professor of Anglo-Irish Literature at University College, Dublin, and has authored critical studies on Seán Ó Faoláin, Thomas

Kinsella, and Austin Clarke. He also edited *No Author Better Served: The Correspondence between Samuel Beckett and Alan Schneider* (Harvard University Press, 1998) and translated the medieval compendium of stories and poems, *Acallam na Senorach*, as *The Colloquy of the Old Men* (Academica Press, 2001). His *When Love Is Not Enough: New and Selected Poems* was published by Salmon Press in 2010.

Seamus Heaney won the Nobel Prize for Literature in 1995. He was former Professor of Poetry at Oxford University and long-time professor of English at Harvard. Author of numerous volumes of poetry, including *Opened Ground: Selected Poems, 1966–1996* (Faber and Faber, 1998; Farrar, Straus and Giroux, 1999), and literary criticism, some of which was collected in *Finders, Keepers: Selected Prose, 1971–2001* (Faber and Faber, 2002; Farrar, Straus and Giroux, 2003). He has also published definitive translations of the medieval Irish epic *Sweeney Astray* (1983) and the Old English epic *Beowulf* (Norton, 2000). His most recent volume of poetry is *Human Chain* (Faber, 2010). He passed away unexpectedly on 30 August 2013 in Dublin.

Joseph Heininger is Associate Professor of English at Dominican University outside of Chicago, Illinois, where he teaches modern and contemporary British and Irish literature. He has published articles on Seamus Heaney's poetic responses to Dante, Eithne Strong's poetry and prose, Joyce's use of advertising fictions in *Ulysses*, and teaching *Ulysses* through the lens of popular culture. He is a former National Endowment for the Humanities Summer Seminar Fellow.

Ed Madden is Associate Professor of English and Women's Studies at the University of South Carolina. He is a poet and scholar of Irish literature who has written *Tiresian Poetics: Modernism, Sexuality and Voice 1888–2001* (Fairleigh Dickinson University Press, 2008) and co-edited *Irish Studies: Geographies and Genders* with Marti Lee (Cambridge Scholars Press, 2008). His poetry includes, most recently, *Prodigal: Variations* (Lethe Press, 2011) and he is currently working on a study, *Quare Fellas: Marginal Masculinities in Irish Literature and Film*.

Derek Mahon lives in Kinsale, County Cork. His published plays include *High Time* (1985), an adaptation of a play by Molière; *The School for Wives: a Play in Two acts after Molière* (1986); and *The Bacchae: after Euripides* (1991). He has also edited *Modern Irish Poetry* (1972) and, with Peter Fallon, *The Penguin Book* *of Contemporary Irish Poetry* (1990). He has translated *Racine's Phaedra* (1996); *Selected Poems* by Philip Jaccottet (1987), which won the Scott-Manriet Translation Prize; and *The Chimeras* by Nerval (1982). His honors include the Irish American Foundation Award, a Lannan Foundation Award, a Guggenheim Fellowship, the American Ireland Fund Literary Award, the Arts Council Bursary, and the Eric Gregory Award. His *New Collected Poems* appeared in 2011 and his *Selected Prose* in 2012 – both from The Gallery Press.

John McAuliffe teaches at Manchester University, where he co-directs the Centre for New Writing and edits *The Manchester Review* and the poetry digest *The Page*. In 2000 he won the *Raidió Teilifís Éireann* Poet of the Future Award and, in 2002, the Sean Dunne National Poetry Award. Author of three volumes of poetry with The Gallery Press, his most recent volume, *Of All Places*, was a Poetry Book Society Recommendation in 2011. He is chief poetry critic at the *Irish Times*.

Medbh McGuckian has published numerous volumes of poetry, many with The Gallery Press. She has been Writer-in-Residence at universities including Queen's (Belfast) and Trinity College, Dublin, and she has been Visiting Fellow at University of California, Berkeley. Winner of The Rooney Prize, the Bass Ireland Award for Literature, the Denis Devlin Award, and the Forward Prize for Literature (2002), her latest volume is *High Caul Cap* (The Gallery Press, 2012).

Pulitzer-Prize winning poet **Paul Muldoon** was born in County Armagh, Northern Ireland and worked for BBC Northern Ireland for many years. Currently Howard G.B. Clark '21 University Professor in the Humanities and Professor of Creative Writing in the Lewis Center for the Arts at Princeton University, he also serves as Poetry Editor for *The New Yorker*. His *Collected Poems: 1968–1998* appeared from Faber and Farrar, Straus and Giroux in 2001, followed by a series of volumes, including his *Wayside Shrines*, which was published by The Gallery Press in 2009. His Oxford Lectures in Poetry were published as *The End of the Poem* (Faber; Farrar, Straus and Giroux, 2006), while his most recent volume is *Maggot* (Faber; Farrar, Straus and Giroux, 2010).

Nuala Ní Dhomhnaill was born in Lancashire, England of Irish parents and moved to the Kerry Gaeltacht at the age of five. Writing exclusively in Irish, she has published a series of poetry volumes. Her *Selected Poems/Rogha Danta* appeared in 1986 (Raven Arts) and her *Selected Essays* in 2005 (New Island). Her most recent volume, *The Fifty-Minute Mermaid* (Gallery, 2007), was translated into

English by fellow contributor Paul Muldoon. She was Ireland Professor of Poetry from 2001–04.

Conor O'Callaghan grew up in Dundalk, Republic of Ireland. He has taught at Wake Forest University and currently teaches at Sheffield Hallam University, United Kingdom. He has published four volumes of poetry with The Gallery Press, most recently, *The Sun King* (2013). He also published *Red Mist: Roy Keane and the Irish World Cup Civil War* (Bloomsbury, 2004). He reviews poetry regularly for the *Irish Times* and the *Times Literary Supplement*. His awards include The Patrick Kavanagh Award in 1993, The Rooney Prize Special Award in 1996, *The Times* Educational Fellowship in 1997. *The History of Rain* (1993) was shortlisted for the Forward Prize in 1994 and *Fiction* (2005) was shortlisted for the *Irish Times* Poetry Now Prize.

Shaun O'Connell is one of the original professors in the English department at the University of Massachusetts, Boston, where he has taught since 1965; he also taught regularly for Harvard Extension School (1963–2005). He wrote and appeared in two film series on prose composition which appeared on WGBH TV. He is the author of two books – *Imagining Boston: A Literary Landscape* (Beacon Press, 1990; paperback edition, 1992) and *Remarkable, Unspeakable New York: A Literary Landscape* (Beacon Press, 1995; paperback edition, 1997) – and has edited an interpretive anthology, *Boston: Voices and Visions* (University of Massachusetts Press, 2010).

Bernard O'Donoghue is professor of medieval literature at Oxford University, and has published several well-received volumes of poetry, most recently *Farmer's Cross* (Faber, 2011), which was shortlisted for the T.S. Eliot Prize. His *Selected Poems* was published by Faber in 2008. He edited *The Cambridge Companion to Seamus Heaney* (2006) and has won the Whitbread (now Costa) Prize for Poetry. He is also an acclaimed translator, having published *The Courtly Love Tradition* (Manchester University Press, 1983), *A Stay in a Sanatorium*, poems from the Czech of Zbynk Hejda (Cork: Southword Editions, 2005), and *Sir Gawain and the Green Knight* (London: Penguin, 2006).

Dennis O'Driscoll worked for the Irish government in both the Stamp Duties adjudication office and Revenue Customs for more than forty years. Author of nine volumes of poetry and the essay collection *Troubled Thoughts, Majestic Dreams* (The Gallery Press, 2001), O'Driscoll was regarded as one of the finest poets and reviewers in Ireland. His *Stepping Stones: Interviews with Seamus Heaney* (Faber; Farrar, Straus and Giroux, 2008) is the definitive 'autobiography' of that poet. Born in 1954 in Thurles, County Tipperary, he died suddenly in Naas, County Kildare on Christmas Eve, 2012. His most recent volume of poetry, *Dear Life*, appeared from Anvil in 2012, while his essay collection *The Outnumbered Poet* will be published by The Gallery Press and his *A Michael Hamburger Reader* will appear from Anvil – both in 2013.

Thomas O'Grady is Professor of English at University of Massachusetts, Boston, and Director of the Irish Studies Program there. He has published poetry and fiction in *Agni*, *Verse*, *Kansas Quarterly/Arkansas Review*, *Poetry Ireland Review*, *Queen's Quarterly*, and *Dalhousie Review*. An expert on Patrick Kavanagh, O'Grady has published articles on Kavanagh and other Irish writers in *James Joyce Quarterly*, *Èire-Ireland*, *New Hibernia Review*, *Studies: An Irish Quarterly Review*, and *Etudes Irlandaises*.

Joyce Peseroff is a distinguished Lecturer in English at the University of Massachusetts, Boston, and has published four books of poetry, most recently *Eastern Mountain Time* (Carnegie Mellon, 2006). She served as Coordinating Editor, Managing Editor, Editor, and Associate Poetry Editor of *Ploughshares*. Editor of *The Ploughshares Poetry Reader*, *Robert Bly: When Sleepers Awake*, and *Simply Lasting: Writers on Jane Kenyon*, she has won a Pushcart Prize and grants from the National Endowment for the Arts and the Massachusetts Artists Foundation.

Justin Quinn teaches at the University of West Bohemia and Charles University in the Czech Republic. Co-founder and editor of *Metre* with fellow contributor David Wheatley, he has published three volumes of poetry with The Gallery Press, including *Close Quarters* (2011). His academic works include *Gathered Beneath the Storm: Wallace Stevens, Nature and Community* (2002) and *American Errancy: Empire, Sublimity and Modern Poetry* (2005), along with the *Cambridge Introduction to Modern Irish Poetry* (2008). He has edited *Irish Poetry after Feminism* (2008) and *Lectures on American Literature*, 3rd ed. (2011).

Thomas Dillon Redshaw is Professor of English Emeritus and Editor Emeritus of *New Hibernia Review*, University of St. Thomas, Minnesota. He also served as Editor of *Èire-Ireland* from 1973–1996 and has been Senior Fellow at the Institute for Irish Studies, Queen's University, Belfast. An expert on Irish book and periodical history, Redshaw has published two books on John Montague, edited *Thomas MacGreevy: The Collected Poems* (Dublin: New Writer's Press, 1971, 1972), and has written articles on the history of Liam Miller's Dolmen Press, on Montague, MacGreevy, James Liddy, and other Irish writers. With Sandra O'Connell, he has recently edited a collection on George Reavey for Lilliput Press.

A native of Paris, Tennessee, **Richard Rankin Russell** is 2012–13 Centennial Professor and Professor of English at Baylor University in Texas, where he teaches modern and contemporary British and Irish literature and directs the Beall Poetry Festival. His publications include *Martin McDonagh: A Casebook* (Routledge, 2007), *Bernard MacLaverty* (Bucknell University Press, 2009), *Poetry and Peace: Michael Longley, Seamus Heaney, and Northern Ireland* (University of Notre Dame Press, 2010), and *Modernity, Community, and Place in Brian Friel's Drama* (Syracuse University Press, 2013). His *Bernard MacLaverty: New Critical Readings* is forthcoming from Bloomsbury, while *Seamus Heaney's Regions* will be published by University of Notre Dame Press, both in 2014.

Gerard Smyth published his third volume, *Orchestra of Silence*, in 1971 with Peter Fallon's Tara Telephone and has served in various capacities at the *Irish Times*, where he currently works as the paper's poetry editor. His work is influenced by the old Liberties area of Dublin, in which he was born and raised, and the rural County Meath landscape where he spent significant time as a child and teenager also features in his poems, such as the one printed in the current volume. *The Fullness of Time: New and Selected Poems* was published by Dedalus Press in 2010.

David Wheatley has published four volumes with The Gallery Press, *A Nest on the Waves* (2010) being his most recent. A founder-editor of the influential poetry journal *Metre* (with fellow contributor Justin Quinn), he has taught at Hull University, England, and currently teaches in the Department of English Literature at the University of Aberdeen, Scotland. He has won the Rooney Prize for Irish Literature and the Vincent Buckley Poetry Prize.

Richard Wilbur is former Poet Laureate of the United States, two-time winner of the Pulitzer Prize, and one of the foremost living poets in America. His *Collected Poems, 1943–2004* appeared in 2004 and *Anterooms: New Poems and Translations* in 2010. Well-known also as a translator of plays by the French dramatists Molière and Racine, he has taught at Amherst College since 2008 as the John Woodruff Simpson Lecturer, a post once held by Robert Frost.

Introduction

RICHARD RANKIN RUSSELL

Irish poet Peter Fallon has run The Gallery Press since 1970, publishing hundreds of titles in Irish poetry, drama and fiction since then, mostly in poetry. He and Timothy Engelland also started The Deerfield Press in Deerfield Massachusetts, where Fallon was Writer-in-Residence from 1976–77 and again from 1996–97. Fallon has also authored many volumes of his own poetry; co-edited, with Derek Mahon, the influential 1990 collection, *The Penguin Book of Contemporary Irish Poetry*; adapted into dramatic form Patrick Kavanagh's novel *Tarry Flynn*; published an acclaimed translation of Virgil's *Georgics* in 2004 that was revised and reprinted by Oxford World's Classics in 2006; and will shortly publish a translation from Hesiod, *Deeds and Their Days*. He won the 1993 O'Shaughnessy Poetry Award from the Irish American Cultural Institute and served as the inaugural Heimbold Professor of Irish Studies at Villanova University in Philadelphia in the spring of 2000. Villanova gave him an Honorary Doctorate at that time. In 2009, he received an Alumni Award from Trinity College, Dublin, and in 2010, was appointed Adjunct Professor of English there. For 2012–13, he was the Burns Library Visiting Scholar in Irish Studies at Boston College. In Ireland, he is a member of the prestigious arts group, *Aosdána*. However, Fallon's own work has garnered relatively little critical attention, even as The Gallery Press's important role as the major Irish poetry publisher has slowly received its due, including a 1995 celebration in the *Irish Literary Supplement* marking its 25th anniversary and a 2010 series of events celebrating its 40th anniversary, culminating with the celebration at the Abbey Theatre on 6 June of that year.[1] Such neglect is a matter of regret, given the high quality of his literary work and the praise showered on Fallon from poets including the American Pulitzer-Prize winner Richard Wilbur, former British Poet Laureate Ted Hughes, and Irish Nobel Laureate Seamus Heaney. Testifying to their continuing admiration for Fallon's poetry, both Wilbur and Heaney have contributions in the present collection.

Given Fallon's crucial importance as the leading publisher of Irish poetry, as editor, as translator, as poet, and the corresponding under-representation of his work and relative failure to recognise The Gallery Press in the anthologies and criticism until very recently, it is high time for a collection treating his various, intertwining vocations. This volume redresses his critical neglect by collecting critical essays on the history of The Gallery Press, on Fallon's own poetry, on his translation of the *Georgics*, on his dramatic translation of Patrick Kavanagh's novel *Tarry Flynn*, on his relationship to other poets, particularly the American poet Wendell Berry, and on Fallon's role as editor by a number of the poets he publishes. A number of poems by the poets he publishes are also included.

I invited Fallon to read his poetry at the Southern regional meeting of the American Conference for Irish Studies, at Chattanooga, Tennessee, in March 2009. Also at that conference, I organised what I believe is the first academic panel dedicated to Fallon's work. There was a lively question and answer session after these presentations and I, along with my fellow panelists Joseph Heininger and Bryan Giemza, whose work features here, quickly realized that a collection on Fallon is warranted.

In 1998, Fallon would look back on nearly thirty years of publishing Irish in his 'Notes on a History of Publishing Poetry' and observe, 'I recognize an imperative and a challenge – that is, to keep open and alert to emerging voices . . . . I like to think I can continue to help nurture their fledgling work by careful attention and to praise it by publishing it alongside the finest work of their older contemporaries'.[2] By the time Gallery turned forty years old in 2010, Fallon could justifiably claim that 'The Gallery Press has enabled what might be recognized not as a Golden Generation but as a Golden Age' in Irish poetry.[3] By 1997, Dillon Johnston, the former editor of the leading North American publisher of Irish poetry, Wake Forest University Press, could note in his respected study *Irish Poetry after Joyce*, that Gallery 'has been the most successful' of all Irish presses in the last twenty-five years, 'with a more extensive list of living poets than any press in Britain and Ireland except Bloodaxe'.[4] More recently, David Wheatley praised Gallery in his edited volume *The Cambridge Companion to Contemporary Irish Poetry*, pointing out 'With its high production standards, Peter Fallon's Gallery Press could legitimately claim to have succeeded the defunct Dolmen Press as Ireland's premier publishers [sic] of poetry'.[5] Seamus Heaney's essay, published here for the first time and delivered originally at the 40th anniversary celebration of The Gallery Press at the Abbey Theatre, suggests not only the staying power of the press, but also how it has fostered the literary careers of dozens of Irish writers.

Fallon has long promoted new and established Irish poets, first from Dublin, then from his family farm, Loughcrew, in Oldcastle, County Meath. Born in then-West Germany in 1951 to Irish parents, he and his family moved to a farm in County Meath, Ireland, in 1957. After attending St. Gerard's School in Bray, County Wicklow, he finished his secondary education at Glenstal Abbey School a year early at sixteen, but Trinity College, Dublin refused to admit him at so early an age. During the year before he entered Trinity, Fallon started the Meath Poetry Group with a reading in Navan in 1968, and he and several of his friends started a poetry magazine called *Capella*. In an interview, Fallon told fellow publisher Dillon Johnston that, 'I started Gallery Books to publish single volumes occasionally between issues of the magazine *Capella*'.[6] Thomas Dillon Redshaw's essay in this collection treats the early history of The Gallery Press, including the genesis and production of *Capella*.

After he matriculated at Trinity, Fallon published the first Gallery Book on 6 February 1970, from his home in South Dublin. When pressed by Johnston for the origin of the name of his press, Fallon pled forgetfulness: 'I don't know. I really have no idea. I presume I wanted something simple and straight. I may have been thinking, that you put some books together and end up with an exhibition of what's going on'.[7] The Gallery Press soon flourished, eventually growing to develop an active list of some 250 titles. Fallon himself points to the publication of Eiléan Ní Chuilleanáin's first book and a selection of Pearse Hutchinson's poems (who defected from Dolmen Press), as well as the decision to publish hardbacks, all in 1972, as the turning point for Gallery: 'It was the first time we had published a handful of books at one time. And, looking back, the move of Pearse Hutchinson from Dolmen in 1972 was significant because subsequently others moved from Dolmen and from other presses'.[8] Gallery's rapid rise in the publishing scene in Ireland *did* attract other poets: both Derek Mahon and Medbh McGuckian left Oxford University Press for the Irish confines of Gallery, as did John Montague later on.[9] In his essay for the current collection, Mahon approvingly discusses how Gallery Press's scrupulous attentiveness makes it a better publisher than his former London publisher. Fallon himself has argued that his publishing of Mahon and McGuckian marks an important moment of cultural reclamation: 'This act of "retrieval" of Irish works I now see as one of the subtle revolutions in Gallery's existence'.[10]

Gallery continued to be run partly from Dublin up until 1988, when Fallon moved the entire operation to his farm in North Meath at Loughcrew, an evocative landscape whose significance is explored by Shaun O'Connell in his essay for the present collection. Despite the competition from other Irish presses, Gallery remains the leading Irish publisher of Irish poetry. Fallon's success as a publisher stems from his knack for spotting literary talent, his considerable editorial skills, and his warm, endearing personality that has enabled him to cultivate the friendship and poetry of many emerging Irish poets.

Fallon has kept a low profile in the Irish literary scene for a number of years, but in 1995, the 25th anniversary of Gallery, he was honored and fêted at a variety of venues throughout Ireland. The Fall 1995 issue of the *Irish Literary Supplement* had a full page of tributes to him, including the lead encomium from just-named Nobel Prize Winner Seamus Heaney. Heaney's comments embody the essence of this poet-publisher who has continually fostered the work of his 'gallery' of poets: 'Averse to hype, true to his own taste, fortified by the long haul, Peter Fallon has watched out for his writers in every sense. He continues to help new talent into the light, and that light is growing stronger now that many of his poets have grown within his orbit . . . .'[11] Poet Medbh McGuckian, whose 'On Cutting One's Finger While Reaching for Jasmine', is included in this collection, warmly notes Fallon's role in her growth as a poet:

> At a point in my development when I could go no further with my British publishers, he had faith in me and nurtured mine in myself . . . . It was also a period when I needed to just feel secure and valuable in an Irish, even a national, context, and Gallery Press through Peter gave me that support . . . . I do not think I would still be writing now if Peter were not at the helm of my life . . . . had a woman editor before who followed me as far as she could, but I have never felt Peter's not being a woman inhibiting, and I know Eiléan [Ní Chuilleanáin] and Nuala [Archer, whose Kavanagh Award-winning first volume Fallon published] feel exactly the same.[12]

That McGuckian, a female poet from Northern Ireland, would so highly praise her male publisher from the Republic – indeed, credit him for keeping her writing – bespeaks the consummate skill which Fallon employs in dealing with the Gallery poets be they male or female, from North or South. In his interview with Dillon Johnston, Fallon is adamant about Gallery's commitment to quality poets, male or female, and points out that 'we have published Eiléan Ní Chuilleanáin for more than twenty years and . . . we now publish Medbh McGuckian, Nuala Ní Dhomhnaill, and Paula Meehan, and recently we have taken on Vona Groarke[;] I feel comfortable we are publishing the best women poets publishing in Ireland'.[13]

Fallon's publishing has not been limited to Irish poets. In 1974, he began to publish drama, including plays by the Irish playwrights Tom Murphy and Marina Carr. In 1979, Fallon approached the leading Irish playwright, Brian Friel, and asked him if he could publish some of his work. Friel allowed Fallon to republish his first stage-play, *The Enemy Within*, as well as his *Selected Stories*. Gallery has kept other early Friel plays in print and has published a selection of original Friel plays, beginning with *Aristocrats* in 1980. The press is also committed to restoring to print the plays of the Irish dramatist Tom Kilroy. Gallery's poetry to drama ratio is roughly three to one. It has also published other works of fiction by Irish writers such as John Banville. Gallery Press volumes are distinguished by their multi-colored designs, their spare but beautiful artwork, and their relatively inexpensive prices, except for its limited editions, which can sell for hundreds of Euros or dollars.

If Fallon had only committed himself to The Gallery Press, his place in recent Irish literary history would be secure, yet he has also long published his own poetry, translations, and adaptations. But besides some scattered reviews and essays, there has been relatively little critical commentary on his work.[14] Fallon's representation in anthologies of Irish poetry has been even more scant until very recently. An exception came in prominent literary critic Declan Kiberd's inclusion of four Fallon poems in his section 'Contemporary Irish Poetry' for the third volume of the *Field Day Anthology of Irish Literature*. In his headnote, Kiberd observes that 'In committing himself to the local and the quotidian in the rural life of County Meath, where he lives as a farmer, poet, and publisher, he is not only heir to Patrick Kavanagh's "parochial" achievements but is inspired by the ecological vision of transatlantic poets like Gary Snyder and Wendell Berry'.[15] This accurate description that attends both to the local intensities and wider influences on Fallon's work was published in what has become a canonical anthology, but besides being included in the collection Fallon edited with Derek Mahon in 1990, his poems were not reprinted in other such books. Dennis O'Driscoll does mention him in his helpful essay, 'A Map of Contemporary Irish Poetry', originally published in an issue of *Poetry* in 1995 and expanded into a longer essay for a collection in 2001.[16] Recent hopeful signs of Fallon's rise in critical esteem come both from his inclusion in Wes Davis's acclaimed 2010 collection from Harvard University Press, *An Anthology of Modern Irish Poetry*, and in Patrick Crotty's 2010 edition of *The Penguin Book of Irish Poetry*.[17] Davis discusses Fallon's importance for Irish poetry and gives a generous selection of his poetry. In his headnote, Davis draws on Fallon's 'Caesarean', about the efforts to deliver lambs from their dying mother, to argue that 'this kind of tenderness toward sacrifice and careful attention to the minutiae of experience – both physical and emotional . . . distinguish[es] Fallon's poetry'.[18] The current volume on Peter Fallon aims to capture the spirit of his combination of tenderness and attentiveness toward his publishing enterprise and in his own work. At the same time, it seeks to convey the gritty particularity of his grounded writing, epitomized perhaps by his poem 'Winter Work', one of the most-cited poems in the essays that follow. Other recurring concerns include the marked 'turn' in his new poetry beginning with *Ballynahinch Postcards* and *The Company of Horses* (both from 2007) that is driven by his energetic verbs and brief verbal snapshots of natural life, along with his concept of poetry and nature – and poems about nature – as 'news' worth relating.

This collection opens with a section entitled, 'Fallon and The Gallery Press', which features Thomas Dillon Redshaw's stimulating early history of the 1960s/early 1970s cultural and literary milieu in Dublin that led to the founding of The Gallery Press and Seamus Heaney's stirring retrospective view of Gallery over its history. Dennis O'Driscoll and Derek Mahon then discuss their particular relationship with Fallon, his work, and The Gallery Press in their insightful essays. A second section, 'The Contours of Fallon's Creative Work', delves into the particular form and contents of his creative writing. Maurice Harmon surveys the entire corpus of the poetry in his essay, while John McAuliffe treats Fallon's intertextual relationship with Seamus Heaney and Paul Muldoon, particularly in his 1983 volume, *Winter Work*; Thomas O'Grady probes Fallon's adaptation of Kavanagh's *Tarry Flynn* and Ed Madden explores the complex question of masculinities in Fallon's poetry, particularly in the poetic sequence 'A Part of Ourselves'. The third section, 'Fallon and the Natural World', seeks to understand Fallon's deep and complex relationship to his environment in County Meath and beyond. Shaun O'Connell offers a moving treatment of Fallon's Loughcrew to begin this section.

In my own essay, I examine the dynamic concept of place in Fallon's writing through the lens of environmental literary criticism, as do Justin Quinn, in his essay on Fallon's husbandry and Joseph Heininger in his exploration of Fallon's translation of the *Georgics*. The fourth section, 'Fallon and America', includes Joyce Peseroff's observations about Fallon's Deerfield poems; Bryan Giemza's reflections on the relationship between the American poet and environmental activist Wendell Berry and Fallon; Berry's own reprinted introduction to Fallon's 2007 chapbook, *Airs and Angels*; and two recent poems by the American poet, Richard Wilbur. The fifth section features a series of poems by poets, many of whom The Gallery Press has published, including Medbh McGuckian, Bernard O'Donoghue, Paul Muldoon, Conor O'Callaghan, Nuala Ní Dhomhnaill, Seamus Heaney, Michael Coady, Alan Gillis, John McAuliffe, Eamon Grennan, David Wheatley, Vona Groarke, Gerard Smyth, and Ciaran Carson.

Peter Fallon: Poet, Publisher, Editor and Translator gives much-needed critical attention to the various aspects of Fallon's life and work, particularly the much-undervalued poetry. The list of contributors suggests Fallon's importance to a huge array of Irish, British, and American poets in Ireland, the United Kingdom, and in the United States. As Fallon's work continues to appear and publish the 'news' of his and our worlds, and as he continues publishing outstanding Irish poets, playwrights, and fiction writers, his reputation will only grow. This collection, then, not only celebrates his profound achievements in poetry, publishing, translating, and editing, but also suggests in its own diversity of genres and writers how Peter Fallon has fostered a living literary community in Ireland that has over-spilled the boundaries of gender and generation, province and nation, and reached the shores of Britain and America.

REFERENCES

Battersby, E., 'The View from Gallery – 25 Years on', *Irish Times*, 7 February 1995, City ed., p.10.

Crotty, P. (ed.), *The Penguin Book of Irish Poetry* (New York: Penguin, 2010).

Davis, W., 'Peter Fallon', in Davis (ed.), *An Anthology of Modern Irish Poetry* (Cambridge: Harvard University Press, 2010), pp.617–18.

Fallon, P., 'That Familiar Quiet: A Poet's Cares in County Meath: Interview with Shaun O'Connell'. Ts. of interview on 3 July 1987. Peter Fallon/Gallery Press Collection, Manuscript, Archives, Rare Books Library, Emory University.

Fallon, P., 'My Feet on the Ground: An Interview with Peter Fallon by Dillon Johnston', in *Irish Literary Supplement*, 14, 2 (Fall 1995), pp.4–5.

Fallon, P., 'Notes on a History of Publishing Poetry', *Princeton University Library Chronicle*, 59, 3 (Spring 1998), pp.547–58.

Fallon, P., 'A Point of Departure', in *Forty: Dublin Writers Festival Presents The Gallery Press 40th Anniversary Poetry Celebration*. The Abbey Theatre, 6 June 2010. (Loughcrew, Ireland: Gallery Press, 2010), n.p.

Heaney, S., 'Tributes to Peter Fallon: 25 Years of Gallery Press', *Irish Literary Supplement*, 14, 2 (Fall 1995), p.6.

Johnston, D., *Irish Poetry after Joyce*, 2nd ed. (Syracuse: Syracuse University Press, 1997).

Kiberd, D., 'Peter Fallon, (1951–)', in S. Deane (ed.), *The Field Day Anthology of Irish Literature*, Vol. III (London/Derry, Northern Ireland: Field Day, 1991), p.1417.

McGuckian, M., 'Tributes to Peter Fallon: 25 Years of Gallery Press', *Irish Literary Supplement*, 14, 2 (Fall 1995), p.6.

McKenna, C., 'The Gallery Press', in Clare Hutton and Patrick Walsh (eds), *The Irish Book in English, 1891–2000: The Oxford History of the Irish Book Vol. V* (Oxford: Oxford UP, 2011), pp.592–611.

O'Driscoll, D., 'A Map of Contemporary Irish Poetry', in *Troubled Thoughts, Majestic Dreams: Selected Prose Writings* (Loughcrew, Ireland: The Gallery Press, 2001), pp.67–79.

Russell, R.R., 'Loss and Recovery in Peter Fallon's Pastoral Elegies', *Colby Quarterly*, 37, 4 (December 2001), pp.343–56.

Russell, R.R., 'Peter Fallon', in Jay Parini (ed.), *British Writers, Supplement XII* (Detroit: Scribner's, 2007), pp.101–16.

Wheatley, D., 'Irish Poetry into the Twenty-First Century', in Matthew Campbell (ed.), *The Cambridge Companion to Contemporary Irish Poetry* (Cambridge: Cambridge UP, 2003), pp.250–67.

NOTES

1. One recent and welcome exception is Colleen McKenna, 'The Gallery Press', in Clare Hutton and Patrick Walsh (eds), *The Irish Book in English, 1891–2000: The Oxford History of the Irish Book Vol. V* (Oxford: Oxford University Press, 2011), pp.592–611.

2. P. Fallon, 'Notes on a History of Publishing Poetry', *Princeton University Library Chronicle*, 59, 3 (Spring 1998), p.558.

3. P. Fallon, 'A Point of Departure', in *Forty: Dublin Writers Festival Presents The Gallery Press 40th Anniversary Poetry Celebration*. The Abbey Theatre, 6 June 2010 (Loughcrew, Ireland: The Gallery Press, 2010), n.p.

4. D. Johnston, Preface to *Irish Poetry after Joyce*, rev. ed. (Syracuse: Syracuse University Press, 1997), pp.xi–xii.

5. D. Wheatley, 'Irish Poetry into the Twenty-First Century', in Matthew Campbell (ed.), *The Cambridge Companion to Contemporary Irish Poetry* (Cambridge: Cambridge University Press, 2003), p.251.

6. P. Fallon, 'My Feet on the Ground: An Interview with Peter Fallon by Dillon Johnston', *Irish Literary Supplement*, 14, 2 (Fall 1995), p.4.

7. Ibid.

8. Ibid.

9. E. Battersby, 'The View from Gallery – 25 Years on', in *Irish Times*, 7 February 1995, city ed.: 10.

10. P. Fallon, 'Notes on a History of Publishing Irish Poetry', p.552. See also, Colleen McKenna, 'The Gallery Press', p.600, who cites Fallon's statement, 'So, there is a deliberate act of repossession or repatriation of Irish poets and I think that we can publish Irish poets as well now, in Ireland, as anyone can' (qtd. in P. Fallon, 'That Familiar Quiet: A Poet's Cares in County Meath: Interview with Shaun O'Connell'. Ts. of interview on 3 July 1987. Peter Fallon/Gallery Press Collection, Manuscript, Archives, Rare Books Library, Emory University).

11. S. Heaney, 'Tributes to Peter Fallon: 25 Years of Gallery Press', *Irish Literary Supplement*, 14, 2 (Fall 1995), p.6.

12. M. McGuckian, 'Tributes to Peter Fallon: 25 Years of Gallery Press', *Irish Literary Supplement*, 14, 2 (Fall 1995), p.6.

13. P. Fallon, 'My Feet on the Ground', p.6.

14. For a comprehensive treatment of Fallon's career through the publication of *News of the World: Selected and New Poems* (1998), see R.R. Russell, 'Peter Fallon', in J. Parini (ed.), *British Writers, Supplement XII* (Detroit: Scribner's, 2007), pp.101–16. For a stimulating survey of the entire corpus of Fallon's poetry through *The Company of Horses* (2007), see Maurice Harmon's essay in the present collection, 'Peter Fallon's Profane Rituals'.

15. D. Kiberd, 'Peter Fallon, (1951–)', in S. Deane (ed.), *The Field Day Anthology of Irish Literature*, Vol. III (Derry: Field Day, 1991), p.1417.

16. See D. O'Driscoll, 'A Map of Contemporary Irish Poetry', in *Troubled Thoughts, Majestic Dreams: Selected Prose Writings* (Loughcrew: The Gallery Press, 2001), p.78. O'Driscoll praises Gallery Press for having discovered a number of poets and 'repatriated other important writers . . . from British imprints', then praises Fallon's poetry for 'the supple and sympathetic way he incorporates the voices and visions of his community into conversational yet highly-crafted poems'.

17. P. Crotty (ed.), *The Penguin Book of Irish Poetry* (New York: Penguin, 2010), includes Fallon's poem 'The Company of Horses', pp.816–17.

18. W. Davis, 'Peter Fallon', in Davis (ed.), *An Anthology of Modern Irish Poetry* (Cambridge: Harvard University Press, 2010), p.618.

Part I

Fallon and
The Gallery Press

The Dublin Arts Festival, 1970:

Capella, The Book of Invasions, and the Original Gallery Books

THOMAS DILLON REDSHAW

From 1969 through 1972, Peter Fallon and Eamon Carr published eight chapbooks of contemporary Dublin poetry under the imprint of Tara Telephone Publications.[1] At the issue of Pearse Hutchinson's *Watching the Morning Grow* (1972), the chapbooks became books published under the now canonical Gallery Press imprint.[2] That beginning commenced under auspices tangential to those some historians of Irish writing and print may allow.[3] It proved also both tellingly distinct, on the one hand, and historically typical, on the other. The ontogeny of The Gallery Press – a name in Irish publishing now to be conjured with – recapitulates some features that mark the origins of prior Irish literary presses dating from, for example, the Salkelds' Gayfield Press in the 1940s to John Deane's Dedalus Press in the 1980s. Even so, the appearance of the earliest 'Gallery Books' catches a particular moment in Dublin's cultural history and in Ireland's literary history – a moment characterised by what Jeff Nuttall then termed 'bomb culture'; a moment bounded by the first and second Dublin Arts Festivals of 1970 and 1971; moment then was overtaken by the contemporaneous flare-up of the 'Troubles' in Northern Ireland.

The first years of the Dublin Arts Festival – its invention, planning, underwriting, events, and consequent criticism – span that moment. These years encompass the period when, in its idiosyncratic fashion, Ireland partly assimilated what Nuttall, writing in 1966–67, anatomised as 'Bomb Culture'.[4] As in France and Germany, Britain and America, the cultural period of the Sixties in Ireland extended from 1963 – marked by the Beatles' concert at the Adelphi Theatre – through the tumultuous finale of the decade into 1972 – a grim year opened by the burning of the British embassy on Merrion Square. Just as those events bracket well-known political events on the world stage – the Civil Rights Movement, *les évenements de Mai*, 1968, across Europe – so they bracket political events in Ireland: the opening of the Irish economy, the rise of ecumenism, the Dáil ministries of Lemass and Lynch, the export of Irish culture, and the outbreak of the Northern Troubles.[5] Looking back, what any experienced reader of Irish culture inevitably notes is the flush of imaginative and performative energies in both popular and 'high' Irish culture. This is the moment of Roddy Doyle's *The Commitments* (1989) as much as it is of Thomas Kinsella's *The Tain* (1969).

Indeed, with the Literary Revival of Yeats and Joyce in mind, some readers have taken the burgeoning of Dublin's literary culture in the 1960s to be a second revival featuring the work of both 'revived' writers such as Austin Clarke or Patrick Kavanagh, among the poets, or new writers like John Montague and Richard Murphy, or Eavan Boland and Brendan Kennelly. Two very public and publicly funded celebrations of Ireland's past seemed to declare that two tides in official Irish culture had run their course and were open to criticism. The 1965 celebration of the birth of W.B. Yeats, orchestrated in Dublin by Liam Miller of the Dolmen Press, capitalised on international Yeats scholarship, established the 'Yeats industry', and provided a forum for the hieratic impulses of Irish cultural self-regard and, not incidentally, matter for Bord Fáilte's efforts to elevate Irish tourism. Immediately following the Yeats centenary, the 1966 commemoration (*cuimhneacháin*) of the Easter Rising – a celebration punctuated by the blowing-up of Nelson's Pillar – provided a display of the accomplishments of the Sinn Féin state: electoral democracy, the reinvention of neutrality, and pride in national self-invention.[6] Neither celebration really proposed the ideology of the Revival or of Sinn Féin as sustainable, on-going critiques of the present. Rather, they seem to have been felt as a release, as a liberation from the past, as signs that Irish culture could now behave differently and, so it then seemed, more freely.

Just returned from his second sojourn in America, John Montague caught the moment of that lift several ways around in *A Chosen Light* (1967), and particularly in 'The Siege of Mullingar' and its often quoted refrain: '*Puritan Ireland's dead and gone, / A myth of O'Connor and O'Faolain*'.[7] Portraying this 1963 weekend festival of traditional music – one of the *fleadhanna* in the period from the 1950s through the 1970s that 'attracted unwelcome attention from alienated city and country youth' – the three septets of Montague's poem have much pertinence in this context.[8] By alluding to the swan and his mate in the canal harbor at Mullingar, Montague sets Yeats and the Revival back into their Romantic context. By noting that the lovers paired on the canal bank listen 'on Sony transistors / to the agony of Pope John', Montague registers both the changing character of Irish Catholicism after Vatican II and Ireland's economic opening to foreign goods – 'Sony transistors' and not Pye wirelesses – as well as the culture's unwary openness to global media.[9] By using the occasion of the 1963 festival of Irish traditional music, Montague underscores the allure not only of Ireland's native ballad and *sean nós* performing traditions, or of dance or *rince* and *céilidh* or concert traditions, but also of the broader social forms of dance and song – the showbands. These years saw the rise of Tommy Makem and the Clancy Brothers and of The Dubliners, of Caitlín Maud and Dolly McMahon, of Seán Ó Riada's Ceoltóirí Chualann and then the Chieftains, and of Thin Lizzy and Horslips. They saw also the coming in force of pop, rock, and blues to Dublin.

To young listeners with a few shillings to spend on singles, or a punt for an LP, transistor radios and record shops brought not only Ireland's home-grown traditions of music-making, but also pop, blues, and rock purveyed by the media-driven culture industries of Britain and America. Looked at askance by the pundits of the Irish Catholic church and of traditional nationalism – and often by distressed parents – the novelty and energy of this music and its public performance served to focus the energies and enthusiasms of young Irish people. Roddy Doyle's *The Commitments,* as well as its lively incarnation on film, offers one sense of this swerve in Ireland's popular culture. The commercial locus for this opening in Dublin was the Art Moderne hall of the Adelphi Cinema on Middle Abbey Street, west across O'Connell Street from Yeats's Abbey Theatre.[10] In November 1963, a few weeks before the Kennedy assassination, the Adelphi was host to the only live concert – two back-to-back performances on Tuesday night, November 4 – in Ireland by The Beatles.[11] The crowd in Abbey Street tested the resources of the Gardaí.[12] Two years after, The Rolling Stones appeared twice at the Adelphi in January 1965, and again in September 1965.[13]

Of equal importance was Bob Dylan's concert May 5 1965, in advance of the release of *Blonde on Blonde.* Dylan performed an acoustic first set, came back with a badly miked and amplified electronic second set, and was booed by his

Dublin audience for this ethical and aesthetic lapse. Like folk audiences in the United States, Dubliners had come to see him as an icon of protest, and the poetic charge in his songs seemed compromised by his swerve toward electronic instrumentation.[14] Then the jazz critic for the *Irish Times*, George Hodnett, forgivingly observed that the Dylan concert was not 'music but something else; something sociologically interesting'.[15] What Hodnett homed in on was the stature of Dylan's words: 'Mr Dylan is a poet, and though he might be a minor one were he to publish in slim volumes, without the assistance of guitar, harmonic and publicity machine, it is something to sell poetry to a mass-audience at all'.[16] Younger Dubliners heard Dylan not so much as a rocker, but more as a bluesman, as a protest singer, a peoples' poet, as did Phil Lynott.[17] Now a legendary figure, Lynott was the guitarist, singer, and writer for Thin Lizzy, 'a band for whom the song has been the musical unit', as Peter Fallon recalled in 1974: 'I remember five or six years ago how he'd come down with his mates to the poetry-reading sessions I ran in Dublin and play some songs he'd written, a little unconfident but glad of a "listening" audience'.[18] Offering his lyrics as poems, Lynott published two chapbooks that were printed together in *Songs for While I'm Away* (1977, 1997), with illustrations by Jim FitzPatrick, whose *Rocker* poster depicts Lynott astride a spiritual Harley-Davidson – an idealized image drawn from American popular culture.

The mass marketing of popular music in the Republic – the ubiquity of 45 rpm singles and LPs, for example – extended to literature and to poetry courtesy of the efforts of Penguin Books. Allen Lane's reinvention of paperback publishing in Britain after World War II created a new venue for poetry when, in 1962, the firms' editors created the Penguin Modern Poets; twenty-seven inexpensive paperbacks presenting in each volume the work of three contemporary poets unencumbered by introductions or notes. The series offered a broad span of British poets, as well as two Irish poets: Richard Murphy and Michael Longley.[19] More notably, the series offered selections from the San Francisco Beat poets: Gregory Corso, Lawrence Ferlinghetti, Allen Ginsberg, and Charles Bukowski, Philip Lamantia, Harold Norse. One title was revised and republished in 1983: *The Mersey Sound*. First published in 1967, *The Mersey Sound* offered poems by Adrian Henri, Roger McGough, and Brian Patten. Now the régisseur of Bloodaxe Books, and publisher of many contemporary Irish poets, Neil Astley recollected that *The Mersey Sound* 'woke us up'.[20] Owing to the easing of protective tariffs, in 1960s and 1970s Dublin these Penguin books, like other artifacts of popular culture, could be purchased new from the well-stocked Penguin Bookshop in Andrew Street, opposite McCullough and Piggott's music shop. They also turned up battered and weary, having been passed round and round, in such used bookshops as Greene's at the back of Trinity College. These editions reached many Arts students, of course, but they also attracted young readers outside of the universities.[21]

Moreover, Penguin also widely published another charismatic anthology of anti-establishment poetry, Michael Horovitz's *The Children of Albion: Poetry of the Underground in Britain* (1969). In his episodic, sometimes exclamatory 'Afterwords', Horovitz claims for the poets in his anthology 'The unfinished work of Blake – of this unfinished poem – is ours to carry on. The legacy of the whole man'.[22] The crucial event that incited Horovitz to compose his anti-establishment anthology was the last-minute creation of the 'International Poetry Incarnation' of June 11 1965, in London's Royal Albert Hall. The promised presence of Pablo Neruda and Andrei Voznesensky attracted some 6,000 followers of poetry 'from the thriving underworld of clubs and musicians and art students'.[23] The crowd was rewarded by the real presence of Allen Ginsberg who embodied 'animating, intermingling and loosening the perimeter divisions between poetry – jazz, blues, raga & modern classical music in the new solar sound-systems of beat caverns, pop charts, and psychedelic "trips"'.[24] Horovitz spins his 'Afterwords' around the armature of William Blake's 'Jerusalem' from *Milton: a Poem* (1808). In so doing, Horovitz unlaces the new patchwork poetic of performance from America or Europe and weaves it into the contrary English tradition of the romantic yet Protestant social sensibility.

Perhaps owing to Yeats's promotion of the Occult and of Blake as a Romantic ancestor, no home-grown Irish anthology of the period attempted such a statement as *Children of Albion* or its American predecessor Donald M. Allen's *The New American Poetry, 1945–1960* (1960). Both John Jordan's *Poetry Ireland* (1963–68) and John Montague's *Poetry Ireland* readings in the Lantern Theatre remained fixed near the academy, as had *The Dolmen Miscellany* (1963) which phrased its stance elegantly but timidly. The stance of Michael Smith's *Lace Curtain*, for example, resolved back to the poets of the 1930s – Beckett, Devlin, Coffey – and second-generation European Modernism keyed by Joyce and Maritain. If James Liddy's *Arena*, Brian Lynch's *The Holy Door* (1965–66), or Hayden Murphy's *Broadsheet III* be taken into account, then Patrick Kavanagh might be counted as Dublin's countervailing figure – the gruff guru of the Bailey. However, after his death in 1967, Kavanagh had become more a totemic absence, rather than a presence like Ginsberg or Bob Dylan. Moreover, despite the memorials of the Yeats centenary in 1965 and the official commemoration of the Easter Rising in 1966, the city saw and heard no inciting event quite like London's 'International Poetry Incarnation'. What may be counted closest in spirit and effect to that legendary 'happening' was the Liberty Hall reading on Tuesday, 7 April 1970, during the first Dublin Arts Festival.

Events of the first Dublin Festival were well reported in the *Irish Times* and other Dublin papers.[25] Like the Belfast Festival begun by Michael Emmerson in 1964, the Dublin Festival originated in the university, in Trinity College, owing to the efforts of Cormac Ó Cuilleanáin. Charles Acton painstakingly critiqued as too casual the management of the first two years of the festival, but he praised the poetry programs for 'reaching new audiences' and connecting the universities with the 'ordinary citizen'.[26] These readings Peter Fallon and Eamon Carr arranged at a tangent to the festival's administration proper. The series ran the week of April 6 1970. Lunch hour readings happened in the Gallery of the department store Brown Thomas then on the east side of Grafton Street. The poets were Des O'Mahony, Eamon Carr, Leland Bardwell, Fallon, Justin O'Mahony, Gerard McCarthy, Donal Sheridan, and two Americans: Eugene Robert Platt and Thomas Tessier. Following the late-night marathon of Liverpool poets at Liberty Hall came the climactic evening reading in Trinity's Examination Hall featuring Brendan Kennelly, Eavan Boland, and Michael Longley.[27] Fallon also organized the readings under the flag of Tara Telephone Publications during the second Dublin Arts Festival, in March 1971, featuring Fallon, Gerard Smyth, Hayden Murphy and Patrick Galvin, in Brown Thomas and upstairs at Sinnot's pub. The climactic reading for the second 1971 festival presented Michael Hartnett, Peter Levi, and Pearse Hutchinson performing translations from Gaelic, Russian, Greek, and Portuguese.[28]

Printed in black and red, the festival programs bear a Celtic Revival symbol created by the Dublin illustrator, illuminator, and artist Jim FitzPatrick. FitzPatrick took a cue from Ireland's store of early creations of the Irish monastic *scriptoria*, like the well-known Book of Kells in the Long Library at Trinity College. Beginning with broad curves to make what appears to be a letter form, FitzPatrick gave it the head of a bird whose beak clasps the interlaced plumage of its own head. Having itself a head, the plumage has a life of its own. Suggesting the shape of the Gaelic letter 'd', this image also suggests that the festival's artworks – symphony or ballad, poem or play – have dual import. Here FitzPatrick adapts Celtic motifs to a modern Irish moment. An avowedly self-taught artist, FitzPatrick acknowledges the influences of, among others, *fin de siècle* illustrations, including those of

Harry Clarke, and of American comics, including visual abridgements of classic novels.[29] One image, and not a directly Irish or Celtic one, links FitzPatrick into the popular culture of the late 1960s. This is his 1968 poster of Che Guevara – his face and beret abstracted as an icon of rebellion, especially during student protests in European and North American universities.[30] Working from his graphic studio Two Bare Feet, FitzPatrick provided the cover art for the two Tara Telephone publications: the broadside series titled *The Book of Invasions* and the little magazine titled *Capella*. Except for *Capella* 4, the covers hint at a science-fiction version of episodes from the *Lebor Gabála Érenn*.[31] *Capella* 3 (December, 1969) was distributed with a small 'poster poem' graphic of 'The Coming of the *Tuatha De Danann*'.[32] The run of *Capella*'s covers offers a fantasy in which the invasion of the Galaxy Master's bubble-wrapped warriors encounters early Celtic heroes, who rebel against the universal eye of the Balor-like Galaxy Master. The four interim issues of *The Book of Invasions* reiterates some of the *Capella* covers, and both make one-time use of montage.

FitzPatrick's Dublin Arts Festival symbol appeared almost a decade later centered on the wrap of *The First Ten Years: Dublin Arts Festival Poetry*, published by the organisers of the festival. Peter Fallon and Dennis O'Driscoll edited this commemorative anthology. Fallon's introductory paragraphs recognise both the particular character of the festival readings, which 'have always operated independently of the festival themes', and his own independence.[33] They remind the reader that *Capella* 4 presented poems by the 1970 Dublin Festival poets. Bearing the neo-Celtic Dublin Festival symbol by Jim FitzPatrick, *Capella* 4 contains poems by the festival readers: Brendan Kennelly, Michael Longley, and Seamus Heaney among the Irish, Roger McGough, and Adrian Henri, Mike Evans, and Brian Patten from the Merseyside. These offer a taste of the texts performed at the festival readings that had evolved from readings in Parnell Square, College Lane, and Sinnott's pub. The festival booked daytime readings by 'less well-known writers' into Brown Thomas on Grafton Street: '[I]t was the procession of hundreds of people each lunchtime that was astonishing!'[34] Of particular interest here is Fallon's recollection of the evening readings during the first years of the festival:

> Those were the days of more experiment with poetry and music,
> of more interaction between the arts, and one evening in Liberty
> Hall found members of the Liverpool Scene – poet Adrian Henri,
> singers/songwriters Mike Hart and Andy Roberts and saxophonist/

poet Mike Evans–sharing the stage with Pete Morgan and Brian
Patten and Tara Telephone.[35]

Present-day web sources treat Tara Telephone as an Irish 'beat group' and an
antecedent to Horslips, chiefly owing to the role that Eamon Carr played in the
latter. Yet, because Tara Telephone rose out of loosely organised poetry workshops
and open reading sessions, the group had literary aspirations, albeit 'underground'
ones, and so Tara Telephone publications had self-identifying importance equal
to the group's performances. Carr recalls that the group started out as a trio –
himself, Peter Fallon, and David Costelloe – then added a guitarist, Paul Kennan,
and the singer Lucienne Purcell. In 1970 the group expanded to include Declan
Sinnott, Bernie Barrett, and Andrew Robinson, who recalls that 'Some poems were
read with musical backing, some set to tunes and sung'.[36] Robinson also recalled
the lines whose pronunciation gave George Hodnett pause:

> Pale Aphrodite carries the light
> That will ignite our journey
> Born of the sun, she is the one
> Who always brings sympathy . . . [37]

Having interviewed Carr and Fallon in the spring of 1970, Brian Darcy identified
the challenge of Tara Telephone's populist aspirations as an essentially literary
one: 'the performance of a poem in the context of "modern pop" so that some of
the poetry would rub off'.[38] Tara Telephone 'recitals' were well reported in Ireland,
while the open reading sessions – first in 51 Parnell Square, then in the Trinity
Arts Society – gained an underground reputation that attracted Dublin poets,
visiting Americans, and singer-songwriters from the 'Irish beat' milieu. Phil Lynott
recited with the poets, and 'was well nervous about it', in the words of Eamon
Carr, 'but it sort of validated what he was doing'.[39] Validation constituted, in part,
the purpose of Tara Telephone publications and performances.

The national moment for Tara Telephone came during the first Dublin Arts
Festival early in 1970. By booking the Liverpool poets into the venue of the Liberty
Hall auditorium, the festival made a statement by associating their energies and
novelty with the voice of Irish labor. Like the Abbey Theatre, Liberty Hall can
be counted as a cradle of modern Ireland. Like the Abbey Theatre, the present
building is modern, a modest Modernist glass and steel tower on Eden Quay. The

site was the political home of the Irish Transport and General Workers' Union, of native Irish socialism, and of Connelly and O'Casey. Performing past midnight, the musicians – sometimes amplified, sometimes not – and the readers provided a 'real feast [or *fleadh*] of music as backing poetry'.[40] Adrian Henri brought to Dublin the poets he had anthologized in *The Mersey Sound*: Pete Morgan, Mike Evans, Brian Patten. Peter Fallon and Eamon Carr read with Tara Telephone. In a memorial memoir for Tara Telephone's guitarist David Costelloe, Eamon Carr recalls the group's origin:

> Inspired by the poetry reading scene in Liverpool (and throughout Britain in the late 1960s), Peter Fallon and I set up a poetry workshop – called Tara Telephone – in Dublin around 1968. A bit like today's singer songwriter open mic [mike] nights, it enabled 6 young writers to try out their work on an enthusiastic and helpful audience.[41]

From those workshop evenings and 'open mic nights', Tara Telephone Publications and then Gallery Books emerged. Interviewing Peter Fallon in 1991, Peter Denman wanted to know when The Gallery Press 'actually' started, and Fallon replied, 'In February 1970' with *Answers*, by Des O'Mahony and Justin McCarthy.[42] This collection, however, bears the imprint of Tara Telephone Publications, and a number of hallmarks – typed setting, offset printing – of the Dublin print milieu at the turn of the decade. Moreover, in an afterword Fallon and Eamon Carr observed that *Answers* 'is the first of a series of short representative collections of "unpublished" Irish poets'.[43] In 1991 Fallon posed the upper boundary of the print milieu in which the first Tara Telephone Publications appeared. That upper boundary was Liam Miller's Dolmen Press, which 'commanded a position of excellence and elegance, [though] there was something lofty and removed about it'.[44] The starting line was readings in pubs and university rooms, their ephemeral printings, and the small magazines. Though it became the stuff of legend and Bord Fáilte prose, this 'underground' and partly undergraduate literary milieu has only lately come to be anatomized from memory and in memoir. Writing back in 1969 for John Mulcahy's *Hibernia*, Roy Lisker surveyed the now-legendary Thursday readings at Sinnott's organised by Leland Bardwell and Eiléan Ní Chuilleanáin and refereed sometimes by Pearse Hutchinson and sometimes by Hayden Murphy.[45] The Sinnott's readings had supplanted the more formal *Poetry Ireland* readings arranged by John Montague at, among other venues, the Lantern Theatre, which was run by Patrick Funge, of the Elo Press, and Liam Miller.

From the pub and the academy came the poetry broadsheets of the time, Dolmen produced the University College Dublin broadsheet (1967–70), edited by Richard Ryan.[46] Hayden Murphy hawked his *Broadsheet* (1967–1978) – printed offset and visibly pasted up from typewritten copy – in pubs, at readings, and to bookshops like Parson's and the Eblana. In his *Irish Literary Magazines* (2003), Tom Clyde observes that the broadside or broadsheet belongs to the 'guerrilla tradition'.[47] Inexpensive to produce and hard to market, such *feuilletons* served the purpose of announcing the presence of new groups of writers with an agenda set oblique to the prevailing culture.[48] From James Liddy, the originator of *Arena* (1963–65), and from the Funge Art Centre in Gorey came *Poetry Broadside*.[49] From the universities came *St. Stephen's* and *Icarus*, both vying for Dublin readerships and not just an undergraduate audience. Into this context came the magazine *Capella* (1969–70) and the broadside *Book of Invasions* (1969). These offset printings register the sea-change in Dublin printing technology – from Letraset to offset – that made print democratically available. Even expatriate American poets joined in with typewriter-set pamphlets from a short-lived Seafront Press.

More sophisticated sources of print had been consolidated by entrepreneurs like Jefferson Smurfit. Old firms, like Cahill's after its quayside premises burned, abandoned linotype for computer drive filmsetting, like Smurfit's Richview Press. Even so, shops like the Elo Press served literary production with hot type. Not all new publishing efforts began in offset. Michael Smith's *The Lace Curtain* (1969–78) was commercially printed, but the early productions of Smith's New Writers' Press followed the handset craft example of the evolution of Dolmen Press. Smith is well known for his sharp critical support of the Irish poets of the 1930s and for his early advocacy of Michael Hartnett. Even so, his early printings aspired to the condition of the 'book beautiful' that Liam Miller had championed since 1951. Like Miller, Smith began at home with a hobbyist's press, set and printed his editions by hand, and cut his own cover decorations. Like Miller, Smith came to use Dublin job printers and binders – the Dorset Press, in this instance – for his Zozimus Editions, like *The Collected Poems of Thomas MacGreevy* (1971) or August Young's *On Loaning Hill* (1972). Macdara Woods' *Decimal D. Sec. Drinks in a Bar in Marrakesch* (1970) catches the transition: the eight-page text was set and printed at the Dorset Press, but the hand-printed wrap bears a green linocut by Smith. Like Miller, he began to exploit the design options that commercial printing offered, as when he eschewed the craft chapbook for his series of 'versheets', edited by Trevor Joyce. These slimmest of pamphlets consist of broadsides of single-author texts folded and pasted into a cover. In terms of critical pertinence, the most notable of them remains James Liddy's *Homage to Patrick Kavanagh* (1971).[50]

Along with posters and programs, 'poet cards', 'versesheets', and broadsides constituted the printed ephemera of the Dublin Festival performances. Bookshops like Parson's and the Eblana had the patience for them – flat, folded, and flimsy – but it was in the halls and pubs where they were most fittingly peddled as souvenirs of readings or promotions of performances to come. *The Book of Invasions*, edited by Eamon Carr and Peter Fallon, served those purposes. The broadsheets also served to, as the editors declared with the first issue, 'bridge the gap between [issues of] the quarterly Capella [*sic*] magazine'.[51] Fallon and Carr titled their broadsheet after the twelfth-century telling of the myths of Ireland's settlement, the *Lebor Gabála Érenn*, up to the coming of the Sons of Míl in the time of Alexander the Great. Jim FitzPatrick's covers repeat the mythological 'invasion' motif by deploying the comic book imagery of science fiction. *The Books of Invasions* distinguishes itself at a glance from Hayden Murphy's *Broadsheet* (March, 1970), typewriter set, decorated by Pauline Bewick, and containing poems by well-known figures – John Montague, Seamus Heaney, and Brendan Kennelly. To take another example, the telling contrast between *The Book of Invasions* and the *Broadsheet* of the Poetry Workshop, University College Dublin, is plain: no art work, chaste typesetting from the Dolmen Press, and contributions by established poets: Ted Hughes, Richard Murphy, John Montague and Desmond O'Grady.

Printed only on one side and published folded so as to provide eight pages of text, the four issues of *The Book of Invasions* keep the projects of Tara Telephone before the group's audience and readership. For example, the second 'chapter' of *The Book of Invasions* closes with notes announcing: the contents of the forthcoming issue of *Capella*; the start of the Tara Telephone 'open reading' sessions; and the availability of the Tara Telephone 'poetry/music group' for performances. The third 'chapter' notes, for example, that the December 1969 issue of *Capella* 'will again contain contemporary Irish poets and some selected British writers'.[52] Like *Capella*, *The Book of Invasions* features poems in the lower-case, 'Pop' mode by those who attended the workshops and open readings in 1969. The poems resemble song lyrics or protest poetry: protest against the police and for Wole Soyinka; protest against social conformity to national myths and for Judy Garland. The later 'chapters' contain poems by Leland Bardwell and Brendan

Kennelly, and by the Liverpool poets who appeared during the first Dublin Arts Festival. In hindsight, the iconography of *The Book of Invasions* casts its pages in a nimbus of irony. Even so, visually and textually, the ambitions of these broadsides and of *Capella* express the period's newly freed energies striving for invention.

Like the 'chapters' of Tara Telephone's *Book of Invasions*, the issues of *Capella* do not display accomplished print craft. Up through the fourth issue, they are the product of offset printing from copy set in a 'Mod' sans serif font. Through the eighth and last issue, they bear the declaration 'Published by the Tara Telephone', as if to suggest a communal enterprise arising out of the Tara Telephone 'open-reading' sessions'.[53] Edited by Eamon Carr and Peter Fallon through issue 5/6, *Capella* sought to present 'the work of the "younger" Irish poets and a cross-section of contemporary British poets'.[54] Up through issue 5/6, what distinguishes *Capella* from the other Dublin little magazines of the day is the presence of the younger British poets featured during the 1970 Dublin Festival. Even so, *Capella* 3 (December 1969) opened by announcing Tara Telephone's ambition 'to start a series of representative collections of local unpublished poets', and closed by announcing the publication, for 10 February 1970, of 'Gallery Books No. 1'.[55]

Among the Irish poets represented early in *Capella* are Fallon and Eamon Carr, along with Leland Bardwell, Brendan Kennelly, and Pearse Hutchinson. After *Capella* 4 (April 1970), which includes Seamus Heaney, the presence of Irish poets becomes more pronounced: Hayden Murphy, James Simmons, Eileán Ní Chuilleanáin, Gerard Smyth, Paul Murray, and Frank Ormsby. Here and there appear poems by Americans: Allen Ginsberg, Knute Skinner, and Thomas Tessier. After the fourth issue, the editing of *Capella* becomes less self-conscious about its workshop origins and more discerning. *Capella* discovered its critical stance by practice and example; its pages never featured reviews. Only once did *Capella* offer anything like criticism: in advance of Pete Morgan's reading in Trinity College, *Capella* reprinted Adrian Henri's introduction to Morgan's *A Big Hat or What?* (1968). *Capella*'s shift to more formal editorial discipline also finds expression in the presentation of those last three issues. The covers are printed on coated card, the pages are laid out securely, the texts are set by linotype, and, despite uneven inking, each page bears the kiss of type.

Aside from representing the poets who read during the first Dublin Festival, *Capella* 4 again announced the publication of *Answers*, by Justin McCarthy and Des O'Mahony, as 'Gallery Books 1'. In their notes to this pamphlet, Fallon and Carr observe that the two poets came out of 'a group of formidable young writers' who attended the open readings organised by Tara Telephone.[56] The purpose of the first of the Gallery Books was to give readers a chance to see more from *Capella* writers, and this holds true for Liam Murphy's *occasion of wordshed: a collection of wordisms* (1970).[57] While Murphy begins with an epigraph in Irish from Seán Ó Ríordáin, he continues on in lower case and in the populist mode of the 'Mersey Sound' poets.[58] With this collection the Gallery Books acquire durability by acquiring card covers with French flaps. While the titles and lines of these three poets sometimes refer to Irish locales and literary figures, little of their structural display on the page refers to either the long verse tradition in either Gaelic or high English tradition that the poets might have assimilated from their Arts curricula in the universities. Indeed, the stylistic stance taken is 'non-U'. Often declarative, romantic, easily ironic, the diction and pacing of these poems have an orality founded in the venue of the workshop and 'open-reading' and a lyric character founded in the venue of the cellar club and music stage. These are the beginning poems of, to borrow from Blake, if not Horovitz's Children of Albion then of their cousins across the Irish Sea – James Liddy's Children of Erin.

In June 1971, just after Tara Telephone issued the last 'chapter' of *The Book of Invasions*, Peter Fallon began to explore the challenge of rendering the Irish poem in less demotic forms of print by issuing Broadside I, *A Kind of Trust*, by Brendan Kennelly, an early poem that survived the cut for *The Essential Brendan Kennelly* (2011).[59] This broadside was the first in a series of Tara Telephone broadsides printed at Mary 'Paul' Pollard's St. Sepulchre's Press (1964–92). Edited by Fallon, these broadsides were set and printed by hand on a Columbian 'Eagle' press in Marsh's Library.[60] The making of these broadsides connects the start of Fallon's exploration of print craft through Pollard to Liam Miller and to the standards of handwork that Dolmen exhibited in the 1960s and that Miller attempted to reassert in his brief engagement with revival of the Cuala Press in the early 1970s. In one sense, these broadsides are as demotic as the 'chapters' of *The Book of Invasions*, for their physical format recalls the narrow ballad sheets of the early 1800s. Unlike either of those, these broadsides were not peddled on the road or hawked in Dublin's pubs. Word of mouth sold these broadsides, as it did the often satirical and scurrilous St. Sepulchre's broadsides. Producing these broadsides offered Fallon an introduction to a craft-conscious readership both aware of the 'book beautiful' and mindful of national tradition.

Pointedly devoid of FitzPatrick's 'New Age' imagery, these Tara Telephone broadsides betoken an evolution in Fallon's editorial practice toward the fixed presence of print and away from the evanescence of live performance – readings, readings with music, singing the text – linked into the unpent energies of popular music. Tara Telephone's starting purposes included giving Irish poets and poetry access to a new audience outside of university venues. As issues of *Capella* and the intervening *Book of Invasions* issued from Fallon's family home in Rathgar, enquiries and submissions both solicited and not prompted practical instruction in the pages of *Capella* and in Fallon's return correspondence. Interest in Tara Telephone Publications proved so demanding that Fallon took to including in his replies typed sheets giving the addresses of other Irish magazines, thus also asserting *Capella*'s place amid the established literary publications in Ireland.[61] In tune with the musical term *a capella*, the title of Tara Telephone's magazine suggests the poetic voice without accompanying instruments, whether bass viol or bongo drums. As issues throughout the first Dublin Festival years of 1970 and 1971, the magazine's improving print craft improved in standard ways. *Capella*'s pages came to emphasise the presentation rather than the performance of the poem. Likewise, the short span of the first Gallery books emphasises with increasing confidence the presentation of the poems and their printerly display as in a 'gallery'. The curatorial term 'gallery', of course, implies a selective rather than a populist editorial stance. Moving away from the immediacy of the workshop or open reading, Fallon sought collections from a well-practiced, but younger generation of poets than those served in the mid-1960s by Liam Miller's Dolmen Press, beginning with Brendan Kennelly.[62] With Pearse Hutchinson's *Watching the Morning Grow* (1972), Gallery Books claim their distinctive idiom in the linocut cover by Michael Kane, whose images and lettering visually define the second period of Gallery Press publishing.

REFERENCES

Acton, C., 'Poetry and Music in Liberty Hall', *Irish Times*, 8 April 1970, p.8.

Acton, C., 'Dublin Arts Festival Repeated Previous Errors', *Irish Times*, 9 April 1970, p.10.

Anonymous, 'Adelphi Cinema', www.beatlesbible.com/1963/11/07/libe-adelphi-cinema-dublin-ireland (accessed 26 July 2012).

Anonymous, 'Adelphi Cinema', www.en.wikipedia.org/wikiAdelphi_Cinema (accessed 26 July 2012).

Anonymous, 'The Rolling Stones', www.en.wikipedia.org/wiki/The_Rolling_Stone_tours (accessed 6 August 2012).

Astley, N., 'Bile, Guile, and Dangerous to Poetry (2005)', www.stanzapoetry.org (accessed 9 October 2012).

Ballin, M., *Irish Periodical Culture, 1937–1972: Genre in Ireland, Wales, and Scotland* (New York: Palgrave Macmillan, 2008).

Brown, T. and M. Longley (eds), *The Essential Brendan Kennelly: Selected Poems* (Winston-Salem, North Carolina: Wake Forest University Press, 2011).

Campbell, M., *The Cambridge Companion to Contemporary Irish Poetry* (Cambridge: Cambridge University Press, 2003).

Carr, E., 'Tara Telephone', www.irishshowbands.net/bgtaratele.html (accessed 26 July 2012).

Clyde, T., *Irish Literary Magazines: An Outline History and Descriptive Bibliography* (Dublin: Irish Academic Press, 2001).

Darcy, B., 'Dial Tara for Talent', *Musical Gazette* (May 1970), p.8. Peter Fallon/Gallery Press Archive 817, Box 176, Manuscript, Archives, and Rare Book Library, Emory University.

Decurtis, A., 'Bob Dylan as Songwriter', in K.J.H. Dettmar (ed.), *The Cambridge Companion to Bob Dylan* (Cambridge: Cambridge University Press, 2009), pp.42–54.

Dowd, M., 'The Gaelic Guerrilla', *New York Times*, 4 July 2012, p.A19.

Fallon, B., *An Age of Innocence: Irish Culture 1930–1960* (Dublin: Gill and Macmillan, 1998).

Fallon, P. and E. Carr, *The Book of Invasions*, 1 (August 1969), recto.

Fallon, P. and E. Carr, *Capella*, 2 (September 1969), p.1.

Fallon, P. and E. Carr, *The Book of Invasions*, 3 (November 1969), recto.

Fallon, P. and E. Carr, 'Editorial' and Announcements, *Capella*, 3 (December 1969), pp.1, 36.

Fallon, P., 'List of Literary Magazines', Peter Fallon/Gallery Press Archive, Box 176, File 18, Manuscript, Archives, Rare Books Library, Emory University.

Fallon, P. and E. Carr, 'Notes', in D. O'Mahony and J. McCarthy, *Answers*, Gallery Books, Number 1 (Dublin: Tara Telephone Publications, 1970), p.27.

Fallon, P. and D. O'Driscoll (eds), *The First Ten Years: Dublin Arts Festival Poetry* (Dublin: Dublin Arts Festival, 1979).

Fallon, P., 'Peter Fallon and The Gallery Press: An Interview with Peter Denman', *The Poetry Ireland Review*, 34 (Spring 1992), pp.32–7.

Fallon, P., 'Introduction', in Philip Lynott, *Songs for While I'm Away* (London: Boxtree Books, 1997), p.1.

FitzPatrick, J., 'Biographical Notes', www.jimfitzpatrick.ie/biography-2.html (accessed 18 February 2003).

Gillespie, E., 'The Funge Fun Centre', *Irish Times*, 14 July 1972, p.10.

Hodnett, G., 'Bob Dylan at the Adelphi', *Irish Times*, 6 May 1966, p.10.

Horovitz, M. (ed.), *Children of Albion: Poetry of the Underground in Britain* (Harmondsworth, UK: Penguin Books, 1969).

'International Poetry Incarnation Flyer', http://realitystudio.org./bibliographic-bunker/45th-anniversary-of-the-international-[poetry-incarnation-at-royal-albert-hall/ (accessed 12 October 2012).

Larmour, P., *Free State Architecture: Modern Movement Architecture in Ireland, 1922–1949* (Kinsale, Ireland: Gandon Editions, 2009).

Kennelly, B., 'A Kind of Trust', in T. Brown and M. Longley (eds), *The Essential Brendan Kennelly: Selected Poems* (Winston-Salem, North Carolina: Wake Forest University Press, 2011), pp47-48.

Lee, J.J., *Ireland 1912–1985: Politics and Society* (Cambridge: Cambridge University Press, 1989).

Lisker, R., 'Poetry and Literary Pubs', *Hibernia*, 24 October 1969, p.22.

Lynott, P., *Songs for While I'm Away* (London: Boxtree Books, 1997).

MacAvock, D., 'Poets Read Own Works at T.C.D', *Irish Times*, 9 April 1970, p.10.

McKenna, C., 'The Gallery Press', in Clare Hutton and Patrick Walsh (eds), *The Irish Book in English 1891–2000: The Oxford History of the Irish Book*, Vol. V (Oxford: Oxford University Press, 2011), pp.592–611.

Montague, J., *A Chosen Light* (London: MacGibbon and Kee, 1967).

Montague, J., *A New Siege: An Historical Meditation*, Poet Card 1 (Dublin: The Dolmen Press, August 1970).

Murphy, H., 'Festival's Last Poetry Reading', *Irish Times*, 6 March 1971, p.15.

Murphy, L., *Occasion of wordshed: a collection of wordisms*, Gallery Books, Number 2 (Dublin: Tara Telephone Publications, 1970).

Negus, K., *Bob Dylan* (Bloomington: Indiana University Press, 2008).

Nuttall, J., *Bomb Culture* (New York: Dell Publishing, 1970).

O'Mahony, D., *Man and his Spaceship, Earth: in the Beginning* (Dublin: School and College Services, 1976).

O'Mahony, D. and J. McCarthy, *Answers*, Gallery Books Number 1 (Dublin: Tara Telephone Publications, 1970).

Quinn, J., *The Cambridge Introduction to Modern Irish Poetry, 1800–2000* (Cambridge: Cambridge University Press, 2008).

Redshaw, T.D., '"We Done Our Best When We Were Let": James Liddy's *Arena*', *South Carolina Review*, 38, 1 (Fall 2005), pp.269–82.

Redshaw, T.D., 'Conversation with Charles Benson', Keeper, Early Modern Books, Long Library, Trinity College, Dublin, 12 March 2010.

Robinson, A., 'Musician Andrew Robinson Recalls . . .', www.taratelephone/tara/introduction.html (accessed 26 July 2012).

Shovlin, F., *The Irish Literary Periodical, 1923–1958* (Oxford: Clarendon Press, 2003).

Smyth, G., 'How Many Words Must a Man Write Down', *Irish Times*, 16 April 2011, p.B7.

Tessier, T., 'E-mail to Author', 10 August 2012.

Templeton, L., 'Publications List', www.taratelephone.com/tara/introduction.html (accessed 26 July 2012).

Tobin, F., *The Best of Decades: Ireland in the 1960s* (Dublin: Gill and Macmillan, 1984).

Vallelly, F. (ed.), '*Fleadh Cheoil*', in *The Companion to Irish Traditional Music* (Cork: Cork University Press, 1999), p.134.

Whitney, K., 'An Irish Man's Diary', *Irish Times*, 18 November 2008, p.15.

NOTES

1. I dedicate this essay to the sweet memory of the poet and polymath Dennis O'Driscoll (1954–2012), who gave me, during our many Dublin conversations, telling reminders of literary Dublin in the distant 1970s.

2. Sources like Matthew Campbell's *Cambridge Companion to Contemporary Irish Poetry* Cambridge: Cambridge University Press, (2003) or Justin Quinn's *Cambridge Introduction to Modern Irish Poetry, 1800–2000* Cambridge: Cambridge University Press, (2008) tend to scant the milieu – technical, economic, and social – in which the poets and their books reached their audiences. *The Oxford History of the Irish Book* begins to address that lack. For views of the milieu of Ireland's literary periodicals just before the 1970s, see M. Ballin, *Irish Periodical Culture, 1937–1972: Genre in Ireland, Wales, and Scotland* (New York: Palgrave Macmillan, 2008) and, especially, F. Shovlin, *The Irish Literary Periodical,1923–1958* (Oxford: Clarendon Press, 2003).

3. C. McKenna, 'The Gallery Press', in *The Oxford History of the Irish Book*, V (Oxford: The Oxford University Press, 2011), p.592.

4. J. Nuttall, *Bomb Culture* (New York: Dell Publishing, 1970), p.ix, offers several schema that pertain to Ireland in the late 1960s, among them: 'What has happened is that the pressure of restriction compelling the leftist element in the young middle class to join with the delinquent element in the young working class for the reaffirmation of life by orgy and violence'.

5. See B. Fallon, *An Age of Innocence: Irish Culture 1930–1960* (Dublin: Gill and Macmillan, 1998); J.J. Lee, *Ireland 1912–1985: Politics and Society* (Cambridge: Cambridge University Press, 1989), pp.329–410.

6. F. Tobin, *The Best of Decades: Ireland in the 1960s* (Dublin: Gill and Macmillan, 1984), pp.34–5, 138.

7. J. Montague, *A Chosen Light* (London: MacGibbon and Kee, 1967), p.60.

8. F. Vallelly (ed.), '*Fleadh Cheoil*', in *The Companion to Irish Traditional Music* (Cork: Cork University Press, 1999), p.134.

9. See Montague, *A Chosen Light*, p. 60.

10. Seating some 2,300 spectators, the Adelphi Cinema was built in 1939 on the eve of World War II. In 1970, the auditorium was divided into three viewing rooms, later four, and was demolished in 1995, though the façade was preserved. See Anonymous, 'Adelphi Cinema', www.en.wikipedia.org/wikiAdelphi_Cinema (accessed 26 July 2012). For a survey of Art Moderne architecture in Ireland, see P. Larmour, *Free State Architecture:Modern Movement Architecture in Ireland, 1922–1949* (Kinsale, Ireland: Gandon Editions, 2009).

11. J. Nuttall, *Bomb Culture*, p.136, asserts that the Beatles were 'the biggest single catalyst in this whole acceleration in the development of the subculture. They robbed the pop world of its violence, its ignorant self-righteous drabness, its inferiority complex. They robbed the protest world of its terrible self-righteous drabness, they robbed the art world of its cod-seriousness'.

12. K. Whitney, 'An Irish Man's Diary', *Irish Times*, 18 November 2008, p.15. See also Anonymous, 'Adelphi Cinema', www.beatlesbible.com/1963/11/07libe-adelphi-cinema-dublin-ireland (accessed 26 July 2012).

13. See Anonymous, 'The Rolling Stones', en.wikipedia.org/wiki/The_Rolling_Stone_1965_tours (accessed 6 August 2012).

14. T. Tessier, T. 'E-mail to Author', 10 August 2012. Tessier recalls that Dylan's repertoire included acoustic renditions of 'Don't Think Twice' and 'Blowin' in the Wind' and electric versions of 'Mr. Tambourine Man' and 'Like a Rolling Stone' backed by the Hawks, later The Band. See also, Gerry Smyth's appreciation of Dylan as poet, 'How Many Words Must a Man Write Down Before You Call him a Poet?' *Irish Times*, 16 April 2011, p.B7.

15. G. Hodnett, 'Bob Dylan at the Adelphi', *Irish Times*, 6 May 1966, p.10.

16. Ibid. G. Smyth, 'How Many Words Must a Man Write Down', p.B7, recalls that the Irish 'folkies' were well aware of Dylan's early acoustic repertoire and that he made a 'big impact' in Irish rockers with *Highway 61 Revisited* (1965) and *Bringing it all Back Home* (1965).

17. In a plain-spoken chapter on Dylan's lyrics, Keith Negus, *Bob Dylan* (Bloomington: Indiana University Press, 2008), p.99, observes that Dylan reached 'an educated, mildly bohemian, middle-class audience eager to elevate popular songs as a new poetic art'. See also A. Decurtis, 'Bob Dylan as Songwriter', in K.J.H. Dettmar (ed.), *The Cambridge Companion to Bob Dylan*, (Cambridge: Cambridge University Press, 2009), pp.42–54.

18. P. Fallon, 'Introduction', in Philip Lynott, *Songs for While I'm Away* (London: Boxtree Books, 1997), p.1.

19. This series lasted until 1979, and was followed by thirteen more volumes in the 1990s, which presented selections from three Irish poets: Eavan Boland, Matthew Sweeney, and (again) Michael Longley.

20. N. Astley, 'Bile, Guile, and Dangerous to Poetry (2005)', www.stanzapoetry.org.uk (accessed 9 October 2012).

21. In Britain, Penguin had also become the leading mass-market publisher as represented, chiefly, in the now canonical works of Raymond Williams such as *The May Day Manifesto 1968.*

22. M. Horovitz (ed.), *Children of Albion: Poetry of the Underground in Britain* (Harmondsworth, UK: Penguin Books, 1969), p. 377. *Children of Albion* answers A. Alvarez's often reprinted and now famous introduction 'Beyond the Gentility Principle', which first appeared in Penguin's *The New Poetry* (1962).

23. Vosnesensky and Neruda did not appear, though they were listed on the mimeographed flyer describing the program, http://realitystudio.org./bibligraphic-bunker/45th-anniversary-of-the-international-poetry-incarnation-at-royal-albert-hall/ (accessed 12 October 2012).

24. M. Horovitz (ed.), *Children of Albion,* pp.325, 327. Among the other readers were William S. Burroughs (on tape), Lawrence Ferlinghetti, Anselm Hollo, Adrian Mitchel, George MacBeth, and Tom McGrath.

25. The turn of the decade – 1969 through 1971 – saw the start of many arts festivals in the Republic, among them:the Wexford Festival of Living Music, the Gorey Arts Festival, the People's Festival for a Socialist Ireland (at the Project Arts center, itself founded in 1967). Other events – like the Human Rights Day Concert against Apartheid (1971) and the well-published international arts show ROSC '71 – also display the period's energy, confidence, and purpose.

26. C. Acton, 'Dublin Arts Festival Repeated Previous Errors', *Irish Times,* 11 March 1971, p.10.

27. D. MacAvock, 'Poets Read Own Works at T.C.D.' *Irish Times,* 9 April 1970, p.10. MacAvock noted that Brendan Kennelly read 'a poem born of his experiences as Junior Dean of [Trinity College] faced with a group of fashionable protesters, all loud of voice and phrase'.

28. H. Murphy, 'Festival's Last Poetry Reading', *Irish Times,* 6 March 1971, p.15.

29. FitzPatrick's extensive web site offers examples of his work over the decades as well as useful biographical notes. See www.jimfitzpatrick.ie/biography-2.html (accessed 18 February 2003).

30. FitzPatrick's image of Guevara is the iconic poster recalled by J. Nuttall in his preface to *Bomb Culture:* 'It is the violence of Che Guevara, his life, his rapacious good looks,

his fabulous death, which constitute his appeal. Nobody decorates a bed-sitter with posters of Bolivian Miners' (p.ix). See also M. Dowd, 'The Gaelic Guerrilla', *New York Times*, 4 July 2012, p.A19.

31. See FitzPatrick's rendering of the *Lebor Gabála Érenn*, www.jimfitzpatrick.ie/biography-2.html (accessed 18 February 2003), which could absorb darts of political commentary, as in the star warrior's orders on the cover of *Capella* 3 referring to 'C.I.A. Labour Camps. Irlandia Nord 2'.

32. Measuring 29.2 x 21 cm., this graphic is printed in black on vanilla paper and is dated January, 1970. Tara Telephone offered two 76 x 51 cm. 'poem-posters' designed by FitzPatrick at Two Bare Feet: 'No Exit', a poem by Peter Fallon printed in silver and black and 'A Tale of Love', a poem by Eamon Carr, printed in day-glo pink and silver. Both were screen printed in editions of fifty. *Hibernia* reproduced the latter in February 1969, above a note describing Tara Telephone in advance of a 'recital' in Liberty Hall. Peter Fallon/Gallery Press Archive 817, Box 176, Manuscript, Archives and Rare Book Library, Emory University. See also L. Templeton's Tara Telephone publications list at www.taratelephone.com/tara/introduction.html (accessed 26 July 2012).

33. P. Fallon and D. O'Driscoll (eds), *The First Ten Years: Dublin Arts Festival Poetry* (Dublin: Dublin Arts Festival, 1979), p.9.

34. Ibid., p.7.

35. Ibid.

36. Andrew Robinson, 'Andrew Robinson Recalls . . . ', www.taratelephone/tara/introduction.html (accessed 26 July 2012).

37. Andrew Robinson only partially quotes this lyric in his recollections. See Ibid.

38. B. Darcy, 'Dial Tara for Talent', *Musical Gazette* (May 1970), p.8, Peter Fallon/Gallery Press Archive 817, Box 176, Manuscript, Archives, and Rare Book Library, Emory University.

39. E. Carr, 'Tara Telephone', www.irishshowbands.net/bgtaratele.html, accessed 26 July 2012.

40. C. Acton, 'Poetry and Music in Liberty Hall', *Irish Times*, 8 April 1970, p.8.

41. E. Carr, 'Tara Telephone', www.irishshowbands.net/bgtaratele.html (accessed 26 July 2012).

42. P. Fallon, 'Peter Fallon and the Gallery Press: An Interview with Peter Denman', *The Poetry Ireland Review*, 34 (Spring 1992), p.33.

43. P. Fallon and E. Carr, 'Notes', in Des O'Mahony and Justin McCarthy, *Answers*, Gallery Books, Number 1 (Dublin: Tara Telephone Publications, 1970), p.27.

44. P. Fallon, 'Peter Fallon and the Gallery Press: An Interview with Peter Denman', p.32.

45. R. Lisker, 'Poetry and Literary Pubs', *Hibernia*, 24 October 1969, p.22. 'The Whiskey House' in South King Street, Sinnott's, placed newspaper advertisements about the readings: 'Poetry Reading Every Thursday'.

46. Numbered consecutively, these were printed at the Dolmen Press works in North Richmond Street, and were published for the poetry workshop at University College, Dublin, in editions of one thousand copies. Gerard Fanning revived *Broadsheet* for two issues dated 1975 and 1977.

47. T. Clyde, *Irish Literary Magazines: An Outline History and Descriptive Bibliography* (Dublin: Irish Academic Press, 2001), p.249.

48. Murphy's editorial policy favoured writers connected to Pearse Hutchinson and Eileán Ní Chuilleanáin who, with Macdara Woods, founded the long-running poetry magazine *Cyphers* in 1975. See Ibid., pp.249–50, 273–4.

49. See T.D. Redshaw, "'We Done Our Best When We Were Let": James Liddy's *Arena*', *South Carolina Review*, 38, 1 (Fall, 2005), pp.269–82. On the Gorey Arts Festival, see E. Gillespie, 'The Funge Fun Centre', *Irish Times*, 14 July 1972, p.10. The art center in Gorey was the creation of the painter Paul Funge (1944–2011), whose brother Patrick ran the Elo Press and, with Liam Miller, the Lantern Theatre on Merrion Square.

50. Liam Miller tried a related form with John Montague's *A New Siege: an Historical Meditation*, Poet Card 1 (Dublin: The Dolmen Press, August 1970). While this format failed in the shops, Montague's poem successfully exemplified a number of traits delineated in Michael Horovitz's introduction to *Children of Albion* (1969).

51. P. Fallon and E. Carr, *The Book of Invasions*, 1 (August 1969), recto.

52. P. Fallon and E. Carr, *The Book of Invasions*, 3 (November 1969), recto.

53. P. Fallon and E. Carr, *Capella,* 2 (September 1969), p.1.

54. Ibid.

55. P. Fallon and E. Carr, 'Editorial' and Announcements, *Capella,* 3 (December 1969), pp.1, 36.

56. See Fallon, P. and E. Carr, 'Notes', in D. O'Mahony and J. McCarthy, *Answers*, Gallery Books, Number 1 (Dublin: Tara Telephone Publications, 1970), p.27. D. O'Mahony later published *Man and his Spaceship, Earth: in the Beginning* (Dublin: School and College Services, 1976).

57. L. Murphy, *Occasion of wordshed: a collection of wordisms*, Gallery Books, Number 2 (Dublin: Tara Telephone Publications, 1970).

58. Still based in Waterford City, Liam Murphy remains active as a poet and storyteller under the aegis of Cuala Verbal Art.

59. 'A Kind of Trust', in T. Brown and M. Longley (eds), *The Essential Brendan Kennelly: Selected Poems* (Winston-Salem, North Carolina: Wake Forest University Press, 2011), pp.47–48.

60. Of American manufacture, this press came from Browne and Nolan's Richview Press in Clonskea and was set up in the basement of Marsh's Library in January 1964. The Library School, University College Dublin, bought the press in February 1984. See T.D. Redshaw, 'Conversation with Charles Benson', Keeper, Early Modern Books, Long Library, Trinity College, Dublin, 12 March 2010.

61. P. Fallon, 'List of Literary Magazines', Peter Fallon/Gallery Press Archive, Box 176, File 18, Manuscript, Archives, Rare Books Library, Emory University.

62. Like Eavan Boland, with *New Territory* (1967), Kennelly's *Collection One / Getting up Early* (1966) and *Good Souls to Survive* (1967) was published by Allen Figgis; neither was ever published by Liam Miller at Dolmen.

Gallery at the Abbey:

An Introduction to the
40th Anniversary Reading

SEAMUS HEANEY

John Keats once called a poem 'a little region to wander in', so when I consulted the *Shorter OED* to check out 'gallery', I was glad to find that Keats's definition was echoed in the first of the eleven entries provided. The primary meaning for 'gallery' is given as 'a covered space for walking in'. Then there follow several variations and extensions of this, such as 'a projecting platform', and in a theatre, 'the highest of such platforms', or indeed 'the occupants of the gallery portion, or the gods'.

Here, of course, in this recently refurbished Abbey Theatre, there is no such high platform, but the place is still not without its gods – household gods, that is – and tonight it is hard not to think of them, hard not to imagine W.B. Yeats and Lady Gregory and John Millington Synge looking down on this celebration by Irish poets of their Irish publisher, and feeling a renewed faith in the epoch-making literary movement they established just over a hundred years ago.

'A man ... innocently dabbles in words and rhymes and finds that it is his life'. So wrote Patrick Kavanagh in a famous sentence that is as true to the experience of Peter Fallon the publisher as it is true of him as a practicing poet. For Peter found his way to crediting publishing by crediting poetry, crediting the poetry of others as much as his own, and in his introduction to this evening's souvenir booklet he provides a moving statement of trust in those twin callings. Essentially he reveals the link between the growth of his poet's mind and the responsibilities as well as the rewards of keeping going as a publisher. Care, company, community have been fundamental concerns of Peter's writing in and about the world: care for people and place, for planet earth and the poetry of earth, for the values espoused by Virgil in the *Georgics* which he has translated, values kept alive in our time by the eco-poetry of contemporaries like Gary Snyder and Wendell Berry whom he reveres. And the seriousness of that caretaking has developed over the years to a point where the artistic and the moral have converged. The second paragraph of the introduction to the souvenir booklet where he speaks about the origins of The Gallery Press has the clarity and conviction of truthful personal witness. Referring to the celebration of the house's twenty-fifth anniversary, he reasons:

> Fifteen years ago I wrote that it began in innocence. Part of that innocence, perhaps, was a perception that there was something escapist about the arts. Bohemian 'values' still lingered. There was a sense that the arts were an addendum to 'ordinary' life, a luxury parallel to quotidian acts and thinking. But . . . the fractures in society and the world were less grievous [then] than now.

From this, it is clear that Peter Fallon understands the function of the arts in society in much the same way as it was once understood by the Czech poet, Miroslav Holub. For Holub the function of the arts in the body politic – and the function of theatre in particular – was analogous to the function of the immune system in the human body: the arts, like the system, worked for good. Even though they might not be fit to conquer the noxious elements, they were a force that fortified resistance to them. And our poet-publisher has continued to operate on the basis of a similar conviction, one that is bound to have been strengthened by the presence on his list of playwrights of such imaginative faith and artistic resource as Marina Carr, Brian Friel, Tom Kilroy, Frank McGuinness, and Jim Nolan. And that same conviction, imaginative faith, and artistic resource will be evident in the work of the poets who read here this evening.

The work of those poets, individually and collectively, prompts me to quote a couple more of those *OED* definitions. The first is of a gallery as 'a space for the exhibition of works of art', which meaning applies most obviously to Gallery as the home-based publisher of works of Irish poetic art over the past four decades, although it applies also to the important place the Press holds in our national life – holds because it has consistently earned it. But there are older, more arcane meanings that fit the work done by our poet and his house: these constitute entry number 8 in that same *OED*. There I found the following intriguing meanings for a gallery: 'a passage made by deer etc. through brushwood; also a passage made by an animal underground'. These senses of the word and others relating to underground mine shafts are also powerfully suggestive. They remind us of the way poetry can wear out secret channels for itself and operate below the surface of consciousness in an individual and ultimately in a society; they remind us indeed of something the poet Eugenio Montale once referred to as 'the second life of art', art's 'obscure pilgrimage' as he called it, 'through conscience and memory . . . its entire flowing back into the very life from which it took its first nourishment'. Or to put it as Peter does, art and artists are situated and negotiate between the mundane and the mysterious.

The poets on the Gallery list are indispensable to the art of poetry as an ongoing endeavour in Ireland; indispensable to the honour in which that art is held at home and to the honour which it earns for us abroad. Obviously there are other constellations and fixed stars in our poetic firmament besides those published by this Press, but we can grant that easily and thankfully, yet still go on to say – without sounding either exaggerated or sycophantic – that the people who will read here this evening have extended and enhanced a tradition that goes back a millennium, and then another half millennium, back to that moment when Irish poetry becomes part of the written record. Already at that point we find poems and poets doing what lyric poems and poets continue to do to this day, which is to take snapshots of the individual consciousness and thereby provide an intimate swift glimpse of the spiritual and cultural state of their place and times.

It has been my privilege for the best part of a lifetime to have enjoyed the friendship of Peter and Jean and their family, Adam and Alice. Ever since a certain December day in 1971 when Peter arrived on our doorstep in Belfast, carrying a limited edition of poetry broadsides that had to be signed, Marie and I have watched with admiration and gratitude as he got started and then kept going, first on his own and eventually with Jean, as partners and publishers, undaunted and devoted. So it has been a special pleasure to introduce this formal and timely celebration of them and their work in the national theatre, in the certain knowledge that they will be back on the job tomorrow morning, getting started all over again, making their presence felt in the lives of our poets and playwrights and us, their lucky audience.

So I can think of no better way to get this show on the road than to quote the second-to-the-last paragraph of Peter's introduction to the souvenir booklet where he says of the Press:

> We uphold twin imperatives – to keep the art of poetry (and its relationship with its audience) alive and in good health, and to celebrate it because its tradition is essential to our culture, and because, by participating in it, we may refine our capacities to think and feel. We may, in short, learn to think and feel better. We may thereby improve our chances of fulfilling ourselves individually and collectively as a human, decent, kind society.

And that, ladies and gentlemen, says all that needs to be said.

7 June 2010

Peter Fallon Revisited

DENNIS O'DRISCOLL

Peter Fallon was my first poet – the first I met, the first I heard read poems in public. When I moved to Dublin in 1970, unlettered in the ways of the poetry world, Peter (born in 1951, barely three years my elder) was already well on his way to becoming a man of letters. Ringleader of every worthwhile poetry plot, he was rejuvenating and regenerating the art, dusting it off, stirring it up with the whirlwind stamina of a young Yeats or Pound. His dashing dress code and exuberant spillage of ink-black hair lent him an aura that was as dandyish as it was hippyish, as mystical as it was modish. I was aware that he had a musical side, with prominent rock group affiliations; but my congenital deaf spot for rock music left me ignorant of that dimension of Peter's life. To me, he was primarily a poet, irrespective of any alterative persona – Trinity College student, arts impresario, band associate – he might present to the world. And he remains for me what then he was. Poet first and foremost. Editor. Man on a sacred mission: passionate, driven, resolute.

Peter's energising omnipresence lit a neon torch for a generation that had had its fill of staidness and – appetite freshly whetted by *Lunch Poems* and *Howl*, by the Beat school and the Liverpool Poets – was hungry for an Irish poetry with more pizzazz, more jizz, more jazz, one likelier to appeal to the metalhead music fan than the egghead academic. As performer, festival organiser, magazine editor and book publisher, he expanded Ireland's poetry constituency, making the art accessible to an audience that had felt excluded from this 'elitist' pursuit. His Tara Telephone readings in 1970 were credited by the *Evening Herald* newspaper with bringing poetry 'to the people – where it belongs'.[1]

In about 1974, I was purportedly the warm-up reader for Peter in a Lantern Theatre reading, but I merely chilled the audience with my then-ghoulish poems. It was left to Peter to clear away my cadavers, thaw out our listeners, and skillfully pilot them towards the more congenial climes of his far warmer, far more proficient poems. Around that time also, he and Daniel Reardon allowed me to host a lunchtime reading of their work in University College. Their fee – whatever voluntary pennies were tossed in the circulated mortar board by the penurious student audience – would scarcely have covered the cost of a Guinness fill-up in the campus bar, much less a fill-up for Peter's Guinness-black Morris Minor.

For all his associations with pop poetry and Beat poetry, Peter was independent of poetry schools and groups, camps and campuses. 'Trendy' though the young man may have seemed, in the John Lennonist mode, the young poet was fashioned in the John Clare mode (minus the madness), setting out on a lone rural journey that steered clear of trends and fads. His poems were neither flared nor tie-dyed. 'Solitary' is the final word in his accomplished first collection, *Among the Walls* (1971), and the book as a whole – containing poems written for the page rather than performance, and devoid of the twee side of Sixties verse – is the work of a poet seriously committed to his art. The same may be said of *Co-Incidence of Flesh* (1972).

That his dedication had yielded early dividends was evident by the time his third collection, *The First Affair* (1974), appeared, its taut, well-crafted poems flourishing both in performance and in print. Peter's plangent readings of poems like 'If She's Your Lover Now', redolent of young love and perennial pain, linger in the memories of his audiences: the mood music of a generation. In 'Shillings', another retrospect on lost love, he coined three priceless lines that bring 'the time and the place and the loved one together', recreating – in about twenty thrifty words – a bygone phase of twentieth-century Irish life: 'My pockets are full of shillings. // I used save them for the meter in your flat; / Such habits are not easily broken.'[2]

Part II of the collection saw the poet mapping out his future path: changing poetical and personal direction, setting his watch to rural time. The development in his work, over so short a period, was as startling as it was impressive. Still only twenty-three, he had found his true voice and his true subject matter had found him, commandeering that voice for poems that have every claim to inclusion in any collected edition of his work. The verse is more disciplined formally; the sonnet, 'A Hungry Eye', could slip unnoticed into his later collections, so fully does it anticipate some of the distinct features of his mature work: the affectionate and sympathetic depiction of neighbours, the acknowledgment of their hardships, the incorporation of demotic speech ('I mind the time we'd snows in May') and proper names ('Joe Lynch').[3]

Fallon's life-changing decision, in the 1980s, to transplant The Gallery Press (which he started 'in innocence' in 1970) from suburban Rathgar in Dublin to rural County Meath was an audacious one – although he had personal ties with Meath, having spent portions of his childhood on the Lennoxbrook farm of his uncle, Peter Mullan. Finding his place there, he is happy to explore, if not explain, local lore and legend. Like Brendan Kennelly ('Proof is what I do not need')[4], an early signing to the Gallery Press list, Fallon believes that 'The man is wise who'll not ask why, / who'll not explain'.[5] He can be simultaneously respectful and ironical towards folk cures:

> my mother would cross
> a sty in your eye
>
> and if that didn't cure it
> it wasn't a sty.[6]

'Mole', one of the pair of Fallon poems selected by Seamus Heaney for his anthology of emerging poets, *Soundings 2* (1974), heralds the splendid imagist to come: 'Thalidomide, earth-seal / of muscle, tail a teat / and nose the sound of stone . . . .'[7] It is among the poems which resurface – some with revisions – in *The Speaking Stones* (1978). One senses that Fallon regards that fourth collection, assured in idiom and secure in locale, as a fresh beginning, his Opus 1. While this implies a harsh judgement on the earlier collections, sidelining them as apprentice work, the discernment is consistent with Fallon's editorial scrupulousness at The Gallery Press; he is doing unto himself as he does unto others. Residence in a Loughcrew landscape of passage graves, many millennia old, has heightened his sense of what 'time' means in that 'test of time' to which all poetry is ineluctably subjected. The rhythm must be right, the structure watertight, the evocation exact, the metaphor striking, the emotion true.

The leap from *The First Affair* to this Opus 1 is undoubtedly a giant one, and the splash made by the collection was appropriately large. *The Speaking Stones* inaugurates the chronicling of community life – its dramas, traumas, customs, challenges and manifold pleasures – that Fallon will set about in earnest in later collections. The faintly discernible influence on *The Speaking Stones* of Paul Muldoon's work is a reminder that Fallon, Muldoon's exact contemporary, was an ardent champion of the Ulster poet's work before it became widely read and admired. Fallon's egg-blowing 'One' –

> I take a thorn and pierce each end,
> blow
> the yolk on the ground like a petal of gorse,
> spilt gold,
> and hold a bubble of bone[8]

– may be read as a companion piece to Muldoon's 'Blowing Eggs', which features such lines as these:

> This is the breathless and the intent
>
> Puncturing of the waste
> And isolate egg and this the clean delivery
> of little yolk and albumen.[9]

The prevailing contemporary exemplar for both poets was Seamus Heaney. Muldoon's first collection, *New Weather* (1973), and Fallon's *Speaking Stones* both include a poem entitled 'Hedgehog', but, for all the outsiderism the prickly creature embodies in each, they are breeds apart: Fallon's mammal is a physical creature, Muldoon's a metaphysical one.

The pivotal influences on Fallon at this time are communitarian more than poetical, and stem from his growing appreciation of the familiar and familial, of cherishing the local in an increasingly globalised world. When the distinguished publisher Liam Miller moved his Dolmen Press office from Dublin to Mountrath, County Laois, he was simply realising his dream of decentralising his work to his home town. No doubt Miller in Laois and Fallon in Meath were glad to have escaped their daily eye-contact and street-corner contact with would-be authors, not to mention the post-rejection antagonism of the same species. But, apart from the practical benefits a tranquil and isolated poetry place and publishing base would confer ('It's doubtful that Gallery could have survived if it were based in Dublin'),[10] Fallon's agenda entailed deeper aspirations: 'some credible version of a life, and some exciting and memorable expression of that version'.[11] Such a life would be marked by responsible husbandry of land, neighbourly cooperation, dedication to the art and craft of poetry, and – as editor and publisher – high editorial and production values. His ultimate hope is that both his smallholding and the art of poetry will be the better for his endeavours: 'The work and the life at the end of the day both add up to some kind of love affair with a particular place'.[12]

Apropos of Fallon in the early Seventies, Seamus Heaney wrote, 'In photographs from that time, he looks a bit like John Lennon, but nowadays he is more likely to remind you of a Berry (Wendell) than a Beatle.'[13] As two poets with practical farming expertise, unafraid to get their writing hands dirty – even dungy – or to lend them to cow-milking as well as lyric-making, there is a natural affinity between the Meath writer and his Kentucky elder. Both poets embrace what Wendell Berry terms 'the community speech, unconsciously taught and learned, in which words live in the presence of their objects'.[14] Berry, looking back to a pre-war rural community in Kentucky, noted that 'It supported itself, amused itself, consoled itself, and passed its knowledge on to the young. It was something to build on'.[15] Many forces – economic, environmental and technological – unravelled such tight-knit communities. Yet, by contributing meaningfully to their respective hinterlands through their physical and literary labours, Fallon and Berry trust that some stable community life may still prove salvageable from the flotsam of 'liquid modernity'. In a 1983 interview with Ciaran Carty, Fallon spoke anxiously of the pressures which now beset communities, and the wasted, damaged lives that result:

> There's been a breakdown in the individual and a breakdown in
> the community. There's this sense of people coming apart and not
> knowing their place anymore, and not knowing where they fit into
> the scheme of things; a sense of not having a relationship to a way
> of life and not having anything to be responsible for, of people
> wanting to care, but having nothing to care about.[16]

In the same interview, he lamented that 'agriculture is changing from being an art to a science. It's turning into just another business . . . It's one of the biggest problems of modern life. We're caught between traditional values and unlimited technology'. Expressing further sentiments to which every Berry-like bosom will return an echo, he concluded, 'My life now is an attempt to go back to my native ground and to hold it'. One way of holding his native ground, of acquiring freehold tenure there, is through his art; he shows the non-metropolitan milieu to be a viable source of twenty-first century poetry, one as pertinent to global village life as to local village life:

> When I looked
> at the mountain
> long enough
> I grew to know
> all manner
> of mountains.[17]

The jacket note on his dramatised version of *Tarry Flynn*, Patrick Kavanagh's autobiographical novel, points to Fallon's 'special intimacy with the world that Patrick Kavanagh's novel delineates'.[18] Ironically, Fallon co-dedicates the play to his uncle and namesake Peter, who initiated him in the mysteries of Meath farm life, whereas in *Tarry Flynn* itself, it is an uncle Peter ('Petey') who prompts Tarry (Patrick Kavanagh in all but name) to abandon his small farm and settle in the city. "'Living in the country", the uncle insists, "is a hard old station. Crooked lanes and little lumpy hills".'[19] Patrick Kavanagh would, in time, reduce Dublin to negotiable village proportions by habitually patrolling the little shops and crooked lanes around whatever lumpy Ballsbridge flat he called 'home'. Fallon, having reversed Kavanagh's hegira from country to city, has no intention of renouncing his backroads and drumlins:

> . . . All I approve persists,
> is here, at home. I think it exquisite
> to stand in the yard, my feet on the ground,
> in cowshit and horseshit and sheepshit.[20]

As this poem ('Winter Work') makes clear, Fallon celebrates his way of life, never pretending to eke out subsistence with the hardscrabble graft of a pioneer. Yet, crucial to the success of Fallon's celebratory style is his refusal to romanticise or sentimentalise farming life. If he does not play up its hardships, neither does he downplay them. Some of his best poems contain graphic depictions of physical work – dipping sheep, performing a caesarean on a ewe, spraying potatoes, saving hay, harvesting grain, foddering cattle ('He is stuck in the mud of four weeks' rain / backing a tractor through a gap').[21] Although ever-tender towards his 'care', he leaves the reader under no illusion about the crueller side of farm life. Lambing time is 'the positive season'; nonetheless, 'loss is expected, / a part of the whole, / the breeches, abortions / accepted . . . '.[22]

The light and humorous touch evident in 'Winter Work' is even more pronounced in the poems where, with a poet's relish, he draws on the colourful words, cunning wisecracks and droll locutions that distinguish and enliven rural speech: the banter of drinking pals, the repartee of neighbours, the earthy ripostes of those who toil and till. These locutions animate his collections – from *The First Affair* in 1974 ('A hungry eye sees far')[23] to *The Company of Horses* in 2007 ('Nearly never bulled a cow')[24]: 'a cut above buttermilk'[25]; he'd take 'the milk from your tea'[26]; 'He ate the pattern off her plate'[27]; 'the wind that peeled potatoes in New York'[28]; 'There's men dying now never died before'[29]; 'A hasky wind. / A hoor . . . .'.[30] In certain instances, entire poems ('Confederates', 'The Late Country') are dramatised with that flair for characterisation and timing he demonstrated in his stage adaptation of *Tarry Flynn*. His re-creation, in 'The Late Country', of a *Garda* raid on a huddle of after-hours drinkers would make for an hilarious stage scene:

> They started
> asking things they knew already,
> 'Name?'
>
> and noted men muttering in Irish
> and forgetting their addresses,
> observed the clumsy pantomime
> of men with drink taken standing
> straight upright, blinded by the light.
> 'Have you any idea of the time?'
>
> 'I suppose it's late.'
> And the guard we knew loomed
> in battle dress beside us like the Prince
> of Darkness. 'I'm surprised at you.
> I thought you knew better . . . ' 'You're
> surprised? Sure I thought I left ages since'.[31]

Only someone who is an outsider as well as insider, someone capable of artistic detachment and attentiveness, could reproduce so vividly what the rest of this drinking fraternity would take for granted. As Patrick Kavanagh, speaking from long experience, noted, 'A poet is never one of the people. He is detached, remote, and the life of small-time dances and talk about football would not be for him. He might take part but could not belong.'[32] Fallon himself acknowledges the inevitable gap between him and his neighbours when he writes, regarding his bilingual life in Co Meath:

> I re-learned, or remembered, the language which surrounded me when I was a boy. I knew again a vocabulary and idiom belonging to the way of life in a local community. But by this time I had been schooled in another language – of literature and the academy. On the one hand, there was a language that I had inherited or absorbed, that I simply *knew*. On the other there was one I'd been attracted to, and studied.[33]

In mediating a harmonious 'mixed marriage' between two disparate registers of language – one highborn, the other of more humble birth – Fallon displays true artistic mettle:

> It's true I chose another course, talk
> in small communities, a hope to sway
> by carry-on people I understand
> and love. I came on a place and had to stay
>
> that I might find my feet, repair
> the mark of human hand, and repossess
> a corner of my country.[34]

His poems revealing the darker side of local life – shootings, incest, a dumped baby – exacted a heavy price, jeopardising his faith in community solidarity by separating him more rancorously from neighbours than two-tier language ever would. In courageously discharging the poet's time-honoured truth-telling role, and refusing to yield to self-censorship, Fallon was abruptly reminded of how readily small communities will close ranks, huddle within their narrow horizons, and collude in conspiracies of silence. His comments regarding the hostile reception meted out to some of the poems in *The News and Weather* (1987) bespeak the severe challenges presented to a poet-in-permanent-residence in a rural area – how unflinching his gaze must be, how steady his nerve, how unassailable his integrity, how immense his fortitude and forbearance:

> They didn't object to the treatment. They just didn't want anything at all written about what had happened. There could be talk about things like that in another parish, but not in their own. But I think these things should be told. . . I'm not certain that telling these truths leads to better things or heals anything, although I have hopes that it may. I am, however, certain that *not* telling them doesn't. . . For twelve years, all my energies had been devoted to a community and to a celebration of that community. It was my place and the place of my poems. That's why the reaction was so disturbing and horrifying. I began to have doubts about the whole project.[35]

In the poem, 'If Luck Were Corn', a man – nauseated by gossip about a girl who consigned her dead baby to a lake – scolds his neighbours: 'if you drained the ponds / in your back yards / you'd find more than you bargained for'.[36] Happily, Fallon's more supportive neighbours and the approbation of strangers allayed his doubts, restored his poetic morale and 'validated the work'.[37] Five years after *The News and the Weather*, a new collection, *Eye to Eye* (1992), contained some of his finest poetry.

'A Woman of the Fields', with which *Eye to Eye* opens, is an invocation of woman as lover, muse and fertility goddess. Fallon's God-like Patrick Kavanagh in the sonnet 'God in Woman' is feminine; Fallon writes unaffectedly, and with disarming directness, 'I love my children / and my wife'.[38] The 'Hail Mary' prayer is among his favourite texts: 'The words are lovely in their pure praise of a woman, a mother – maybe all women – and the phrase which has always delighted me, that is "the fruit of thy womb", for an offspring, a welcomed child, has again and again been submerged in the interminable decades of a million galloping rosaries'.[39]

Eye to Eye closes on a heart-rending note. 'A Part of Ourselves' is a sensitively-judged sequence on the death of the baby son born to the poet and his wife, Jean. Meticulously fashioned, this harrowing poem features the two of them, who

broached the sorrow hoard
of women, tales unmentioned in their marriages,
unsaid to friends, to families.
Fellow feeling loosed their tongues
about unwanted pregnancies, abortions, miscarriages. . .[40]

Violence against women, physical and psychological, appalls this poet, who himself 'grew up in the care of loving women'.[41]

'The Wife' is a blunt, pithy, devastating portrait of a loyal wife who is so belittled by her boorish husband ('she the shadow, he the sun—')[42] and his circle as to be denied even the dignity of her name. More distressing still is 'The Woman of the House'; the violence and violation here are physical, and it is the abused woman herself who haltingly, but poignantly, narrates the poem, observing, 'Sometimes I'd wish I was for death'.[43]

Fallon's irenic impulses extend beyond his own community in Meath to the wider Irish community; terrorist violence dismays him no less than domestic violence. So we find him expressing 'care' not alone for his family and his flocks but – especially when the Ulster 'Troubles' raged at their vicious worst – for his country: '"How's all your care?" I'm asked. / "Grand. And yours?" I don't repeat / my worry for my care, my country'.[44] This public aspect of his work has been downplayed not only by critics but also by the poet himself, who excluded two of his most public poems – 'A Handful of Air' and 'The State of the Nation', one phantasmagoric, the other fierce – from *News of the World* (1998), his 'Selected and New Poems'. For all its stanzaic formality, 'The State of the Nation' can barely contain the poet's anger, as he dishes out invective with uncharacteristic but condign virulence and a scathing irony that borders on sarcasm. Rhyming '*An Phoblacht*' (the title of Sinn Féin's pro-IRA newspaper) with 'fucked' ('If their day comes / the country's fucked'), he also cunningly glosses the Provisional IRA catchcry, '*Tiocfaidh ár lá*' ('Our day will come').[45] Fallon is scornful of 'blather about Ireland' – in particular the hints, nudges, winks of those who lay claim to paramilitary heroism:

They're mad

in the head, brave boys

in the dark, bright sparks
and the blind eye turned.
Draw them out; all they'll say
is, 'Pass no remarks'.

It'd make you spit blood.
If they so much
as shook your hand
you'd have to count your fingers,
limp men leaning on the crutch

of a crippled history.[46]

One bragger about 'all he'd suffered for the Cause, / the blows for Ireland, burning haybarns / and big houses' is brought down to earth by his dismissive sister: "You're great, she'd say, just great, / you'd free the nation late at night / but couldn't clear a downpipe in the light / of day".[47]

    Fallon's own patriotism is literally a love of the land. Builders of a nation, not its wreckers, earn his admiration; his roll of honour includes those ('their sovereign thought was Ireland') who 'fought the Black and Tans / and wintered in damp ditches' in the early twentieth century: 'Without their kind there'd not be / a Republic'.[48] His disillusionment at how that Republic has betrayed its hard-won inheritance is encapsulated in his 1994 poem, 'St Oliver's':

I think of our children, those girls at the cross,
    and entreat a just inheritance:
information, kindness, a chance,
    and then a second chance;

I dream an innocent end to the commonness
    of double talk and single think,
reprisals, revenge,
    the nod and the wink
of parish pump politics–
    jobs for the boys, Euro junkets . . . .[49]

Ultimately, Fallon's 'care' is for the planet as a whole. Without spelling out the ecological tenets that underwrite how he lives, he is heedful of the fact that 'right livelihood' at home will benefit the rest of the globe. What occurs in one location today will impact on other places tomorrow – or the day after:

> Nearly two days after
> the tsunami
>
> an extra ripple where
> the river bumps into the sea.[50]

That pithy message is peeled from his sheaf of *Ballynahinch Postcards,* in which transitory glimpses are rendered permanent through memorably atmospheric and imagistic writing. The West of Ireland is captured in the manner of an Oriental nature poet: 'a passing cloud / bestows / the curtsy of the moon'[51]; trees are 'inclined to the East – / with their prayer mats / of fallen leaves'.[52] Fallon's imagistic gifts are not unexpected in a poet whose appreciation of Irish painting is reflected in his catalogue notes for exhibitions, collaborations with artists, and reproductions of modern Irish art works on Gallery's elegant book covers. The visual appeal of his poetry can be further illustrated by his 'soft stampede'[53] of snow, the combine harvester as a Mississippi paddle boat, the 'brindle bodice'[54] of a hen pheasant, the old man in whose hair 'The spiders of age / have woven grey webs'[55], or this haiku-like gem from 'The Deerfield Series: Strength of Heart': 'Shadows cross / the road; / a row of birches: / barcode'.[56] We savour a waterside view of the 'slow-motion' crane as he revs up for take-off:

> Now he unfolds
> the parcel of himself
> and starts to gather up
>
> the vast contraption of his wings
> and crank himself
> aloft.[57]

'What most poets mean, when they say they're interested in poetry', Peter has attested, 'is that they're interested in their own – or possibly their friends' – poetry'.[58]

One sometimes fears that Peter possesses a rarer, more generous tendency: that of taking so much interest in the poetry of others – devoting so much time and thought, as publisher and editor, to their work – that he may neglect his own. Reassuringly, however, inspiration continues to flow from some deep subterranean source in the midnight oil wells of megalithic Meath, and is refined – who knows when, in his phenomenally busy life? – into high-octane poetry. His translation of *The Georgics* of Virgil was a major achievement also, one reaping the harvest of hands-on experience and – across the great landmass of millennia – timeless empathy.

Millennia ago too, Tara in County Meath was regarded as the centre of Ireland – physically, politically, royally – as Peter Fallon and The Gallery Press are now at the poetical centre of Ireland. Through precept and practice, he has raised the bar of Irish poetry – a poetry that is enjoying an unprecedented level of international attention and acclaim. Such is the extent of Peter's contribution that he is ensured a permanent place in the country's literature and literary history. As Basil Bunting wrote of Ezra Pound's *Cantos*, 'There are the Alps . . . // you will have to go a long way round / if you want to avoid them.'[59]

The abiding note of Peter's work is the celebratory one: 'Celebrate a place for them, / the wildflowers.'[60]; 'I love my life'[61]; '[We] give thanks for our friends, / our children, the good meat'[62]; 'I have loved my term / on earth'[63]; 'Here, where I've been happy / and in my element.'[64] To cite the jacket text of *The Company of Horses*, his 'life-affirming lyrics' celebrate 'the blessings of the whole green force of nature': 'There are hymns to family and friends, to the majesty of trees and other living creatures.' His Gallery Press work, too, has been undertaken (in vital, steadfast partnership with Jean) in the most salutary possible spirit: 'From the beginning, the impulse was praise, and it still is. My understanding of publishing is praising.'[65] 'A Brighter Blue' reverses W.H. Auden's 'Funeral Blues' with its opening admonition to 'Stop all the clocks . . . '[66]:

> Turn up the sun!
> And put the leaves back
> on the trees.
> Let river reins hang slack.

> Wash the sky
> a brighter blue.
> Give back to swans
> their downy retinue.[67]

Intermittent though our meetings necessarily are now, living in different parts of the country as we do, Peter and I always resume where we last left off, adding a further gleaming link to our lifelong conversational chain. Our reunions are invariably warm, frank, free of all dissembling: a friendship founded on mutual trust and an implicit acknowledgment of poetry as a great green force in our lives. Forty years after our first encounter, Peter's devotion to poetry is as unflagging as ever, and his sense of humour just as wicked. 'Daylight Robbery' is a misty, mystical, mischievous four-liner:

> You think you'll dander out
> to look at the mountain
> and find yourself venturing out
> to look *for* the mountain.[68]

REFERENCES

Anonymous, *Evening Herald*, 21 January 1970.

Auden, W.H., *Selected Poems*, expanded 2nd ed., Edward Mendelson (ed.) (New York: Vintage, 2007).

Berry, W., 'Does Community Have a Value?', in *Home Economics: Fourteen Essays* (Berkeley, California: North Point Press, 1987), pp.179–92.

Berry, W., 'Standing by Words', in *Standing on Earth: Selected Essays* (Berkeley, California: Counterpoint Press, 1983), pp.24–63.

Bunting, B., *Complete Poems*, Richard Caddel (ed.) (Tarset, UK: Bloodaxe, 2000).

Fallon, P., *The First Affair* (Dublin: The Gallery Press, 1974).

Fallon, P., *The Speaking Stones* (Dublin: The Gallery Press, 1978).

Fallon, P., '"The Poet Who Knows His Place": Interview with Ciaran Carty', *Sunday Independent*, 27 March 1983, n.p.

Fallon, P., *Winter Work* (Dublin: The Gallery Press, 1983, 1986).

Fallon, P., '"Place Named": Interview with Ciaran Carty', *Sunday Tribune*, 6 December 1987, n.p.

Fallon, P., *The News and Weather* (Dublin: The Gallery Press, 1987).

Fallon, P., *Eye to Eye* (Loughcrew, Ireland: The Gallery Press, 1992).

Fallon, P., 'The State of Poetry: Peter Fallon', *Krino*, 14 (Winter 1993), pp.16–18.

Fallon, P., *News of the World: Selected and New Poems* (Loughcrew, Ireland: The Gallery Press, 1998).

Fallon, P., 'Notes on a History of Publishing Poetry', *Princeton University Library Chronicle*, 59, 3 (Spring 1998), pp.547–58.

Fallon, P., 'Afterwords', in *The Georgics of Virgil* (Loughcrew, Ireland: The Gallery Press, 2004), pp.120–27.

Fallon, P., *The Georgics of Virgil* (Loughcrew, Ireland: The Gallery Press, 2004).

Fallon, P., *Tarry Flynn: Based on the Novel by Patrick Kavanagh* (Loughcrew: The Gallery Press, 2004).

Fallon, P., 'Letter', in Niall MacMonagle (ed.), *Lifelines: New and Collected Letters from Famous People about Their Favorite Poems* (Dublin: TownHouse, 2006), p.77.

Fallon, P., *Ballynahinch Postcards* (Aghabullogue, Ireland: Occasional Press, 2007).

Fallon, P., *The Company of Horses* (Loughcrew, Ireland: The Gallery Press, 2007).

Fallon, P., *Arts Tonight* (RTÉ Radio 1), 5 April 2010.

Fallon, P., 'The Fields of Meath', *Boyne Berries*, 10 (Autumn 2011), p.4.

Heaney, S., 'Tributes to Peter Fallon: 25 years of Gallery Press', *Irish Literary Supplement*, 14, 2 (Fall 1995), p.6.

Kavanagh, P., *Self-Portrait* (Dublin: The Dolmen Press, 1964).

Kennelly, B., *A Time for Voices: Selected Poems 1960–1990* (Newcastle upon Tyne: Bloodaxe Books, 1990).

Muldoon, P., *Poems: 1968–1998* (New York: Farrar, Straus, Giroux, 2001).

NOTES

1. Anonymous, *Evening Herald*, 21 January 1970.

2. P. Fallon, 'Shillings' in *The First Affair* (Dublin: The Gallery Press, 1974), p.13.

3. P. Fallon, 'A Hungry Eye' in ibid., p.27.

4. B. Kennelly, *A Time for Voices: Selected Poems 1960–1990* (Newcastle upon Tyne: Bloodaxe Books, 1990), p.101.

5. P. Fallon, 'Legend', in *The Speaking Stones* (Dublin: The Gallery Press, 1978), p.38.

6. P. Fallon, 'Mare', in ibid., p.58.

7. P. Fallon, 'Mole', in ibid., p.24.

8. P. Fallon, 'One', in ibid., p.11.

9. P. Muldoon, 'Blowing Eggs', in *Poems: 1968–1998* (New York: Farrar, Straus, Giroux, 2001), pp.5-6.

10. P. Fallon, 'Notes on a History of Publishing Poetry', *Princeton University Library Chronicle*, 59, 3 (Spring 1998), p.555.

11. Ibid., p.553.

12. P. Fallon, '"Place Named": Interview with Ciaran Carty', *Sunday Tribune*, 6 December, 1987, n.p.

13. S. Heaney, 'Tributes to Peter Fallon: 25 years of Gallery Press', *Irish Literary Supplement*, 14, 2 (Fall 1995), p.6.

14. W. Berry, 'Standing by Words', in *Standing on Earth: Selected Essays* (Berkeley, California: Counterpoint, 1983), p.33.

15. W. Berry, 'Does Community Have a Value?', in *Home Economics* (Berkeley, California: North Point Press, 1987), p.182.

16. P. Fallon, '"The Poet Who Knows His Place": Interview with Ciaran Carty', *Sunday Independent*, 27 March 1983, n.p.

17. P. Fallon, Geography *Ballynahinch Postcards* (Aghabullogue, Ireland: Occasional Press, 2007), n.p.

18. P. Fallon, *Tarry Flynn: Based on the Novel by Patrick Kavanagh* (Loughcrew, Ireland: The Gallery Press, 2004).

19. Ibid., p.94.

20. P. Fallon, 'Winter Work', in *Winter Work* (Dublin: The Gallery Press, 1983), p.48.

21. P. Fallon, 'Country Music', in *News of the World: Selected and New Poems* (Loughcrew, Ireland: The Gallery Press, 1998), p.30.

22. P. Fallon, 'The Positive Season', in *The Speaking Stones* (Dublin: The Gallery Press, 1978), p.46.

23. P. Fallon, *A Hungry Eye, The First Affair*, p.27.

24. P. Fallon, 'A Want', in *The Company of Horses* (Loughcrew: The Gallery Press, 2007), p.20.

25. P. Fallon, 'Airs and Graces', in *News of the World*, p.34.

26. P. Fallon, 'Neighbours', in ibid., p.40.

27. P. Fallon, 'Big', in *Eye to Eye*, p.47.

28. P. Fallon, 'Windfalls', in ibid., p.19.

29. Ibid.

30. P. Fallon, 'Winds and Weathers', in ibid., p.48.

31. P. Fallon, 'The Late Country', in *News of the World*, p.29.

32. P. Kavanagh, *Self-Portrait* (Dublin: The Dolmen Press, 1964), p.308.

33. P. Fallon, *The Georgics of Virgil* (Loughcrew, Ireland: The Gallery Press, 2004), pp.123–124.

34. P. Fallon, 'The Heartland', in *News of the World*, p.53.

35. P. Fallon, in '"Place Named": Interview with Ciaran Carty'.

36. P. Fallon, 'If Luck Were Corn', in *News of the World*, p.55.

37. P. Fallon, in '"Place Named": Interview with Ciaran Carty'.

38. P. Fallon,' An Easter Prayer', in *News of the World*, p.117.

39. P. Fallon, 'Letter', in Niall MacMonagle (ed.), *Lifelines: New and Collected Letters from Famous People about Their Favorite Poems* (Dublin: TownHouse, 2006), p.77.

40. P. Fallon, 'A Part of Ourselves', in *Eye to Eye*, p.58.

41. P. Fallon, 'Happy. Loving Women', *News of the World*, p.131.

42. P. Fallon, 'The Wife', in *Eye to Eye*, p.33.

43. P. Fallon, 'The Woman of the House', in Ibid., p.14.

44. P. Fallon, 'My Care', in *News of the World*, p.60.

45. P. Fallon, 'The State of the Nation', in *Eye to Eye*, p.23.

46. Ibid., pp.22–3.

47. P. Fallon, 'Big', in Ibid., p.47.

48. P. Fallon, 'The Conny Ward', *Winter Work*, p.32.

49. P. Fallon, 'St Oliver's', in *News of the World*, p.121.

50. P. Fallon,'One World', in *The Company of Horses*, p.34.

51. P. Fallon, 'Chatelaine', in ibid., p.30.

52. P. Fallon, 'A Visiting', in ibid., p.33.

53. P. Fallon,'Whoosh', in *News of the World*, p.127.

54. P. Fallon, 'Morning Glory', in *The Company of Horses*, p.13.

55. P. Fallon, 'The Conny Ward', in *Winter Work*, p.33.

56. P. Fallon, 'Birches', in *News of the World*, p.103.

57. P. Fallon, 'Crane', in *The Company of Horses*, p.28.

58. P. Fallon, 'The State of Poetry: Peter Fallon', *Krino*, 14 (Winter 1993), p.16.

59. B. Bunting, 'On the Fly-leaf of Pound's Cantos', in Richard Caddel (ed.), *Complete Poems* (Tarset, UK: Bloodaxe, 2000), p.130.

60. P. Fallon, 'The Heart's Home', in *News of the World*, p.133.

61. P. Fallon, 'The Heartland', in ibid., p.52.

62. P. Fallon, 'Grace', in *Eye to Eye*, p.50.

63. P. Fallon, 'Day and Night', in *The Company of Horses*, p.63.

64. P. Fallon, 'The Fields of Meath', *Boyne Berries*, 10 (Autumn 2011), p.4.

65. P. Fallon, *Arts Tonight* (RTÉ Radio 1), 5 April 2010.

66. See W.H. Auden, 'Funeral Blues', in Edward Mendelson (ed.) *Selected Poems*, expanded 2nd ed. (New York: Vintage, 2007), p.48.

67. P. Fallon, 'A Brighter Blue (Ballynahinch Postscript)', in *The Company of Horses*, p.38.

68. P. Fallon, 'Daylight Robbery', in *Ballynahinch Postcards*, n.p.

Works and Days

DEREK MAHON

The sun breaks through after days of fog and bathes everything in a warm glow, but it can't compete with my publisher's radiant smile when things come right. Peter Fallon is one of the great publishers, and 'also' a fine poet. Perhaps the publishing obscures the poetry a little, but I doubt if this bothers him; indeed, it may well be a source of satisfaction. The Gallery Press is a cottage industry with a global reach; it spreads afar. Peter's poetry too spreads afar with its 'news of the world' – but, while thinking globally, it acts locally. He makes a point of cherishing the points of departure. The newsy world, for him, is in the first instance what he sees when he steps out of his house: fields, woods, water. There's a morning freshness about his work that recalls the best of Kavanagh, the Kavanagh of *Tarry Flynn*, the fields that are 'part of no earthly estate'; and, that said, no other precedent springs immediately to mind. Ledwidge? Peter too, like them, writes (or seems to write) as the bird sings. The complex demands of publishing, with its online clamour of information (the schedules, the micro-economy) somehow drop away and he stands clear – 'primitively,' miraculously – in a world of simple things and direct speech, with a semblance of that 'naivety,' says Philippe Jaccottet modestly, 'that I for one most certainly acknowledge, not only for poets but for potential readers'. The Gallery list includes, happily, a dual-language Jaccottet selection, *Words in the Air* (1998), just one of Peter's many imaginative choices; and there isn't a single typo there in the French that I can see.

I used to be with a big, difficult London publishing house. The Gallery Press is better, first because they're so scrupulous and, relatedly, both fast and ecologically 'slow.' Slow as in long maturation, fast as in weekly deadlines; a tiny but dedicated workforce helps. They can, if need be, turn something around in days. A thought grows for ages, or strikes in a split second; the cutting edge is kept at hand in the woodpile. Peter knows how to crack the whip when required, but his patience – fortitude, even – when faced with the finicky last-minute revisions of a troublesome author (thank you, Peter) never ceases to amaze. This patience, fortitude, is evident in his poetry too: 'A Winter Solstice,' for example, where a grievous family loss is remembered with stoicism in a bleak landscape that contains, even so, the beginnings of consolation. We must never forget that Loughcrew is home to a famous archaeological site associated with solstices, seasonal renewals: 'A low sun leans across / the fields of County Meath . . . .' 'Meath' rhymes not with 'wreath' but with 'breathe'. He is profoundly engaged with this landscape as a living thing. He reads the signs of Newgrange 'from the Moon' and is at the same time alert and responsive to the life of the locality, its rhythms and idiolect – as when, in troubled times, a sage remarks, 'There's men dying now never died before'. He's attentive to animal life, bird life especially: the heron, the 'judiciary of crows', the cormorants who 'hang out their wings to dry' and 'crashland to their own applause'. At once fast and 'slow', he is both grounded and airborne, on intimate terms with the tractor remains and machinery parts of Conaty's dismantling shed and alive to 'a future past' from where he sees 'the sunlight on our hill' from the window of a plane in transatlantic flight.

'Who lives in the real world?' he asks. He does for one. He lives, in fact, in an even realer world. He quotes the English poet Kathleen Raine (a favourite too with Dolmen Press in its day) on what she called the 'post-real world'. She recommends instead a world where poetry isn't an escape from reality but an enhancement of it, a deepening and expansion of our works and days – as in Peter's 'Ballynahinch Postcards', where a closely observed bush, nothing remarkable, is made remarkable with holistic insight:

> a paradigm
> of active peace,
> where nothing happens
> all the time.

The beautiful phrase 'active peace,' seemingly so slight and quick, carries a freight of philosophical and even religious significance. A Buddhist or Christian mystic would recognize the concept instantly; and the 'nothing' in quiet Loughcrew is rich with event and achievement. This is the old (new?) rural rhythm; following hard on one another, the days seem unimportant yet have the greatest importance, based as they are on the agriculture, and related activities, where cultures start. A student of Hesiod's original *Works and Days* – a 'hymn', as he says of the *Georgics*, 'to peace and people' – he attends to the bird omens, to the calendar and the gods. Gallery's spring and autumn lists ripen with reliable regularity, and I wouldn't be surprised if he washes his hands in a stream before fording it, as ancient piety required, and so wins divine approval. He too, like all the best poets, goes back constantly to the future, as poet and publisher both; long may he do so.

Part II

The Contours of Fallon's Creative Work

Peter Fallon's Profane Rituals

MAURICE HARMON

In 1957, at the age of six, Peter Fallon returned from Germany where he had been raised to live on his uncle's farm in Carnaross, County Meath, Ireland, which was only a few miles from the townland of Loughcrew where he has lived since 1975. In a note to his translation of Virgil's *The Georgics,* 2004, he described that later settling as a recovery: 'I relearned, or remembered, the language which surrounded me when I was a boy. I knew again a vocabulary and idiom belonging to the way of life in a local community'.[1]

Fallon is indebted for his imaginative response to Loughcrew to the highly speculative essay *Discovery of the Tomb of Ollamh Fodhla Ireland's Famous Monarch and Law-maker upwards of Three Thousand Years Ago* by Eugene Alfred Conwell, published in Dublin by McGlashan and Gill in 1873. Loughcrew Hill, south of the village of Oldcastle, which takes its name from *loch na craoibhe* ('lake of the limb') has a commanding view of the surrounding countryside. On one side are the lakes and lowlands of County Cavan, on the other the historic Boyne Valley. Reputed to be a Neolithic passage-grave cemetery, Loughcrew Hill has thirty chambered cairns and many other ancient monuments. It was once claimed incorrectly that some of the monuments on the hill were the tombs of ancient figures, such as Queen *Tailtiu* or *Ollamh Fodhla,* and that the cemetery was the site of *Aonach Tailtean.* The ridge is also known as *Sliabh na Cailli* ('the Hag's Mountain') and has a massive cairn stone known as the Hag's Chair. Loughcrew House, a Palladian mansion situated at the foot of the ridge and close to Lough Creve, was the birthplace of the martyr St. Oliver Plunkett. *Ollamh Fodhla,* Fallon's imaginative source, begins with references to the townland of

Fearan na gcloch (Farannaglogh) whose two stones, probably used for purposes of incantation and divination in the past, were known as 'the speaking stones'. His fourth collection *The Speaking Stones* (1978), in which he deliberately sets his work in the Loughcrew/Oldcastle area, is particularly indebted to this work.

The previous collections, *Among the Walls* (1971), *Coincidence of Flesh* (1972), and *The First Affair* (1974), were published when Fallon was twenty, twenty-one and twenty-three respectively. They are not particularly concerned with Loughcrew. The first is a pamphlet of subjective lyrics on the theme of love; the second continues the theme with reflections on the uncertainties of love; the third begins with musings about love, its longings and set-backs, but develops in its second section a more realistic approach as Fallon replaces romantic yearnings with poems about people, places, and events in County Meath. Six of these reappear four years later in *The Speaking Stones* and are the first signs of that identification with Loughcrew that has characterised much of his work.

'One', the opening poem in *The Speaking Stones,* has a simplicity of language and a delicacy of feeling as Fallon relates the discovery of an egg he found 'among feathers and bone' but it was, he notes, in a balancing of beauty and violence that colours his sensibility, a 'gentler birth' than that of the lamb whose eyes were picked by crows 'before its two feet touched the ground'.[2] Blowing the yolk from the shell, he brings the 'bubble of bone' to the 'you' in the city to whom the poem is addressed.[3] Other poems from the volume such as 'Legend' record local beliefs and superstitions: 'At Fore the water flows uphill, / won't boil and wood won't burn'.[4] In 'Mare', the speaker tells of how 'with her wedding ring / my mother would cross / a sty in your eye'.[5] He is at home with animals, the mole, the hedgehog, the collie, and deals realistically with varied local incidents: a man killed by a beast, a pet goat being mated, castrating a bull, and calving. He likes to report what he observes, as when he muses in 'Herding' that 'Sometimes I watch rabbits for ages',[6] or ponders the evidence of badgers in 'A Dream of Heaven'.

> They mark their range by musking,
> leave known smells to track
> on stumps and stones and fencing-
> posts as they go homing back
>
> to their share of the world,
> their sucking cubs, a murmur

of whelps that surfaced once
when I was there.[7]

He participates in rural pastimes – snaring rabbits, poaching fish, shooting wildfowl. As he sets out the subject matter of his work, the topics have a familiar feel and the poetry reflects this in its sense of closeness to what is described.

When in 'The Positive Season' he and other men look after flocks of sheep, they are, he declares, 'surgeons, saviours, / sorrowers . . .'; they respond to mishaps and injuries.

Midweek she died,
slipped in a stream and drowned.
A goat's stung eye, the cries
that verged on madness rending
the afternoon, the healing sting of
vinegar, the dog packs at the herds,
the obscenities of crows, red water . . .

all, all the pitiful stations.[8]

The lines are starkly expressive – 'cries', 'rending', 'sting', 'dog packs', and the conclusion summing up painful experiences that may happen to sheep: 'All, all the pitiful stations' evokes Christ's walk to Calvary. The poems reveal an awareness of the natural world: the poet thinks about the death of animals, the growth of a herd, and the seasonal cycle. He cannot prevent hares being killed, but does not like it. In 'The Mass-hour', he participates in trespassing on the master's land, poaching and plundering – 'The way we were killing / we might have been gods' – but that apparent indifference does not mean that he approves of the killing.[9] When he comes upon a badger killed on the road and its mate keening, he recalls in 'Moons' that 'We killed to eat or killed to purge / and I condemned the useless slaughter.'[10] His pity has been conditioned by personal experience of hurt. As he moves to touch the dead animal he associates his feelings with reaching shyly to a lover after a quarrel and with the specific memory of reaching out to his father lying 'late that morning turned towards the wall. / My shyness was fear, fear that he'd turn // on me again'.[11]

His feeling for suffering creatures may be connected with residual fear of a threatening father. In his portraits of people, he feels for those who suffer, are abused, or rejected. His need to identify with a quiet place in County Meath and to conduct his business as a publisher there is marked by the desire for belonging and acceptance. His poems, expressive of life in a particular region, see that rural life as one of order and commitment, of engagement with the land and with the community, and with poetic work. But his involvement can be ambivalent. He gives the impression of being engaged but knows that the artist needs to be detached. In addition, as he points out in *The First Affair*, he does not make a living from sheep farming, but from poetry readings. The language of performance and of publishing differs from the vocabulary and idiom of the local community.

Peter Fallon sets his poetry in three different places: the townland of Loughcrew, the town of Deerfield, Massachusetts, and Ballynahinch, County Galway. Of these, Loughcrew is by far the most significant. If we appreciate his love-affair with the region, we respect his repeated avowals of attachment to the scenes, incidents, and people he finds there. His second mature collection, *Winter Work* (1983), signals a serious engagement with Loughcrew, its history, and Irish names and verifies its antiquity in translating lines from the Hag of Bera's lament, quoted in *Ollamh Fodhla*. Different historical and social perspectives establish a sense of change and continuity and contrast the present with the past – the mythic world and the realistic, the aristocratic pastoral and small farm community, the pagan and the Christian, neolithic and contemporary farmers. He illustrates the cover of *Winter Work* with a picture from *Ollamh Fodhla*. Its perspective of two men beside the lake with shrubs, quiet landscape and house in the distance adjusts our eyes to a relaxed focusing. In '*Cailleach*' the hag has many identities, functions and associations: she is the mother of 'tribes / and races'.[12] Its incantatory style celebrates and memorialises the mythic being, her dual aspect, and multiple manifestations.

> Maiden and crone,
> sister and bride of the sun,
> Shape-shifter, mist-eater,
> scarcely seen;[13]

Rhetorical questions affirm her identities, including that of corn goddess:

> Who hides in the last
> swath to be reaped?
> Who stays in the last
> stook to be tied?[14]

The entire poem is an enthusiastic litany of her fertile role and associations with *Sliabh na Cailli*.

The impulse to evoke the mythic and the historical yields to his feeling for actual scenes. But there are different levels. References to the past, both the ancient past of the cairns and the aristocratic past of the Palladian mansion, provide contrasting settings for poems which are firmly realistic and invariably devoid of historical dimensions. Other poems refer to Christian contexts, such as nails in 'Faith' which were said to be real nails from the Crucifixion 'although we knew they weren't'.[15] Fallon is aware of the mythic past and the persistence of superstition but keeps his feet firmly on the ground.

The News and Weather (1987) and *Eye to Eye* (1992) continue to place the contemporary against the historical. The former has a cover design of 'The Hag's Chair' from *Ollamh Fodhla*. The latter has a cover illustration based on 'Loughcrew, formal garden: view through arch to temple c. 1830'; the gate to the garden is open on the cover and closed on the last page of the collection. *News of the World: Selected and New Poems* (1998), the key text, verifies what the poet regards as important. Part One, which concentrates on Oldcastle, is composed of poems from all three previous collections; Part Two dwells upon Deerfield, Massachusetts, and Part Three returns to Oldcastle. In the opening poem the figure in 'A Woman of the Fields' exists in the real world and is central and dependable. In 'The Lost Field' the poet is enthusiastic about what one may do with land – working, clearing, cultivating, building a house. As he muses, 'Imagine the world / the place your own windfalls could fall. // I'm out to find that field, to make it mine'.[16] Passion is based on 'reverence' for all that lasts, for what one might do with a field.[17]

He chose a place, lived its life and out of quotidian engagement became the kind of poet he is. Living in a rural community, he wrote about place and people but what fundamentally excites his imagination is the beauty of the natural world. When he climbed the great cedar in 'The Witches' Corner' he had the liberating experience of feeling the world at his feet. 'Spring Song' celebrates a magical place with light in the chestnut tree's 'candelabra', with 'Bloom and blossom / everywhere'.[18] Beauty has an ordinary face, weeds, grass, bushes; voices in the leaves; pheasants who brace themselves to sing, all of which the poet responds to with, 'And this is heaven: / sunrise through a copper beech'.[19] In 'The Rag-tree, Boherard', when an ancient tree falls Fallon collects fragments of legend and tradition associated with it.

> We heard it stood . . .
> three hundred years, heard tell of the way
> it simply took up roots and walked.
> Anyway it moved. Or so they say.[20]

The 'we' is communal. It speaks of shared activity and of trust in local knowledge. In 'The Meadow', ten years ago two of them built ten thousand bales and climbed Loughcrew Hill. The speaker recalls: 'We gazed down from / a cemetery of cairns // across a stonewalled country'.[21] The Hill is a place of myth but a thistle splinter brings them back to everyday cares and the knowledge that they have gathered enough of earth's plenty 'to fortify our care against the winter'.[22]

Farm work can be tough and a poem such as 'Country Music' mirrors wintry conditions. The language is ritualistic – the cattle 'worship at an altar / of a trailer', 'swish the thuribles of their tails', and 'slap / incense breath on the silage psalter'.[23] The trailer itself, holding the fodder, is 'an altar' and foddering a 'profane / ritual'.[24] Fallon is one with these men, with the work they do, with the conditions, with their casual profanity. Here he elevates language to associate what he values with religious rituals. Ultimately he stands foursquare in what he has chosen. The concluding, titular poem of *Winter Work* is a vigorous, in-your-face assertion of what he values.

> I warm to winter work, its rituals
> and routines, and find – indoors
> and out – a deal of pleasure, alone
> or going out to work with neighbours,
>
> a *meitheal* still. All I approve persists,
> is here, at home. I think it exquisite
> to stand in the yard, my feet on the ground,
> in cowshit and horseshit and sheepshit.[25]

In 'Gravities', reprinted from *The Speaking Stones*, he and other men attend to the birth of two lambs. This could be an occasion for raising the linguistic level, but the manner is reserved, the language terse. The death of a sheep in 'Caesarean' elicits a more complex response. A ewe is about to 'yean'.[26] Realising that she is not likely to deliver successfully, there is only one thing to be done.

No time to doubt
that we would learn what to do by doing.
We did not hesitate or hurry.

This would take its own time.[27]

When they cut her open, they find twin lambs 'perfectly / formed'[28] but too young to live. As the speaker muses, 'We had thought / of everything but this', and the poem becomes a lament: 'Daughters / of death, they'd never know their gifts, / the everyday miracles of which they were part'.[29] The men have done their best and 'Now there / were other things to do'.[30] In that other doing they find the strength to continue. There are setbacks, disappointments, death, and harsh conditions, but in a community living close to nature these losses are bearable. The men interiorise misfortune, are unable to express how they feel, accept what comes without sentimentality or false feeling. They will suffer, register, and move on. Their habitual reticence that Fallon respects and imitates may be restrictive but can be made into a strength.

The persona the poet creates for himself requires this protective mask like the ewe in 'Fostering' who accepts the lamb once it has been enclosed by the skin of her own stillborn.[31] The deception works. It works also in 'Catholics', where in a subtly managed relationship, the poet-narrator asks for the loan of an ass, but has to listen to the owner's sexual yarns. In fact he is put off by the other's male chauvinism but plays a part to get what he needs.[32]

The role is deceptive since the notion that Fallon is within the community is a convenient fiction or part-fiction. There is always a gap between the sheep farmer and his fellow-workers; he can enter local life at one level but he is apart from it as an artist. Traditionally, being a poet sets him apart in a rural community where the poet was regarded with suspicion or even fear. The notion that he was at one with the community was challenged when locals reacted angrily to some of his portrayals of local individuals and events. It was a disturbing experience for a man who had chosen Loughcrew, identified with its life, and devoted himself to expressing it as honestly as he could and with great affection. His role is not straightforward; he speaks through fictive personae, thereby distancing himself from what he says. He overhears, puts bits of information together, interprets, shows understanding and compassion, but remains detached.

The fact that he has chosen to live and work in a rural community rather than in a town or city may limit the subjects that are available but does not mean that

Fallon is unaware of or indifferent to what goes on elsewhere. He may write of life in the country but he also thinks about events elsewhere. His life may look like a pastoral idyll but is not. In 'The Heartland' a co-ed from Minnesota writes to him about the death of her brother in Vietnam; she joins in protests against the war, and accuses the poet for being 'out of touch', 'too contented'.[33] In fact he is not. Outside events – the Vietnam war, troubles in Northern Ireland, and the Kerry Babies inquiry – do indeed intrude, they 'queer / this pastoral'.[34] It is true he has chosen a different 'course'.

> It's true I chose another course, talk
> in small communities, a hope to sway
> by carry-on people I understand
> and love. I came on a place and had to stay
>
> that I might find my feet, repair
> the mark of human hand, and repossess
> a corner of my country. I write to her:
> our lives are rafts; risk happiness.[35]

The girl opens her heart to him and in turn he opens his heart to her. But rural life is not pastoral. In the idealised world of the literary, pastoral babies do not appear but in Fallon's world a baby girl has been found in a lake. Taking up this theme, 'If Luck Were Corn' tells the story of a pregnant girl, not much more than a child herself, the secrecy, the gossip, the ignorance, and the lack of compassion. A neighbour's observation, 'the like of that's gone on to yours / since the year of One', puts a stop to gossip.[36] Underneath these external preoccupations lies the need to 'repair / the mark of human hand'. The retreat to Loughcrew induces the slow process of psychological recovery but Fallon's poems do not turn inward towards personal investigation. His manner is reserved, and his response is objective.

'My Care' also treats the impossibility of shutting out the world. In the pub the customers listen to news of violence and to endless, unproductive talk that makes the violence in Northern Ireland familiar. Questioning his choice of a safe house in the midlands, Fallon is worried for 'my care, my country' and makes the process of thinking and evaluation the substance of the poem.[37] At its centre is the troubled self in a state of fluctuating uncertainty. He is 'shaken' by deeds that disturb his country: 'Soon I'm sitting by a riot / of kindling, the soft explosions of seasoned logs. / They have shaken the roots of that familiar quiet'.[38]

The word 'news' has ambiguous meanings. One might expect it to refer to the world at large; in fact it refers to a small fraction of that world, the area chosen by Fallon for his personal and poetic living. The locals call a hill by a mythic name but they deal with an everyday world and the poems bring news from there. 'The Late Country' is concerned with 'news' in this limited sense. The narrator tells us, 'They'll be waiting, three wise men, / giving and taking all the news'.[39] The 'news' is both inclusive and particular; it happens in the 'late country', that is, during after hours in a pub, a place where they are welcome after they give the right knock and a paradoxical 'silent / password'.[40] There, news is of the everyday, shaped by the local, expressed in its idiom, and in laconic comedy.

The men exchange news, and are a natural part of this world which shapes them and contains their range of activities. The poem has this quality of taking place in a world apart where the relationships and verbal exchanges almost come by rote, in dialogue which is as congenial in its unchanging rhythms as dialogue in a well-known play. Part of the enjoyment is the giving and taking of news – 'all the news' in the sense that the substance of the dialogue embraces the expected and the normal. It is not a question of hearing news of the unknown as of having the familiar verified, '"Were there many at the mart?"'[41] No need to specify which mart or where it has taken place, or when. The answer is satisfying in its homely confirmation, '"There was often more / at the ringing of a pig."'[42]

When the guards raid they are 'asking things they knew already, / Name?'[43] The men's response becomes comical.

> And noted men muttering in Irish
> and forgetting their addresses,
> observed the clumsy pantomime
> of men with drink taken standing
> straight upright, blinded by the light.
> 'Have you any idea of the time?'

'I suppose it's late.'
And the guard we knew loomed
in battle dress beside us like the Prince
of Darkness. 'I'm surprised at you.
I thought you knew better...' *'You're*
surprised? Sure I thought I left ages since.'[44]

Sometimes the news brought by the poetry is shameful and painful. In *Eye to Eye*, 'The Woman of the House' does not refer to the traditional *bean 'n tí*, someone to be admired or celebrated. Fallon firmly sets all such associations aside to create an account of incest, sibling warmth transformed to nightmare when the brother comes home drunk and she feels so trapped that she sometimes wishes she were dead. In this house of violation she is alone. On some nights she has to take refuge in the shed and wait until 'his ravings ended' before she can go back into her 'home' and experience the peace of sleep.[45] The understated manner of the telling and the use of the literal strengthen the account: 'Such thoughts – and me my age', 'and him back from the town', 'And none to tell a thing'.[46] That compressed syntax becomes lyrical in the closing lines as the agitation caused by the man's presence is replaced by the possibility of peace.

The pattern of oppositions recurs in these poems as one situation is balanced against another. The abused woman's agitation is replaced by the ascent of peace; the Conny Ward's life as a political activist in the past gives way to age, blindness, and confinement in the present. In 'History Questions' the narrator is not the man he used to be but remembers that he knew 'famous and good men', including the Conny Ward, and that 'the wood-cutter's daughter / showed me honey on the forest floor'.[37] The skin of a dead lamb enables the strange animal to be accepted; the disappointment in the failed caesarean is replaced by an ability to move on to 'other things'.[48] Gossip about the girl who became pregnant is stopped by the sharp remark of a neighbour. In a judicious reckoning the man who crowed about what he had went astray and had to be removed by the guards. When they assist at the birth of twin lambs, 'the lambs stood up'.[49] In fact, every lamb is a lamb of God, as Fallon says in another poem.[50] His positive and optimistic temperament transcends suffering.

Fallon's studies of individuals in *Eye to Eye* go on to portray a man who murdered his family in 'Possessed'. Typically, the poem moves indirectly into the narrative: a man becomes obsessed with signs of trespass, 'of wrongs done and disputes'.[51] The poet understands how small matters can become magnified and that such attitudes can be inherited from far back in time, but the poem asks, as it winds itself into the man's obsession, 'was he / ever all right in the head?'.[52] His behaviour could be erratic and one morning 'something snapped', 'For', as the poem rightly says, 'the broody mind must hatch'.[53] He prepared for the killing and carried it out on 'an ordinary afternoon',[54] then gave himself up. People wonder and query what it was that 'came over him'.[55] In this customary incomprehension the poem is faithful to known experience. It is not an isolated event. The speaker voices what all feel and expresses their customary questions when such an event happens. What they question is the mystery of human nature itself, depths that are usually hidden.

In a larger pattern the poems that are set in the Oldcastle/Loughcrew region transcend its status as quiet backwater. Out of limited possibilities Fallon creates, records, and celebrates local activities and people. The things you might do with a farm include the things you might do with a poem. The rhythm of the work and of the words not only bring the region alive, but also, they bring them into an aesthetic that is both distancing and immediate. So 'Dipping Day' brings mimicry and music to the mundane activity. The event is so normal, so recurrent, so little considered by artists that it is almost a surprise to see it become the subject of a poem. But in the dipping, the verbal rituals, and gestures associated with it, the poem animates what it describes. Dipping, Fallon says, in amused exaggeration, exceeds the appeal of the Indian rain dance, transcends boredom, is a ritual in which the celebrants have their 'stations', and chant a refrain.[56]

'Windfalls' begins with vivid description of a gale, 'Wild days and wicked weather / cut to the bone'.[57] These are 'troubled times' with men dying now who 'never died before', but nevertheless the man who is foddering cattle at a gap 'has seen it all and lived to tell'; he has the wisdom of experience to see him through.[58] He will not be defeated: 'He'll saw and split / the windfalls when the wind dies down'.[59] Once again one thing offsets another, what destroys is replaced by what endures. Once again the music of the lines, their inner rhythm, affirms what the conclusion confirms. Even the surprising force of the wind, its antic strength that flipped a roof and undressed an outhouse are in themselves evidence of a power that has an attractive vividness.

The farmer who 'worked with / and not against the weather' is a 'happy man' in 'Eye to Eye'.[60]

> He'd grow grass
> on a stone.
> He has humoured a farm
> into fruitfulness.[61]

Not needing signs and wonder, 'he sees the bounty of God in a breeze'.[62] Fallon does not romanticise. In deliberate contrast with John Montague's 'The Water Carrier' he insists on the harsh, unromantic reality in 'Country Music': 'Now I'm dragging water to a frozen trough' and notes he is 'one with them, their muttered Bollocks, Shits and Fuck its, / a cursèd yoke bent beneath a pair of splashing buckets'.[63] Significantly, his portrait poems are of those who live at an angle to the community, misfits, those who suffer, a woman abused, a suicide, a murder, a girl who becomes pregnant outside of marriage, a woman who went crazy. They may speak the idiom of the place, but there comes a time when they feel that they do not belong.

Not belonging is a pervasive theme. The portrait of the man in 'Eye to Eye' is made up of fragments and particular attributes – cleverness, common sense, and the ability to learn from experience. In 'Carnaross 2' the approach is also oblique. Overhearing conversation, the speaker puts two and two together: a man was bothered by superstitions and intimations of trouble; he was suspected of abusing little girls, and he hanged himself.[64] 'Brothers', a poem about poachers, is also about comradeship and freedom. Those engaged in the illegal activities are 'votaries of darkness' who want to 'adhere // to their own laws'.[65] Afterwards they return to their responsibilities, 'to the world and his wife'; like them the poet is 'still in the dark / putting one foot in front of the other' and being independent.[66] 'The AGM' is an account of a man who feels out of place when he is away from the land. He prefers the local, its familiar activities and his own 'undisturbed train // of thought', and furthermore, he has the right language 'where his tongue belongs to the small talk'.[67] 'Himself' portrays a nameless man who was astray in the head, forsook the community, and sought the privacy of nature. Finally he is taken away to the hospital, where he talks about himself as though he were someone else, but as Fallon insists, he had a life before this decline and is a human being. The last few lines warn those who would undervalue the man's achievements: 'Let them sing loudly / when they've harrowed / all he's ploughed'.[68]

Many of Fallon's poems about Loughcrew have a sturdy rhythm of four iambic stresses in a line: 'I've heard men tell and love to tell…';[69] 'The man at the bar is cursing women; he hates his wife and loves his mother';[70] 'They've noted times the bailiffs scout / the bridge and banks; they argue gaffs / and spears';[71] 'I took the stillborn lamb and cleft / with axe on chopping-block its head'.[72] The declarative force of the sentence is arresting and can indicate a confident practicality. At the same time the narrative momentum can be maintained, as the line is shortened to three stresses or less, or expanded to five. Some poems have a greater variation in stress and line length and an ability to include dialogue so that attention is held less by a strict rhythm than by meaning, changes in point of view, or a narrative's pauses and turns. In 'Spring Song', on the other hand, one follows a series of identifying images, 'Weeds on walls; / the long grass / of the long acre'.[73]

Local sayings and expressions, including a habit of blunt assessment, give the language a distinctive flavour. I've heard men say, "He'd take the eye / of your head". Aye, and the milk from your tea.'[74] It is said of a man that he'd drink 'a lough of drinks';[75] another says of himself, 'I'm all spray and no spit'.[76] Homely remarks can have an animating effect in a conversation.

'Your man bought calves? Did he part

with much?'. 'He did. He paid
two prices for them.' 'Well tell me this,
does the same man have a clue
about stock, or does he only know
about everything?' 'He's no daw.'
'He's not.' 'That's a fact and true.'[77]

In such poems Fallon's ear is true to local speech, and his poems have a feeling of reality. Homely expressions flavour the collections from *Winter Work* to *Eye to Eye* where a speaker says describing a packed dancehall, 'You'd need a haircut to get in'[78]; commenting on a woman with only one child, a man says, 'Time you were in second gear'[79]; and of a hungry man, 'He ate the pattern off her plate'.[80] These turns of speech are less frequent in Part III of *News of the World: Selected and New Poems*.

Many of Fallon's poems have a narrative structure that is sometimes slight, at other times more substantial. His narrative strength may be seen in 'Annaghmakerrig: The Avenue' where in an even-paced movement he brings together the grim reaper in the meadow and the woman he meets at the water's edge who shares her story of the dark depression she suffered before her daughter's birth. He feels buoyed with the 'ceremony / of her gift' and as he walks back past his 'tight keeper / of his own counsel' wonders who he might be, one of twin brothers who served time in Portlaoise prison for the murder of a Protestant, or one of the others from the troubled border area now working on a FÁS scheme to restore the old demesne of Annaghmakerrig.[81] The theme is forgiveness and reconciliation after the sectarian/political divisions of the Northern Troubles. The reaper is silent but 'he smiles'.[82] Once again the Northern Troubles form an accompaniment to a narrative that moves from lack of verbal communication to the poet at his desk, aware of that ominous pendulum in the field, the metronome of its movement a reminder of mortality, life's transience against which the artist works. The poem fits together the pieces of its narrative, the scenes and people, to create its perspectives of life and death, love and loss, pessimism and hope.

Eye to Eye explores these issues more closely from 'A Woman of the Fields', always there, in all seasons and conditions, through the complex perspectives of 'Annaghmakerrig: The Avenue' to 'The Woman of the House'. In this last poem, the tone darkens, the mood becomes tragic, the suffering and darkness more immediate, the individual voice of the woman directly appealing and revealing her nightmare of distorted feeling, abused sexuality, marital subversion, isolation and a silence to be endured. Unlike the woman at the water's edge, she has nobody with whom to share her story, except her incestuous brother. The vernacular language brings its distinctive reality to a tale that hardly bears describing: 'We'd been so close / we'd eaten off one plate'.[83] The implications of the situation for a Catholic woman are not mentioned but are subliminally present.

The dark shadows that have converged on his rural retreat descend into personal tragedy. Part One of News of the World ends movingly with poems about the death of Peter and Jean Fallon's baby. 'A Way of the World', heartbreakingly simple, is a series of statements that render the poet's bewilderment and feeling of loss.

> A lost light shines
> in the haggard
> of years. So much begins,
> like a pearl, upon a blemish.
> Some take life hard,
>
> some take the same life
> easy. I'd sooner sing
> heartbreak nor cry it.

But a baby's born, the baby
dies. Who knows anything?[84]

'A Part of Ourselves' is a restrained contemplation of the death of John Fallon,
born 7 December, died 8 December 1990. The parents exist in the middle of
conflicting feelings.

. . . . Now the minutes are grief
or grief postponed – not to remember
seems to betray; laughter would be sacrilege.
We will find a way to mind him as a leaf

who fell already from the family tree,
crushed. He hadn't a chance.
We pray at best for the open wound
to grow a scar.
We welcome him his deliverance.

There are things worse than death.[85]

'Grief', 'betray', 'sacrilege', 'crushed', 'wound', 'death' – the terms are stark.

News of the World, Part Two, which contains seventeen poems, is called 'The
Deerfield Series: Strength of Heart'. First published in 1997, they were written in
the year Fallon was a visiting writer for the second time at the Deerfield Academy,
Massachusetts, from 1996–97. In Oldcastle he skirted history and mythology; in
Deerfield, the frontier outpost of the English settlement of New England, he tries
'to enter history, geography and mythology to comprehend a place and its fate'.[86]
He is the outsider who observes his surroundings, explores local history, and
learns of 'the human / heart's potential'. The titles bear the flavour of the work:
'Stillwater', 'Bloody Brook', '29 February 1704', 'The Street', 'The Stone Grove', and
so on.

The series is an affectionate consideration of a particular location. He responds
to historical associations – settlers, craftsmen, fights with native Americans, and
the story of Mehuman Hinsdale, the first white baby born in the shade of Beaver
Ridge whose story has the haphazard outline of history and

whose father, uncles, and grandfathers
were killed that noon at Bloody Brook,
whose own new son was slaughtered
in the Leap Year massacre,
who with his wife was captured
and held two years in Canada
before his first redemption.[87]

'The Burying Ground' resounds with the voices of stone makers, its rhyme scheme is an echo chamber of the past 'in the pined, birched, and oaken / grove on Albany Road'; the hosts above ground and below are joined in this villanelle.[88]

Nature is the dominant presence in the sequence, which begins in 'Beaver Ridge' with the detail of the sun rising again over the Pocumtuck Range 'as it has done so often', clearing the mist from the valley and showing the still water 'as it meanders / at the edge of meadows / near a street . . .'.[89] White settlers came to a land teeming with plants and animals, with berries, fish and game in profusion. They set to work, cultivating, planting, harvesting; 'they tended the seed of future promise'.[90] It is a time of prosperity, peace, and apparent promise. 'Could there be an end to weeping?'[91] No, for there is treachery, ambush, bloodshed and widowhood.

As bad as slaughter,
as bad as torture–
a body stripped of all
including skin – was capture.

The pitying pines expressed a groan.[92]

In its adumbration of historical events the poem constantly returns to the theme of settlers at work, their skills as craftsmen – 'the miller, the cartwright, / the ropemaker;'[93] – the recurrence of spring, 'fresh water and wild grapes'.[94] The affectionate naming of trees in 'A Shiver' is evidence of the flow of feeling that Fallon now freely expresses.

aspens, beeches,
walnuts, willows,
magnolia, dogwood,

hazels, and sloes;
birches, birches
and crab-apples,
silver-, swamp-
and sugar maples;

birches and maples,
maples and birches,
and all the other lovely trees
shiver in a human breeze.[95]

In their reflective force the poems commemorate achievement and lament inevitable losses. The legacy of violence is never eradicated.

The series ends with the meditative 'Strength of Heart', which affirms man's capacity to grow and survive, despite suffering and grief. The best choose to grow, not to wilt. Fallon's final injunction emerges from the historical evidence of the spirit's ability to deliver itself, 'Be worthy of this life', he says, 'And, Love the world.'[96]

'The Deerfield Series: Strength of Heart' marks a significant change in mood and language from the earlier poetry of Fallon. The poems are fresh and lyrical, while the language is adjusted to convey this lyricism; the poetic forms vary from full description to haiku-like summary, and the tone, a mixture of eulogy and lament, conveys the changing moods of events and places. In this small corner of New England he perceives a representative sample of human history. In some respects what he finds and how he responds continue what he has done in the earlier collections about Loughcrew. The difference is in the language and the release of feeling that enables the poet to move lightly and confidently.

News of the World, Part Three, 'The Heart's Home', returns to Oldcastle where in 'Our Lives Now' he resumes the role of reflective observer, wondering how the 'shreds and shards' of life of the area will be judged in the future.[97] They are not evaluated by what they have discarded – tractor remains, machinery parts, a hill of tyres, or even by the day they looked for a fossil or an arrowhead, or by 'the apparition / of an osprey and egret instead'.[98] They will be judged by the legacy of a life honestly lived. As he observes, 'The worn thread / was woven honestly and served its while'.[99] In the broken homestead the hearth was once warm and the boy who died 'will not be dead'.[100]

Fallon's appreciation of the beauty of nature continues. 'The Bandon Road: Sight of It' testifies to 'this array of wonder' in the natural world.[101] 'An Easter Prayer' salutes the season in the simplest of language.

> Spring in our steps.
> I love my children
> and my wife.
> Rise all again and again.[102]

'Again' is another poem of praise in language that illuminates the ordinary. Going out to check a ewe in labour, he describes what he sees: 'Along the road / gale forces bend and burst / the sails of ivy in the masts of ash'.[103] The energised relationship in the metaphor of 'gales', 'sails' and 'masts', is reinforced by the predominance of monosyllabic words. His sense of wonder that appears in joyous perception in the eight-line second stanza continues in the images of 'the tide of night's gone out', leaving thistles exposed like 'starfish', a sunrise that has 'suppressed the mist / around a padded nest' where the ewe has given birth to twins.[104] On that high note he can end with the insouciant rhyming couplet: 'The herd of gorse is grazing still / halfway up the hilly hill'.[105]

Poems about actual life have a philosophical basis. In 'St Oliver's' the poet overhears the talk of schoolgirls 'filtered through the hedge'.[106] They are, he reflects, on the threshold of adulthood when they will have to make decisions. They talk now about the usual topics, but what, he wonders, will happen when they have to choose between emigration or staying in Ireland. Adults have serious concerns. The poem remembers the journey he and Jean made across the border to pray in a troubled city that their unborn child would have no 'defect'; it was 'the longest journey / we'll ever undergo'.[107] In this evaluation he declares his preference for a 'just inheritance: information, kindness, a chance, / and then a second chance':

> I dream an innocent end to the commonness
>   of double talk and single think,
> reprisals, revenge,
>   the nod and the wink
>
> of parish pump politics—
>   jobs for the boys, Euro junkets.
> Where they'll soon park in the desperate dark
>   used condoms litter St Oliver Plunkett's.[108]

The poem is dated 1994, the year of the first IRA ceasefire, but it addresses the greed and cheapened morality of modern Ireland. He dreams of an end to shallow values, to the violence of the Northern Troubles, the racket of jobs for the boys, the misuse of public money. The example of the martyred Saint Oliver Plunkett stands behind the account of a better world, which he knows is but a dream.

One of the values he espouses is the readiness to proceed. 'Gate' describes a gate in the middle of the field which seems to have no purpose since it 'stops nothing / and points nowhere'.[109] The field is a symbol. When you come to the gate at the centre, what do you do?: 'Then you pause. And open it. And enter'.[110] The readiness is all and the openness.

Several poems in this section including 'Whoosh', 'Harvest in Spring', 'Meeting in Maine', and 'The Heart's Home' centre on the natural world. In 'Meeting in Maine' the poet comes upon a herd of moose. He had seen signs of their presence and for years had hoped to see them. He has stood and looked around and wondered if one was watching him 'in equal awe'.[111] Then he names what they like to eat.

> Bog rush, pond weed and water lily.
> Dogwood and willow, birch and balsam
> Alder, aspen, mountain ash—
> leaf, twig, shoot and stem—

and is 'reconciled' to never seeing these great creatures of the wild.[112] Then suddenly they appear: 'moose // everywhere and then more moose'.[113] The poem is magnificent in its rapt intensity and respect for the animals. It is a portrait of the self as pilgrim in the wilderness, another version of Fallon's response to nature in County Meath, but in more elevated language. The poem quickens with the warmth of its appreciation. He wants 'room for everything', a world devoid of violence and treachery.[114]

'The Heart's Home' is another poem of total, heartfelt celebration of nature, as part of the ease and wonder of love. Beginning and continuing in the same vein, it gathers together a multiplicity of objects that he would celebrate.

> Let there be animals
> and other wildlife there.
> Let teasel charm gold finches
> beside bracken, where ivy inches

> along branches and a drystone edifice.
> Let it be a healing place,
> where the heart releases care.
>
> Long live the weeds
> and, yes, long live the wilderness.[115]

But there are things which he deplores. The earlier poem, 'The State of the Nation', published in *Eye to Eye*, but not included in *News of the World*, condemns the men of violence, unreservedly: 'If their day comes / the country's fucked'.[116]

Fallon's political poems are unambiguous in their condemnation of violence, the assassinations, the cruelty, the excuse of patriotism, the self-deceiving justifications, and the secrecy with which they move and the secrecy in the community that gives them security. 'The State of the Nation' expresses all of this through the voice of a nameless man who explains why they 'stick a tape across the eyes / before they pull the trigger'.[117] The indignation and disgust in his voice as he tells of such deeds makes the account credible, persuasive and revolting in its stories of killing and mutilation. The poet despises the so-called patriotism and maintains that contact with them contaminates. By the end he condemns not only the men of violence but those who protect them with silence and are themselves implicated in the horrible deeds.

> Too much, too long,
> their carry on as if it's playing
> or play-acting. And you mean to say
> no one knows who they are?
> I mean to say no one's saying.[118]

Fallon's rejection of violence and pseudo nationalism is courageous. He may speak through the mask of the anonymous speaker, but the poem is clear in its condemnation. He may live in a cul-de-sac, an apparent rural idyll, but tragedy in all its shapes and disguises nonetheless enters that world.

Many of the poems in *News of the World* bear witness to the life he chose. In the process of writing about it he verified its values and related them to his life as a poet. Farm work became a metaphor for the work of poetry so that the two sides of his life were joined, one mirroring the other. Three earlier collections, *The*

Speaking Stones, *Winter Work*, and *Eye to Eye*, show his development. In some poets the imagination feeds off memory, while in Fallon experience itself gives imaginative nourishment.

It is no surprise that Fallon translated Virgil's great poem of the land, *The Georgics*. 'I felt,' he writes, 'an affinity with its actual, practical world and with Virgil's description of the griefs and glories of a place in which people tried to establish their lives while their days were adumbrated by a civil war. In Meath I was participating in a farming life while my country worked to find ways to advance in the tender aftermath of "Troubles".'[119] The subject matter of *The Georgics* could not have been more congenial. The hero is an anonymous, conscientious farmer and it is a nature poem about the nature of a place. Virgil describes with realistic fidelity the annual round of labour in which the Italian yeoman spends his life and suggests the delight in heart and mind which he himself drew from such labour. 'The sureness of their knowledge', Fallon observes, 'was the fruit of observation. They were a people who could believe their eyes . . . they preserved room for mystery; and learned the benefits of both'.[120] His translation is faithful to the spirit of the original but is looser than one might have expected.

The poems in *Ballynahinch Postcards* (2007) are also hymns of praise to nature. Written while the poet was staying at Ballynahinch, County Galway, they are openly responsive to the natural world. These haiku-like poems are characterised by exact detail resulting from the poet's observations of particular scenes and incidents. Sometimes they itemise a static scene: 'Sharp frost. Bright sun. / The sky all blue', where each monosyllabic word, undemanding and familiar, carries its full weight.[121] Sometimes they provide a more developed picture, as of trees in the wind 'with their prayer mats / of fallen leaves'.[122] Sometimes they become a descriptive narrative that moves from the objectivity of 'Three mountainy ewes / at grass' to the metaphor of ewes 'on the upper deck / of the mountain' who are

> swept overboard
> by the fury of flash floods
>
> and pushed and pulled downwards
> to snag below the falls—[123]

The force of active verbs and of alliterative words defines an action begun, carried through and completed, in two couplets, while the definite article ensures the scene's immediacy.

The last four lines create stark visual images in the simile that compares the empty eye-socket of the drowned sheep to a burnt-out holiday home. In the quiet ordering of the last line, 'tucked behind a quiet chapel',[124] all the simple words bring peace and calm after the turbulence, terror, and violence of the poem's central drama. He speaks of these poems as 'glances and glimpses' but they are more than that.[125] The glance lingers, and it takes in what it sees; it records, celebrates, and has the capacity to be eloquently affirmative.

Satisfaction in the discovery of fresh images when the intensity of the vision is projected in an original and accurate image is one of the delights of the small gathering of postcard poems. The collection concludes in enthusiastic and affirmative imperatives.

> Turn up the sun!
> And put the leaves back
> on the trees.
> Let river reins hang slack.
>
> Wash the sky
> a brighter blue.
> Give back to swans
> their downy retinue.[126]

In the intensity of the moment's rapture the mood is transformative.

> Resurrect, resuscitate.
> Refresh and renovate.
> Retrieve, regain and re-install,
> translate
>
> everything again.[127]

The call for renewal reflects the refreshment of spirit that has come about from this remove to Connemara; it embraces nature's capacity to flourish again and includes the poet's own creative energies.

The Company of Horses (2007) is also informed by Fallon's relationship with the natural world. The opening poem, 'Go', begins with an injunction to attend to nature's 'shards and shatters' and argues that in this attentiveness one may derive insights into human nature.[128] 'Opera' celebrates springtime days of 'lightsome delight'.[129] All the elements are invoked to create metaphors in which to affirm the power of growth, the 'aria' of birdsong,[130] the swoops and arcs of swallows in 'a renewed rhapsody'.[131]

The fighting cock in 'A Holy Show' is a profane embodiment of male power, self-pride, sexual vigour, and defiance. He is an unrepentant heretic burning on the pyre,

> a blaze of glory
> howling like a heretic
> in the bonfire of his infidel
> and ruffled feathers.[132]

The poetic tributes to natural creatures – starlings, sheep in the Orkneys – are often sounded through a succession of rhymes. In 'Depending on Water' the cheeky chiming of 'bends' with a whole variety of words is a playful declaration of satisfaction and delight.[133] There is also the feeling that like the fighting cock, Fallon does what he wants and takes pleasure in it.

The title poem is a tribute to horses whose company 'is a quiet blessing'. They respond to 'the mere sound or smell / of us ... all neighs / and nickerings'.[134] 'The Company of Horses' moves with ease and fluency, accumulating images, so that the entire poem, gathering the sum of its parts, becomes a glorification.

> And growing out of morning
> mists the ghosts of night
> form silhouettes along the ridge,
>
> a dun, two chestnuts
> and a bay.[135]

Invited to stretch a hand towards her head-collar, he whispers endearments; the moment of intimacy as evocative as Cuchulain's with the old grey mare:

> hearing that her hero
> joined the sleep
> of death, spread her mane
> across his breast and began to wail and weep.[136]

Mythic evocation also appears in Fallon's recreation of the way 'the great assembly' of trees came to comfort Orpheus in 'The Second Sorrow'.

> the great assembly
> of the trees – beeches,
> box, limes and laurels,
> the motley splash of maples,
> parades of cheering palms,
> a poplar guard of honour,
> the water-loving lotus,
> willows too, those staples
>
> of the river bank, all congregated
> to console him . . . .[137]

The vividness of Fallon's perception shines and shimmers throughout the collection. 'The tarmac streams like precious ore / beside wrapped bales bright in the glare'.[138] Nature yields its harvest of beauty in all weathers and that plenitude 'insists a choice – to live; to thrive'.[139] No matter what the circumstances or the setbacks Fallon's tone remains positive, as though he is endlessly sustained and renewed by contact with nature. 'I have', he declares in 'Day and Night', the volume's last poem, 'loved my term / on earth'.[140] The collection rounds to outspoken expressions of belief, sometimes poignant in the larger perspectives of human experience. It is the spirit of uncomplicated joy and faith that the entire collection reflects: love of wife, children, friends, nature. The poet's universe accommodates sorrow and affirms the presence of love.

Having now entered his sixties, Fallon has entered a time in a man's life which may be characterised by re-evaluation of what has been accomplished and consideration of how he wants to live in whatever time is left. In *The Company of Horses*, he moves away from the preoccupations of his life in Loughcrew, from portraits of individuals, from objectively recording the vocabulary and idiom of the area, from what he overhears. Now he is intent on celebration. With short forms and short lines the poems live in the music of their saying. Each recent poem attempts a condition of praise. He revels in the delights and possibilities of language, in the pleasure of making rhymes that connect through each stanza; sometimes he sends the chimes of their association the entire length of the poem. He creates a persona who is attentive to the sights and sounds of the countryside, who knows the names of tree, birds, and animals, and who has an embracing affection for the animals. Even when the poems speak of change and loss, the ravages of winter, age and death, they are refreshingly positive. The entire collection has a generous fluency.

REFERENCES

Fallon, P., *Among the Walls* (Dublin: Tara Telephone Publications, 1971).

Fallon, P., *Coincidence of Flesh* (Dublin: The Gallery Press, 1972).

Fallon, P., *The First Affair* (Dublin: The Gallery Press, 1974).

Fallon, P., *The Speaking Stones* (Dublin: The Gallery Press, 1978).

Fallon, P., *Winter Work* (Dublin: The Gallery Press, 1983, 1986).

Fallon, P., *The News and Weather* (Dublin: The Gallery Press, 1987).

Fallon, P., *Eye to Eye* (Loughcrew, Ireland: The Gallery Press, 1992).

Fallon, P., *News of the World: Selected and New Poems* (Loughcrew, Ireland: The Gallery Press, 1998).

Fallon, P., *The Georgics of Virgil* (Loughcrew, Ireland: The Gallery Press, 2004).

Fallon, P., 'Afterwords', *The Georgics of Virgil* (Loughcrew, Ireland: The Gallery Press, 2004), pp.120–27.

Fallon, P., *Ballynahinch Postcards* (Aghabullogue, Co. Cork: Occasional Press, 2007).

Fallon, P., *The Company of Horses* (Loughcrew, Ireland: The Gallery Press, 2007).

NOTES

1. P. Fallon, 'Afterwords', *The Georgics of Virgil*, trans. Fallon (Loughcrew, Ireland: The Gallery Press, 2004), p.123.

2. P. Fallon, *The Speaking Stones* (Loughcrew, Ireland: The Gallery Press, 1978), p.11.

3. Ibid.

4. Ibid., p.38.

5. Ibid., p.58.

6. Ibid., p.45.

7. Ibid., pp.26–7.

8. Ibid., p.46.

9. P. Fallon, *Winter Work* (Loughcrew, Ireland: The Gallery Press, 1983), p.17.

10. Ibid., p.28.

11. Ibid., pp.28–9.

12. Ibid., p.14.

13. Ibid.

14. Ibid.

15. Ibid., p.12.

16. P. Fallon, *News of the World: Selected and New Poems* (Loughcrew, Ireland: The Gallery Press, 1998), p.17.

17. Ibid., p.16.

18. Ibid., p.18.

19. Ibid., p.19.

20. Ibid., p.25.

21. Ibid., pp.26–7.

22. Ibid., p.27.

23. Ibid., p. 30.

24. Ibid.

25. Ibid., p.51.

26. Ibid., p.38.

27. Ibid.

28. Ibid.

29. Ibid.

30. Ibid., p.39.

31. P. Fallon, *Winter Work*, p.23.

32. Ibid., pp.34–5.

33. P. Fallon, *The News and Weather* (Loughcrew, Ireland: The Gallery Press, 1987), p.24.

34. Ibid.

35. Ibid., p.25.

36. Ibid., p.27.

37. Ibid., p.11.

38. Ibid.

39. Ibid., p.40.

40. Ibid.

41. Ibid.

42. Ibid.

43. Ibid., p.41.

44. Ibid., pp.41–2.

45. P. Fallon, *Eye to Eye* (Loughcrew: The Gallery Press, 1992), p.15.

46. Ibid., p.14.

47. P. Fallon, *The News and Weather*, pp.38, 39.

48. Ibid., p.21.

49. See '9 Nativity' from 'Gravities', in P. Fallon, *Winter Work*, p.25.

50. See P. Fallon, 'The Herd' from *The News and Weather*, p.23.

51. P. Fallon, *Eye to Eye*, p.25.

52. Ibid., p.26.

53. Ibid., pp.26, 27.

54. Ibid., p.27.

55. Ibid., p.28.

56. P. Fallon, *The News and Weather*, p.22.

57. P. Fallon, *Eye to Eye*, p.19.

58. Ibid.

59. Ibid.

60. P. Fallon, *News of the World: Selected and New Poems* (1998), p.22.

61. Ibid., p.23.

62. Ibid.

63. P. Fallon, *The News and Weather*, p.28.

64. P. Fallon, *News of the World* (1998), p.24.

65. Ibid., p.49.

66. Ibid.

67. Ibid., p.50.

68. Ibid., p.67.

69. See 'Acts of Restoration', in P. Fallon, *Winter Work*, p.21.

70. P. Fallon, *News of the World* (1998), p.44.

71. See 'Confederates', in P. Fallon, *Winter Work*, p.44.

72. See 'Fostering', in ibid., p.23.

73. P. Fallon, *News of the World* (1998), p.18.

74. See 'Neighbours', in ibid., p.40.

75. See 'Hay', in P. Fallon, *The News and Weather*, p.36.

76. See 'History Questions', in P. Fallon, *News of the World* (1998), p.68.

77. See 'The Late Country', in P. Fallon, *The News and Weather*, p.40.

78. See 'Eye to Eye', in P. Fallon, *Eye to Eye*, p.16.

79. See 'One Day', in ibid., p.32.

80. See 'Big', in ibid., p.47.

81. P. Fallon, *Eye to Eye*, pp.12, 12–13.

82. Ibid., p.13.

83. Ibid., p.14.

84. P. Fallon, *News of the World* (1998), p.72.

85. Ibid., p.74.

86. P. Fallon, 'Notes and Acknowledgments', in ibid., p.138.

87. See 'Mehuman Hinsdale', in ibid., p.98.

88. Ibid., p.102.

89. Ibid., p.85.

90. Ibid., p.87.

91. Ibid., p.89.

92. See '29 February 1704', in ibid., p.95.

93. See 'The Buttonball', in ibid., p.91.

94. See 'Bloody Brook', in ibid., p.93.

95. Ibid., pp.104–05.

96. Ibid., p.108.

97. See 'Our Lives Now', p.115.

98. Ibid.

99. Ibid.

100. Ibid.

101. Ibid., p.116.

102. Ibid., p.117.

103. Ibid., p.118.

104. Ibid.

105. Ibid.

106. Ibid., p.120.

107. Ibid., pp.120, 121.

108. Ibid., p.121.

109. Ibid., p.124.

110. Ibid.

111. Ibid., p.128.

112. Ibid., p.129.

113. Ibid.

114. Ibid.

115. Ibid., p.133.

116. See Fallon, *Eye to Eye*, p.23. The Republican slogan was 'Tiochfaidh ár lá' (our day will come).

117. Ibid., p.22.

118. Ibid., p.23.

119. P. Fallon, 'Afterwords', p.124.

120. Ibid., p.125.

121. P. Fallon, *Ballynahinch Postcards* (Aghabullogue, Co. Cork: Occasional Press, 2007), n.p.

122. Ibid.

123. Ibid.

124. Ibid.

125. Ibid.

126. Ibid.

127. Ibid.

128. P. Fallon, *The Company of Horses* (Loughcrew, Ireland: The Gallery Press, 2007), p.12.

129. Ibid., p.14.

130. Ibid.

131. Ibid., p.15.

132. Ibid., p.16.

133. Ibid., pp.52–3.

134. Ibid., p.18.

135. Ibid.

136. Ibid., p.19.

137. Ibid., p.21.

138. See 'A Winter Solstice', in ibid., p.49.

139. Ibid.

140. Ibid., p.63.

Double Vision: Peter Fallon's Landscapes with Figures

JOHN MCAULIFFE

Martin Gale's paintings, some of which feature on the covers of Peter Fallon's Gallery Press books, are well-known for their combination of photorealist techniques with more traditional realist concerns. His paintings mark the Irish landscape with its inhabitants, often anonymous workers, whose recognisably casual clothing seems to act as a challenge to the landscapes they look at. Gale, a contemporary of Fallon's, is a useful counterpart for readers considering the ways in which Fallon has developed a particular style and subject which is broadly pastoral and recognisably modern. Richard Rankin Russell has written about Fallon as a pastoral poet, usefully placing him in relation to earlier pastoral modes in Irish poetry and to American pastoral poets, including Wendell Berry, Robert Frost and the Agrarians, but not extending his reading of Fallon to account for his relation to contemporaries, as this essay will do with particular reference to his poems' engagement with and response to the work of Paul Muldoon and Seamus Heaney.[1] This essay will examine *Winter Work*, where Fallon's serious engagement with pastoral traditions is first evident, in particular considering how his poems move with increasing confidence, through their consideration of ideas about home and history, towards William Empson's idea of pastoral as a form 'reflecting a social background without obvious reference to it'.[2]

Fallon's fourth collection, *Winter Work*, begins with a poem called 'Home' which is dedicated to Paul Muldoon, Fallon's exact contemporary, whose fourth collection *Quoof* also appeared in 1983. 'Home', like much of *Winter Work*, is interested in establishing a new territory for Irish poetry, in terms of the particular place it describes and the ways in which it describes that place, in poems that are formal *and* idiomatic, stringing a series of remarks across a nicely turned sonnet. 'Home' begins:

> The faraway hills are green but these
> are greener. My brother roamed the world
> and seemed to know everything. He boasted it
> until I burst, 'Well you don't know John Joe Farrell',
>
> the butcher's son, my friend'.[3]

The opening quatrain's opposition of the brother's idea of the 'world' to the speaker's fixed and local situation is a defining opposition for Fallon's poetry, and for his particular reinvention of the pastoral mode. Is knowledge of the 'world' dependent on worldliness? The poem will go on to enact a recalibration of what the 'world' might mean. Fallon's refusal of the faraway hills is decisive – and the local knowledge he celebrates is edged, across the enjambed stanza break, with a certain menace, 'the *butcher's* son, *my* friend' (emphasis added).

If this seems like familiar opposition, we might identify it with another sonnet, Patrick Kavanagh's 'Epic', with its opposition of Ballyrush and Gortin to the 'Munich bother', a poem whose importance is clear to Fallon.[4] But Fallon's following lines explicitly point in the direction of another surprising antecedent, Major Robert Gregory, as apostrophised by Yeats in 'An Irish Airman Foresees His Death' as he contemplates existence from a great height and thinks:

> A lonely impulse of delight
> Drove to this tumult in the clouds;
> I balanced all, brought all to mind,
> The years to come seemed waste of breath,
> A waste of breath the years behind
> In balance with this life, this death.[5]

Now, Fallon contemplates different kinds of world with a different kind of vertiginous drop: 'I balanced all beside / a field in County Meath, its crooked acres falling / south'.[6] The enjambed 'south' here signals a decision which the poems of *Winter Work* abide by, which is to establish a world which can include but not be defined by the pressing, immediate concerns of the larger world, which in 1983 looks north, across the border, to the Troubles. Fallon's poems do register the north, but only as one element of his world. William Empson suggests why pastoral is useful in this context when, in his essay on Andrew Marvell, he observes, 'to take a simple thing and imply a hierarchy in it can then only be done in a strange world like that of Milton's Adam or a convention like that of pastoral'.[7] Fallon's approach, with its balancing of pastoral and political themes, is dramatically and instructively different to Muldoon's.

In his book, *To Ireland, I*, Muldoon concentrates our attention on how 'the matter of Ireland' finds its way into the work of the poets he analyses, seeing the comma between 'Ireland' and 'I' as a poor barrier for the solitary poet who will be hoovered up by national traditions.[8] Sidestepping Muldoon's notion of a devouring tradition, and the example of his hallucinatory narratives, Fallon's pastoral poems aim to be both rooted and cosmopolitan:[9] circumspect in their references to contemporary Northern Ireland, they wryly attempt to move 'Ireland' towards the margins of his poems, or to represent it on his own terms. The hunger strikes and cataclysmic violence of the North in the early 1980s are the specific subjects of Muldoon's 'Gathering Mushrooms', the opening poem of *Quoof*. Such references, clear in Muldoon, are buried deeper in the corners of Fallon's poems, which are informed by the Troubles even as they frame them in relation to other histories and other narratives. Fallon's particular use of pastoral modes is clear in the rest of this opening poem, which manages to balance rooted and cosmopolitan perspectives. After its modern opening lines, 'Home', like many other poems in *Winter Work*, dips into another era and also takes on another aspect as the original dialogue between the speaker and his brother morphs into a plural voice:

We called a hill *Sliabh na Cailli*, the hag's mountain,
but that's the way it is for lowlanders will call

a small incline a mountain and mountain-men mention
a hill and point at Everest. Things were themselves.[10]

The speaker's relation of size to context, of admitting a particular rather than a universal perspective, a lowlander's rather than a mountain-man's or even a 'world . . . roam[er's]' makes us think again of Homer's ghost conjuring the Iliad out of a 'local row'.[11] However, the gnomic phrase, 'Things were themselves', presents different ways of reading this idea, suggesting perhaps that the people are comprised of the things that make them, the hills around them, but also remembering a simpler time when language could more justly and convincingly be said to represent the places, the 'things' it referred to. At this point the poem takes a couple of more detours, 'divagations' as Elizabeth Bishop calls them in 'The Moose', her unsettled poem with its own inhabitation of in-between places and overheard, half-grasped conversations, subjects to which Fallon is naturally attuned in this and subsequent collections.[12] In 'Home', the detour moves from landscape to family identity, with a graceful and witty pirouette after the line-break which suggestively muddles ideas of paternity or inheritance: 'We bore them as the Cuckoo Clarke bore his origin, / humbled, naturally. We were masters of reserve'.[13]

Many poems might end at that point, with the cuckoo as an unsettling, ironic model for how we may be said to inhabit or bear a particular place. But Fallon sets a different compass for the poem's direction in the closing couplet. He begins again with a highly compressed exchange of dialogue, '"Why?" "That's the way". "Ah why?" "Because . . . "', which calls into question the 'reserve' of which the speakers are master, before spinning the poem in another direction with a 'beggars-can't-be choosers' closing rhyme: 'When all fruit fails we welcome haws'.[14] There is something wily and capacious about the poem's ending with an aphorism, an acknowledgement of the largeness to which the lowlander's speech can aspire even as the line itself admits that its lot is not as immediately fruitful as might be wished. It seems to acknowledge the critique of the 'local' as a limited subject for a poet, even as it finds a way of framing that critique on its own terms.

The doubleness of 'Home', the way in which it enacts meaning in spite of its own objections, is also present in the book's second poem, 'Faith', which explicitly observes in its consideration of religious relics, 'We said they were / the real nails although we knew they weren't'.[15] What is implicit in 'Home' is how it establishes the grounds for how *Winter Work* will engage with contemporary Northern Irish poetic contexts, in particular through its imagination of place, a subject at the heart of the work of his contemporaries. Fallon's poems react in part to the kind of reserved and masterful but curiously abandoned lore of place (in 'Broagh', 'Anahorish', 'Toome') Seamus Heaney used especially in his 1972 collection *Wintering Out*, populating and dramatising the landscapes that Heaney describes, and glossing too Heaney's title, turning its idea of 'survival', of wintering something *out*, into the permanent if still seasonal idea of winter *work*.[16]

Paul Muldoon, too, insists on populating the fields: when places, Irish or otherwise, appear in his poems, they fragment, or appear on a collision course with something else, as when he introduces the misleading 'Eglish' of 'The Right Arm',[17] the 'here' of 'Anseo',[18] the bomb-threatened Belfast office block of 'A Trifle',[19] or the Ballygawley 'roundabout' inscribed on an uncle's forehead in 'The Sightseers'.[20] In the title poem *Quoof*, when Muldoon shifts from his 'childhood settle' to 'an hotel room in New York City' describing a 'red-hot half brick / in an old sock', he expects a reader to understand the poem he has not written, one which would find more natural, ruder, fuller rhymes for 'sock' and 'brick' than he does when he describes his father's 'quoof' *and* the difficulties that trouble communication.[21] That doubleness is something *Quoof* shares with *Winter Work*. Fallon's 'Home' is not as homeless, temporary or solitary as the hotel room of 'Quoof' (or the poem we might imagine as its ruder, inferred but unwritten sibling), but it *is* also a balancing act which responds subtly to its particular historical moment: *Winter Work* may occupy a different, non-urban and seemingly more homogenous world but it too adopts a distinctive, wideframe worldview (much as Fallon will later do in his translation of the *Georgics*).

Fallon's place-name poem, 'Loughcrew', is also clear in the way it stakes out a position distant from Heaney's myths of place (and, to a lesser extent, from Muldoon's ironic displacements).[22] 'Loughcrew' combines elements of different poetics, glossing Loughcrew as '*loch na craoibhe*, lake of the limb / of the oak on the island', but complicating any identifications with place as it says 'I wasn't born here but I came / to be at home near my home place', acknowledging local identity as a gradual, chosen process in his case.[23] Checking the maps against actual coordinates he finds 'a pair of islands. Now there's one', the latter sentence a plain statement of fact *and* a wondering remark. The poem ends with a brief translation of the Hag of Beare, 'Many a wonder have I seen / I have seen Carnbawn a lake / and now it's a mountain green', a riddle whose contrary rhyme finds the ground moving beneath its feet and seems, like the earlier phrase '*came* / to be at home' (emphasis added), to suspect any atavistic relation of identity to place.[24] The poem's combination of personal reminiscence, translation and research (of other maps) suggests exactly how difficult it is to speak simply or directly of a place: triangulated, partial, the place of the poem remains a thing apart from its speaker.

Fallon's poem foregrounds his intermediary status and this perspective opens up a distinctly historical version of pastoral. A related 'local' poem, 'The Hares', describes how hares are captured ahead of a hare coursing meeting. Dedicated to Seamus and Marie Heaney, the poem responds to Heaney's animated translation of the Middle English 'The Names of the Hare' (1981), which fancifully finds 72 names for 'the jumper, / the rascal, the racer'.[25] Fallon's poem grounds the hare in a story, mentioning how he had once broken open the hares' enclosure to set them free ahead of a meeting but now just fed them 'oats and carrots under pines, / away from crows' as the day approached.[26] Literal and matter-of-fact, the poem's last stanza imagines the coursing meeting itself and Fallon's language shifts, the hares suddenly taking on their proper, imaginative weight, their enclosure a 'safe house' (a phrase Fallon uses powerfully in the later poem, 'My Care') and their squeals 'like birds, like babies'.[27] Here, Fallon's poems' acceptance of country traditions does not preclude his critique of those traditions. The poem's shifting tone, like the portmanteau effect of 'Loughcrew', reference to precedent, its ease crossing from one era to another, again reflects Fallon's intermediate position, intent on acknowledging differences, on clearly detaching itself from some aspects of its contexts rather than forcing or forging an identity onto it.

The artificiality and/or consequences of spatial borders and boundaries are recurring themes in Paul Muldoon's poems, which return again and again to rivers, bridges, stairways, customs posts and unapproved roads. The border occasionally surfaces in Fallon's poems too, but he is even more interested in looking at temporal borders in his poems, finding that history – the creation of the new Irish state, for example – may be just as artificial *and* consequential as the physical border and just as likely to falsify or abolish identities. Time and again the poems locate continuities in Irish life which override the historical markers of the new state: these continuities belong to institutions which doubt the relevance or, at any rate, revolutionary consequences of the Irish republic. 'The County Home' rings another change on what we might mean by 'home' and describes some of that institution's residents. It begins,

> They were born in the other century,
> almost all of them, and several are over
> a hundred years old. Parnell was alive,
> a member for Meath. Theirs was the future . . . .[28]

The poem catches something terrible and timeless about its scene. The final speaker is 'doting. He must go to the funeral / of one long dead', and dreaming of getting home, the speakers tell him, '"Yes. / Yes", we lie, "when the weather's right"'.[29] In *Quoof*, Muldoon's ekphrastic depiction of madness, 'Edward Kienholz *The State Hospital*', is also interested in how madness sets the individual adrift, imprisoning its subject in an imperviously solipsistic state, a 'neon-lit, plastic dream bubble'.[30]

Muldoon seals this poem by beginning and ending his poem with the same line, 'where a naked man, asleep, strapped'.[31] Fallon's poem, in three parts and with its historical opening lines, grants some perspective to the reader, placing us outside the world of its residents.

Fallon returns to a state institution in 'The Conny Ward' and national history again provides a context, as he depicts a now-elderly man whose father 'knew the faction fights / and saw evictions in the famine' and who himself 'fought the Black and Tans / and wintered in damp ditches. / Without their kind there'd not be / a Republic'.[32] This poem's gentleness doesn't interfere with its trenchant portrait of a character and a world that has much in common with Patrick Kavanagh's 'The Great Hunger' and Tom French's later poem, 'Pity the Bastards'.[33] Again, though, it is Paul Muldoon who offers a usefully illuminating counterpoint to Fallon's poetics: Muldoon's 'Anseo' imagines another 'Ward', Joseph Mary Plunkett Ward, and offers a tale so over-determined that it becomes allegorical and purely national in a way that Fallon's poem does not. Muldoon's poem connects the child's humiliation by a savage teacher, who sends him out to find the stick (a 'hazel rod') with which he will be beaten, to his eventual role 'just over the border . . . fighting for Ireland', an IRA quartermaster who now terrorises his own recruits when he takes the roll and, alluding to Auden, '[makes] things happen'.[34] This is another sealed narrative, one which the individual protagonist cannot escape. Fallon's poem about Tom Ward, unlike Muldoon's, refuses allegory, insisting on registering a particular scene and certain phrases, not presenting its characters in a heroic *or* anti-heroic scheme or argument, returning to Tom Ward after his battles have been fought: 'now he's in the hospital / and made wear silly spectacles. / He's 94', at which point the poem does some typically swift, telling work with voices and tenses:

> The eyes that spotted Granard Spire
> know visitors by voices.
> Still 'you're a great man, Tom'.
> 'I was, I was'.[35]

Fallon withdraws his poem from the kind of narrative that Muldoon presents as total and inescapable (even as his poems try to turn them inside out). There is room for manoeuvre, for awareness and for other concerns, outside the matter of Ireland, in Fallon's uses of the national narrative. Like Edward Thomas's 'Lob', whose will-o-the-wisp protagonist's traces make up what the poem knows of his country, Fallon's open-ended encounters track alternate, almost evanescent histories.[36]

The logic of Fallon's historicised version of pastoral, with its privileging of the act of poetry as a kind of safe house, is clear too in poems which omit explicit public or national narratives. If he is explicit about the remit of his work in 'The Conny Ward', 'Loughcrew' and 'The County Home', the same ambition is implicit in the pronouncedly dark pastoral turn of other poems. 'Fostering' uses 'deft / skill and rough strength' as it cloaks a living lamb in the skin of a stillborn, fooling its mother 'who sniffed and smelled and licked / raiment she recognised. Then she gave suck'.[37] This powerful poem is grounded in farm work but it is also open to resonant, allegorical readings – about its trying on of the sonnet form, about the fraternal rivalry of 'Home' addressed now from a different, maternal point of view. Another pastoral poem 'Brothers', begins as an account of night-time poaching, brilliantly catching the silent trek to the river.

> A word,
> a glance could put an end to shadows
> in moonlight and lamplight
> on water, flickering here, there,
> moving upriver.[38]

But the poem's account of night work, of these 'votaries of darkness', seems to invite too a reading of the secret, buried life of writing, especially with its closing lines' affirmation: 'I'm at it still, I'm still in the dark / putting one foot in front of the other'.[39] A similar turn marks 'The Lost Field', which begins again with problems of inheritance, with an account of 'outlying land we couldn't find', which might be read as an allusion to Northern Ireland.[40] The poem shifts then towards a more liberating and utopian idea of the lost field as a site of discovery and growth rather than recovery, an idea which might be identified with the contemporary development of the metaphor of the 'fifth province' by the The Crane Bag journal and the Field Day Day Theatre Company, for whom such imagined spaces offer potential futures in which political conflicts are if not resolved then somehow controlled or held in balance.[41] Fallon's poem, dedicated to Tanya and Wendell Berry, may also be read as a parable of the 'return to the land' but readers must be alert too to the way the poem engages with its Irish context, the way it begins 'somewhere near Kells', a location that will put the reader in mind of both the Book of Kells and the Hill of Tara: the poem's story of an imagined world might be said to encompass both green/ecological and Irish contexts as it locates 'the place your own windfalls could fall'.[42] That place, the discovered territory of the poems of *Winter Work*, would become increasingly recognisable as Fallon's own.

The English poet Roy Fisher wrote of his home place, 'Birmingham's what I think with. It's not made for that sort of job, but it's what they gave me'.[43] Sheep farming in Meath, in addition to the working life as Ireland's leading publisher, are more usually full-time occupations and are not obviously rich resources for a working poet. Like Fisher with Birmingham, Fallon has turned his other work into a continuing advantage. This is very clear in the closing, title poem of *Winter Work* that brings together many of the collection's concerns. Its first quatrain reframes the book's engagement with history, again advancing on terms we might recognise from Kavanagh's 'Epic':what, the poem seems to ask, is the price of a belief that 'history / happens to others, elsewhere'?[44]

> Friends are unhappy; their long night
> finds no day, their lane no turn. They wait
> for things to change, as if history
> happens to others, elsewhere. They hibernate
>
> in dreams and fear.[45]

And if *they* 'hibernate' through the winter, Fallon has an alternative approach: 'I warm to winter work, its rituals / and routines', he writes before concluding:

> All I approve persists,
> is here, at home. I think it exquisite
> to stand in the yard, my feet on the ground,
> in cowshit and horseshit and sheepshit.[46]

The rhyme of 'exquisite' with 'sheepshit' brilliantly and ironically keeps the poem's feet on the ground, but this final stanza is ingenious in other ways. The idea of 'home', the place where the book began, returns now with a difference. The phrase 'at home' brings with it a more relaxed and dialogic sense of belonging. And the parenthetical phrase 'is here' also does interesting work, altering our sense of the poem and asking us to consider that 'here' may refer to the poem itself and to a *poet* who has clearly found his feet as much as it refers to the actual physical location of the farmer's winter work. Like Martin Gale, the poem's photorealist modernity, all that *shit*, gives new purchase to older, newly viable ways of thinking about the art and its uses.

Formal self-consciousness is often a defining characteristic of late twentieth-century poetry, often occupying too much of the writer's, reader's and critic's attention. One of the striking features of Gale's paintings is how they address this issue: in his landscapes with figures, the human figures rarely face the viewer, turning away and looking at something just out of shot. It is a dramatic technique, i.e., it dramatises the act of looking, and it encourages the viewer to look more closely at the painting, to figure out how to read these usually solitary figures in their worked landscapes. Fallon's poems, I would argue, are similarly doubled, clearly and unobtrusively drawing on the pastoral tradition but warily addressing, as Empson put it, 'a social background without obvious reference to it'[47], to which I would add that this finely constructed book, in its treatment of how the public world of history impresses itself on the private home of the individual, is also notable for its critical connection of everyday concerns to the prevailing political pressures of the time, a connection made too by the other classic collections of this period.

REFERENCES

Appiah, K.A., 'Cosmopolitan Patriots', *Critical Inquiry*, 23, 3 (Spring 1997), pp.617–639.

Bishop, E., *Elizabeth Bishop: Poems, Prose and Letters* (New York: Library of America, 2008).

Empson, W., *Some Versions of Pastoral* (Harmondsworth: Penguin, 1995).

Fallon, P., *Winter Work* (Dublin: The Gallery Press, 1983).

Fallon, P. and Mahon, D., *Penguin Book of Contemporary Irish Poetry* (Harmondsworth, UK: Penguin, 1990), pp.xvi–xxii.

Fisher, R., *Birmingham River* (Oxford: Oxford University Press, 1994).

Heaney, S., 'The Names of the Hare', in Heaney and Hughes (eds), *The Rattle Bag* (London: Faber, 1982), pp.305–306.

Heaney, S., *Opened Ground: Selected Poems 1966–1996* (London: Faber, 2002).

Kavanagh, P., *Complete Poems* (Newbridge: The Goldsmith Press, 1984).

Kearney, R., 'Editorial / Endodermis', *The Crane Bag*, 1, 1 (Spring 1977), pp.3–5.

Mahon, D., *New Collected Poems* (Loughcrew, Ireland: The Gallery Press, 2011).

Montague, J., *The Rough Field* (Loughcrew, Ireland: The Gallery Press, 1989).

Muldoon, P., *Why Brownlee Left* (Winston-Salem, North Carolina: Wake Forest University Press, 1981).

Muldoon, P., *Quoof* (Winston-Salem, North Carolina: Wake Forest University Press, 1983).

Muldoon, P., "'Wonder-birth'", *To Ireland, I* (Oxford: Oxford University Press, 2000), pp.1–31.

Potts, D., *Contemporary Irish Poetry and the Pastoral Tradition* (Columbia, Missouri: University of Missouri Press, 2011).

Rodensky, L.A., 'Prefatory note', *Some Versions of Pastoral* (Penguin, 1995), pp.vii–xxviii.

Russell, R.R., 'Loss and Recovery in Peter Fallon's Pastoral Elegies', *Colby Quarterly*, 37, 4 (2001), pp.343–356.

Thomas, E., *The Annotated Collected Poems* (Tarset, UK: Bloodaxe, 2008).

Yeats, W.B., *Collected Poems* (New York: Scribner, 1997).

NOTES

1. Richard Rankin Russell, 'Loss and Recovery in Peter Fallon's Pastoral Elegies',*Colby Quarterly*, 37, 4 (2001), p.350, argues '[Fallon] subverts the romanticized rusticism common to earlier examples of the genre'. Pastoral has sometimes been defined by recent English critics as a conservative, nostalgic and escapist mode, but in post-colonial Ireland the generative, utopian possibilities of the mode are more apparent. Donna Potts's recent study *Contemporary Irish Poetry and the Pastoral Tradition* (Columbia, Missouri: University of Missouri Press, 2011) discusses Fallon's translation of Virgil as part of its general overview of pastoral poetry, although her description of pastoral as a 'retreat' (p.13) is complicated by Fallon's pastoral strategies.

2. Quoted in Lisa A. Rodensky, 'Prefatory note', *Some Versions of Pastoral* (Penguin, 1995), p.vii.

3. P. Fallon, *Winter Work* (Dublin: The Gallery Press, 1983), p.11.

4. See P. Fallon and D. Mahon, *The Penguin Book of Contemporary Irish Poetry* (Harmondsworth, UK: Penguin, 1990), p.xvii: 'One poem, the sonnet "Epic", gave single-handed permission for Irish poets to trust and cultivate their native ground and experience'.

5. W.B. Yeats, *Collected Poems* (New York: Scribner, 1997), p.135–6.

6. P. Fallon, 'Home', *Winter Work*, p.11.

7. L. Rodensky, *Some Versions of Pastoral*, p.117.

8. See Paul Muldoon, "'Wonder-birth'", in *To Ireland, I* (Oxford: Oxford University Press, 2000), p.4: 'I'd like to suggest that the figure of Amergin is crucial to any understanding of the role of the Irish writer. . . . The bard Amergin has a mandate, it seems, from the *Míl Espáin* to speak on national issues, to "speak for Erin"'.

9. For an interesting discussion of cosmopolitan rootedness (and the problems attendant on identifying a nation with the state, as many critics of Irish poetry do),

see K.A. Appiah's 'Cosmopolitan Patriots', *Critical Inquiry*, 23, 3, (Spring 1997), pp.617–639.

10. P. Fallon, *Winter Work*, p.11.

11. P. Kavanagh, *Complete Poems* (Newbridge: The Goldsmith Press, 1984), p.238.

12. E. Bishop, 'The Moose', in *Elizabeth Bishop: Poems, Prose and Letters* (New York: Library of America, 2008) pp.158–162.

13. P. Fallon, *Winter Work*, p.11.

14. Ibid.

15. Ibid., p.12.

16. See S. Heaney, *Opened Ground: Selected Poems 1966–1996* (London: Faber, 2002), pp.55, 47, 54.

17. P. Muldoon, *Quoof* (Winston-Salem, North Carolina: Wake Forest University Press, 1983), p.11.

18. P. Muldoon, *Why Brownlee Left* (Winston-Salem, North Carolina: Wake Forest University Press, 1981), p.20.

19. P. Muldoon, *Quoof*, p.30.

20. Ibid., p.15.

21. Ibid., p.17.

22. In this poem Fallon's approach to place may in fact be closer to the poems of John Montague's *The Rough Field* (Loughcrew, Ireland: The Gallery Press, 1989 [rpt. of 1972 ed.]).

23. P. Fallon, *Winter Work*, p.13.

24. Ibid.

25. Seamus Heaney, 'The Names of the Hare', in Heaney and Hughes (eds), *The Rattle Bag* (London: Faber, 1982), pp.305–306.

26. P. Fallon, *Winter Work*, p.27.

27. Ibid.

28. Ibid., p.30.

29. Ibid., p.31.

30. P. Muldoon, *Quoof*, p.21.

31. Ibid.

32. P. Fallon, *Winter Work*, p.32.

33. Its history-from-below of the Republic is also a subtle companion to the poems and plays of contemporaries for whom history and not myth was a prevailing concern.

A foundational poem for this historical turn may well have been Derek Mahon's 'A Disused Shed in Co Wexford', *New Collected Poems* (Loughcrew, Ireland: The Gallery Press, 2011), pp.81–2, but hidden or under-valued histories are central to the contemporary work of Sebastian Barry, Eavan Boland, Harry Clifton, Gerald Dawe, Michael Hartnett, Brendan Kennelly, Tom McCarthy and others. Fallon's poems register history but also insist on privacies, on noticing things so that a reader is not so much persuaded about as brought to hear and see. While I focus on only a few poems in this essay, many other fine poems in *Winter Work*, including 'Bill', 'Confederates', and 'The Heart of Ireland', also link the personal to the public in understated, convincing ways.

34. P. Muldoon, *Why Brownlee Left*, p.20. Fallon's poem 'Bill', *Winter Work*, p.43, slyly alludes to the same poem: 'landlords / of the long acre, sky-farmers. // We know the way it is. We live / our lives; things happen'.

35. P. Fallon, *Winter Work*, p.33.

36. E. Thomas, *The Annotated Collected Poems* (Tarset, UK: Bloodaxe, 2008), pp.76–9.

37. P. Fallon, *Winter Work*, p.23.

38. Ibid., p.46.

39. Ibid., p.47.

40. Ibid., p.18.

41. According to Richard Keaney's editorial, with its suitably Meath-oriented explanation, in the first issue of *The Crane Bag*, 'Modern Ireland is made up of four provinces, whose origin lies beyond the beginning of recorded history. And yet, the Irish word for a province is *cóiced*, which means a "fifth". This fivefold division is as old as Ireland itself, yet there is disagreement about the identity of the fifth. There are basically two traditions. The first claims that all five provinces met at the Stone of Divisions on the Hill of Uisnech, which was believed to be the mid-point of Ireland. The second is that the fifth province was Meath (*Mide*), "the middle". . . . Although Tara was the political centre of Ireland, this second centre was just as important and acted as a necessary balance. It was a non-political centre. It was sometimes described as a secret well, known only to the druids and the poets. . . . It seems clear to us that in the present unhappy state of our country it is essential to restore this second centre of gravity in some way. . . . This province, this place, this centre, is not a political position. In, fact, if it is a position at all, it would be marked by the absence of any particular political and geographical delineation, something more like a dis-position. What kind of place could this be?' Kearney continues by emphasising the rootedness of perspectives in terms that would be familiar to Yeats's airman, Kavanagh's Homer, and Fallon's homecomer: 'In Ireland one may still be confronted with the riddle:

"Where is the middle of the world?" The correct answer to the riddle is "Here" or "Where you are standing"'. Another version of the same idea is the division: North, South, East, West and Here'" See 'Editorial / Endodermis', *The Crane Bag*, 1, 1 (Spring, 1977), pp.3–5, 4.

42. P. Fallon, *Winter Work*, p.19.

43. R. Fisher, 'Six Texts for a Film', *Birmingham River* (Oxford University Press, 1994), p.17.

44. P. Fallon, *Winter Work*, p.48.

45. Ibid.

46. Ibid.

47. W. Empson, *Some Versions of Pastoral*, p.vii.

'This blooming place':
Peter Fallon's *Tarry Flynn*

THOMAS O'GRADY

At a glance, Peter Fallon's adaptation for the stage of Patrick Kavanagh's novel *Tarry Flynn* appears to sit anomalously among the volumes of poetry on the shelf of his published work. In an afterword to the version of the play published by his own Gallery Books, Fallon acknowledges as much, explaining that he undertook the project of adaptation in 1994 mostly as 'a way of re-reading a novel, first published in 1948, by a poet whose works had continued to weave their spells since I read them as an undergraduate . . . more than twenty years earlier'.[1] Fallon then set aside the manuscript for ten years, returning to it only when George B Miller, director of the Selkie Theatre Company based in Pennsylvania's Lehigh Valley, queried him about whether he had ever written plays or stories: 'My answer was no – and yes. Time to dust down the script, I thought, to see if it might interest him'.[2] Obviously it did interest Miller and his Selkie co-producer Kate Scuffle, and on 10 September 2004 the play had its world premiere performance in The Ice House, a theatre in Bethlehem, Pennsylvania.

Yet while the happenstance by which it came to be staged might seem to underscore its anomalousness within Fallon's body of work, an attentive reading of the adaptation reveals that in the same way that the original novel dovetails neatly with Kavanagh's poems – his true forte – the play actually fits comfortably with Fallon's poems both in their own right and in their relationship to the precursory poetry of Kavanagh. In fact, Fallon's *Tarry Flynn* is as much a distillation as an adaptation, a processing and a filtering of not only the plot but also the themes of Kavanagh's novel: the play finally illuminates both the poetic sensibilities and the rural sensitivities of Peter Fallon himself. Fallon admits in his 'Afterword' that by the time his play received its premiere production, the so-called Celtic Tiger, a span of unprecedented economic prosperity and resultant social change in Ireland, had rendered certain of Kavanagh's themes obsolete: 'I was conscious . . . that the Ireland it depicted had suffered seismic changes: the economic excesses of the last decade – along with shifting attitudes in, and to, the Church, and an ever-widening urban/rural division – had dispatched its particular kind of poverty and hungers to a suddenly historical past.'[3] Still, the play transcends the limitations of a mere period piece. Reflecting his assertion that 'Kavanagh's vision, and version of a life, are founded in enduring verities',[4] Fallon's adaptation – no less than his own poems – registers the complexity of an individual's relationship to a place, specifically a rural place, that even while capturing the heart also has the potential to imprison the soul.

THE NOVEL

Indeed, the central theme of the novel involves the ambivalence that Tarry Flynn, in many respects a stand-in for Patrick Kavanagh himself, feels toward the family farm in County Cavan, a stand-in for Kavanagh's own County Monaghan. In typically self-confident fashion, Kavanagh himself declared *Tarry Flynn* 'not only the best but the only *authentic* account of life as it was lived in Ireland this century',[5] a claim that the thematic richness of the novel certainly supports. He also asserted: 'I have closed the door on that class of novel – no one for a generation will attempt to write about the Irish countryside'.[6] While still working on the manuscript, early in 1948, Kavanagh wrote to his brother Peter: 'A novel's story is of no consequence unless it illustrates a theory of life'.[7] Tellingly, the theory that emerges from *Tarry Flynn* illuminates Kavanagh's ultimate questioning of his other extended treatment of rural Ireland, his long poem *The Great Hunger*, published in 1942. Introducing the poem for a broadcast on BBC radio in 1960, Kavanagh explained that 'it is far too strong for honesty', elaborating that 'the poem remains a tragedy because it is not completely born': 'Tragedy is underdeveloped comedy; tragedy fully explored becomes comedy. We can see it and are not afraid'.[8] For bachelor farmer Patrick Maguire, sexual frustration (the cause of scandal when the poem was first published) is matched by a social and economic impotence imposed on him by his domineering mother:

Maguire was faithful to death:
He stayed with his mother till she died
At the age of ninety-one.
She stayed too long,
Wife and mother in one.
When she died
The knuckle-bones were cutting the skin of her son's backside
And he was sixty-five.[9]

In contrast, Tarry Flynn is a capable citizen of the self-contained world of the townland of Drumnay and the parish of Dargan. Twenty-seven years old, Tarry endures, like Paddy Maguire, the daily labours, travails, disappointments and indignities of a small farmer in a provincial backwater in the 1930s: the drudgery of land and animal husbandry, the petty meanness of neighbors, general domestic squalor, the conjoined poverties of purse and of spirit, sexual repression embedded in the teachings and the preaching of the Catholic church. But the crucial distinguishing factor between *The Great Hunger* and *Tarry Flynn* involves Kavanagh's own evaluation of the earlier work: 'there's no laughter in it'.[10] By the time he completed the novel six years later, Kavanagh appears to have developed a different 'theory of life': 'You can escape from anywhere by laughter – levity, levitation. This is the implacable laughter of the gods – not whimsy'.[11]

To the extent that Tarry's circumstances in the novel resemble Kavanagh's own conflicted experience of growing up in and around the village of Inniskeen, County Monaghan (preceding his more or less permanent relocation to Dublin by the late 1930s), the author's capacity to laugh at his protagonist's predicament affirms a point asserted decades later by Seamus Heaney in his book *The Place of Writing*. Borrowing an elementary schoolbook definition of 'work' (in the scientific sense) – 'To work is to move a certain mass through a certain distance' – Heaney clarifies both the nature of and the necessary response to the challenge of distancing oneself artistically from one's personal raw material:

the distance moved through is that which separates the historically and topographically situated place from the written place, the mass moved is one of the writer's historical/biographical experience, and each becomes a factor of the other in the achieved work. The work of art, in other words, involves raising the historical record to a different power.[12]

In *Tarry Flynn*, Kavanagh appears to have discovered for himself how 'distance, either of the actual, exilic, cross-channel variety or the imaginary, self-renewing, trans-historical and trans-cultural sort, can be used as an enabling factor in the work of art'.[13] First by locating the action in County Cavan and secondly by removing himself from immediate identification with his protagonist by finding ways to laugh (at least occasionally) at Tarry's at-times dire situation, he writes a novel that more than a dozen years after its publication continued to give him particular satisfaction: '*Tarry Flynn* is terribly funny and true in most places. No one but me could have done it, and only when I did'.[14]

Much of the humor intrinsic to the novel emerges from its episodic structure – from Tarry's various interactions with his tart-tongued mother and his slovenly sisters, with scheming and litigious neighbors, with unctuous priests, and with the young women of the parish whom he is so easily enamored of yet also so easily unnerved by. Combined with what Peter Kavanagh described as his brother's initial object in undertaking the novel as early as 1940 – 'to set down the authentic speech of the people'[15] – the humor intrinsic to Kavanagh's telling of Tarry's story makes the novel a ready candidate for dramatic adaptation. But just as important in that regard, the novel traces the truly 'dramatic' arc of Tarry's slowly evolving recognition that he would ultimately have to leave Drumnay and Dargan if he were to find enduring happiness in his life. Kavanagh once admitted that *Tarry Flynn* is 'nearer the truth' of his own early manhood than his purported autobiography, *The Green Fool*,[16] and he endows his protagonist not only with a poetic sensibility but also with an incipient poetic talent. In fact, Kavanagh interpolates into the novel, as Tarry's musings, several poems that have endured as part of his own body of work, including the novel's final passage, an eight-stanza ballad that concludes both wistfully and resonantly:

> Maybe Mary might call round . . .
> And then I came to the haggard gate,
> And I knew as I entered that I had come
> Through fields that were part of no earthly estate.[17]

But even beyond the poems, Tarry experiences 'life' with a heightened sensitivity throughout the novel:

He had faith in the day and faith in his work. That was enough.
Without ambition, without desire, the beauty of the world poured
in through his unresisting mind . . . All day he sprayed the potatoes,
and nothing was happening except his being. Being was enough, it
was the worship of God.[18]

Yet, eventually he declares to his friend Eusebius Cassidy, 'I'm chucking the
whole damn thing':

'. . . Chucking what?'
'Drumnay.'
'You are in me arse?'
'I am,' said Tarry, without really meaning what he was saying – at
least he did not think he meant it. 'And then you can have all the
women to yourself, and all the land as well. I don't give a tuppenny
damn for the whole thing'. . .
That day passed and another day and something was wrong in
Tarry's life, something was driving him – where he did not know.
Something was pulling him back, but he did not know what that
was, and he was seeing it now when he lifted his eyes to the lonely
hills.[19]

Tarry's decision to leave – the climax of the novel – is thus ultimately fraught
with emotion that crystallises into a revelation of what is truly at stake for him.
The arrival of his reprobate Uncle Peter provides him with both the impetus
and the rationalisation to depart; responding to Tarry's declaration of love for
Drumnay and environs, his uncle says: 'Haven't you it in your mind, the best
place for it? If it's as beautiful as you imagine you can take it with you. You must
get away'.[20] Nonetheless, Tarry remains conflicted even after he bids his sobbing
mother goodbye and heads down the lane: 'He didn't want to go. If, on the other
hand, he stayed, he would be up against the Finnegans and the Carlins and the
Bradys and the Cassidys and the magic of the fields would be disturbed in his
imagination'.[21] Made manifest to Tarry only as he takes a backward look at the
life and the world that he is abandoning, this is the central tension of the novel,
literally from start to finish.

THE PLAY

Not surprisingly, it is also the central tension of Peter Fallon's adaptation of the novel as a play. Fallon establishes this concern immediately, in a brief Prologue devised, as the stage directions indicate, to emphasise Tarry's *'other-ness'*: *'he can stand aside, look only half-interested, etc . . . .'*[22] Set at the junction of Drumnay lane and the main road, an evening gathering place for local men to posture self-importantly, to gossip, and to harass passersby, the scene in the Prologue culminates with Tarry's frustrated outburst at the news that a young woman who has been somehow interfered with in the townland has reported the incident to the parish priest:

> EUSEBIUS: (*Relishing*) There'll be sport about this, there'll be sport alright.
> TARRY: (*Abruptly*) They can all go to Hell![23]

Clearly, while Fallon essentially fillets out Tarry's identity as an aspiring poet, he nevertheless invests him with the marginal status that Kavanagh, in his early signature poem 'Inniskeen Road, July Evening', associates explicitly with the poet-as-artist in relation to his community. Comparing the poet's social plight to that of Alexander Selkirk, the real-life model for Daniel Defoe's shipwrecked Robinson Crusoe, Kavanagh laments: 'A road, a mile of kingdom, I am king / Of banks and stones and every blooming thing'.[24] Obviously well-versed in Kavanagh, Fallon has Tarry echo that rich equivoque – half curse, half blessing – in evaluating his complex relationship to his native townland: "'I love every step of this (*quiet, hesitant*) blooming place"'.[25]

Thus Fallon develops Tarry not as a poet but simply as a young man drawn by the mystical allure of landscape intimately known – the hills and the fields of Drumnay. Setting the stage (as it were) for the complicating action of Act Two, Fallon gives his protagonist a telling soliloquy toward the end of Act One:

> Is it natural, this need, this hunger I have to be near these whitethorn ditches, the lush nettles and docks and tufts of grass? All that's food and drink to me – the rutted lane banked with wild carrot like girls in their communion dresses in the May procession, and the dandelions like little golden stars in a big green sky, and that full four acres of potatoes coming into blossom. Even if I work

from stars to stars, living from hand to mouth, I'm – happy. You'd
go to the fair and come back thinking the whin bushes ought to
know you . . . .[26]

To that point, most of the action in the play has served simply to introduce the
texture of Tarry's daily life in Drumnay and Dargan: his give-and-take (sometimes
playful, sometimes hurtful) with his mother and his sisters Bridie and Aggie, his
not-fully-trusting friendship with Eusebius Cassidy, his awkward relationship
with the flirtatious Mary Reilly, his coping with the overarching influence within
the community of the Catholic church in the person of Fr. Markey. But at the very
end of Act One, Fallon lifts almost verbatim from the novel a passage of dialogue
that foreshadows what will ultimately affect Tarry's engagement with the land
that has so sustained him; mentioning that the farm of a neighboring family, the
Carlins, may soon be available through foreclosure, Tarry's mother declares, "'It's a
terrible pity you wouldn't take a better interest in your work and you could be the
independentest man. Oh yes, the independentest man, and then you could tell all
the beggars in Ireland to go and kiss your arse!'"[27]

Sure enough, before the end of Act Two Mrs. Flynn announces to Tarry that
she has purchased the Carlin property. But in the meantime the plot has thickened
with several knotty developments. Ironically spurred into action by a Mission in
the Catholic church preaching sexual abstinence, Patsy Meegan, a "'crooked oul'
bachelor'" according to Tarry, starts to show interest in Bridie who, "'within a kick
of thirty'",[28] will soon be beyond easy marrying age for a woman of her station
in rural Ireland and thus will become a liability to Tarry someday bringing his
own wife into the house. At the same time, the winsome Mary Reilly continues
to befuddle Tarry even as his mother suggests that he consider a match with the
physically unappealing, but much better propertied, Molly Brady (an off-stage
presence) – "'There's seven of as nice a field up there as there is in the parish'".[29]
As it turns out, in the narrow world of Dargan, Patsy is a cousin of Joe Finnegan
who, as a cousin of the disenfranchised Carlins, initiates a physical altercation
with Tarry over property boundaries. In Fallon's reworking of plot elements from
Kavanagh's novel, the land that Tarry loves so much and the additional land that
his mother insists will make him independent become increasingly entangled
with each other in Tarry's mind.

In *Sacred Keeper*, his unapologetically admiring biography of his brother, Peter
Kavanagh proffers an insightful evaluation of *Tarry Flynn* as a novel: 'There was

something fundamentally wrong with it which neither of us could put a finger on. I never really liked it: it was not the Patrick Kavanagh that I knew, not really the poet. He was out of his element writing something that bordered on social science'.[30] He may have had in mind a passage in which the narrator explains the complexity of Tarry's response to his mother's bringing home the news of her purchase of the Carlins' farm:

> Tarry was at first tremendously excited over the purchase, but as his mother spoke and he thought the matter over he began to pity himself. Even with the eleven or twelve acres added to their present farm what would they still be but poor? . . . The new acquisition only set him up firmly among the small farmers – fixed him forever at the level of the postman and the railway porter. The farm only drew attention to their real state. A tramp poet would be above him.[31]

In his adaptation for the stage, Peter Fallon has no such vantage point from which to dissect the implications of this complication in Tarry's life. Instead, he rightly relies on plot – or on a twist of plot involving a dubious deed for the Carlin property – to carry his play's thematic weight. Coincidentally, while taken directly from the novel, this twist – utterly plausible in the 'throughother' parceling of lots in Irish townlands – is one that Fallon attests to personally in his poem 'The Lost Field':

> Somewhere near Kells in County Meath
> a field is lost, neglected, let by common law.
>
> When the Horse Tobin went to the bad
> and sold a farm and drank the money
> there was outlying land we couldn't find.
>
> The maps weren't marked.
> My people farmed the farm.
> They looked and asked about.
> They kept an ear to the ground.[32]

For Peter Fallon the poet, that missing acreage is more emblematic than actual, a symbol of life's quest: 'Imagine the world / the place your own windfalls could fall. // I'm out to find that field, to make it mine'.[33] For his character Tarry Flynn, it is all too real, and its loss – or nonexistence – marks the climax of the play. Coinciding with his sisters experiencing their own disappointments, Tarry's '*disaster*' (as the stage directions indicate) – the social embarrassment as much as the financial ruin – leaves him with the difficult task of consoling his mother . . . until the sudden arrival of her brother, whose name Mrs. Flynn had muttered disparagingly throughout the play. As in the novel, Uncle Petey becomes the literal vehicle (he has a car calling for him shortly) for Tarry's becoming independent of the double hold – both spiritual and dispiriting – that Drumnay has on him. Briefly, Tarry attempts to resist his uncle's invitation to leave with him: '"(*Confused*) I love this place, the dunghill and the muddy haggard and the gaps–"'.[34] Ultimately, of course, like Tarry in the novel before him and like Patrick Kavanagh himself before Tarry, Fallon's protagonist acts on Uncle Petey's observation that 'we love most what makes us most miserable': '"You know you could do worse than leave Drumnay with me"'.[35]

Interestingly, as Tarry and Uncle Petey head out the door, Fallon creates a tableau of female stoicism quietly reminiscent of the ending of John Millington Synge's iconic drama *Riders to the Sea*:

> MRS FLYNN *resumes her crouched position at the fire, mumbling prayers. Alone in the world.* BRIDIE *and* AGGIE *re-enter. The three women resume abandoned positions at the hearth.*[36]

Perhaps more interestingly, however, and consistent with his eliminating the Tarry-as-poet dimension of the novel, Fallon ends his play not with the poem that closes the novel but with the final stanza of Kavanagh's Dublin-centered poem 'On Raglan Road', a ballad conventionally sung to the tune of the old Irish air 'The Dawning of the Day' whose wistful strains, according to the stage directions, introduced the Prologue at the start of the play.[37] The effect is that of a curtain call for Patrick Kavanagh, the poet-farmer original of Tarry Flynn who concludes his remarkable sonnet sequence 'Temptation in Harvest', written in 1945–46 while he was working on *Tarry Flynn*, with a description of his own departure from Inniskeen to follow his muse:

> Now I turn
> Away from the ricks, the sheds, the cabbage garden,
> The stones of the street, the thrush song in the tree,
> The potato-pits, the flaggers in the swamp;
> From the country heart that hardly leaned to harden,
> From the spotlight of an old-fashioned kitchen lamp
> I go to follow her who winked at me.[38]

POET AS PLAYWRIGHT

Peter Fallon's adaptation of *Tarry Flynn* as a play is actually not the first. That distinction goes to P.J. O'Connor's version staged at Dublin's Abbey Theatre in November of 1966. In some respects, O'Connor's play may be more 'true' to Kavanagh's novel than Fallon's: certainly it adheres much more closely to the plotline of the original; it is also fully faithful to Kavanagh's attention to Tarry's poetic aspirations, and it includes verbatim many more and much longer passages of dialogue from the novel than Fallon borrows. (Curiously, though, O'Connor omits – or excises – the character of Uncle Petey.)[39] Having fewer on-stage characters and fewer twists and turns of plot, Fallon's version is transparently more compact.

It is also more distilled, as clearly Fallon's adaptation is informed by his personal experience of growing up in a place and a time – a farm in County Meath in the late 1950s and 1960s – not very far removed from Kavanagh's County Monaghan and Tarry Flynn's County Cavan in the 1930s. Evidently, Fallon recognises in Tarry's dilemma a textbook instance of the tension described by John Wilson Foster, in his essay 'The Geography of Irish Fiction', between 'that recurring Irish topophobia, hatred of the place that ensnares the self' and 'what Gaston Bachelard calls "topophilia"', an individual's imaginative appropriation of a specific place that he or she holds personally sacred.[40] But whereas Wilson sees this 'love of place' as 'really a love of self which only in the short run contravenes the theme of self-escape',[41] Fallon's reading – and re-writing – of *Tarry Flynn*, while consistent with Foster's estimation of that novel's 'uneasy balance between rural naturalism and poetic fantasy',[42] reflects his ongoing engagement with the sheer complexity of 'place' in his own writerly imagination. Perhaps his adaptation of the novel is not so anomalous after all. No less than Patrick Kavanagh and his protagonist Tarry Flynn, Fallon knows the unsavory side of rural life:

Neighbours

If your sheep strayed they mightn't be returned.
His? They'd be collected
and maybe more along with them.

He was known to all and nodded to
in company when others talked,
he whose flock grew overnight
and not by buying or breeding,
whose brands were smudged, and who sheared early.

I've heard men say, 'He'd take the eye
of your head.' Aye, and the milk from your tea.[43]

In his afterword to the play, Fallon expresses gratitude to his own Uncle Peter: 'One clear day in 1957, the day we arrived to stay permanently in Ireland, he took this then five-year-old boy by the hand and had me "help" him with a lambing. On that February afternoon he put before me what has turned out to be a crucial, sustaining part of my life.'[44] Small wonder that he should end his poem 'Winter Work' with lines that Kavanagh might have given to Tarry Flynn:

I think it exquisite
to stand in the yard, my feet on the ground,
in cowshit and horseshit and sheepshit.[45]

REFERENCES

Bellman, The (Larry Morrow), 'Meet Patrick Kavanagh', in Peter Kavanagh (ed.), *Patrick Kavanagh: Man and Poet* (Orono, Maine: The National Poetry Foundation, 1987), pp.117–22.

Fallon, P., *News of the World: Selected and New Poems* (Loughcrew, Ireland: The Gallery Press, 1998).

Fallon, P., 'An Afterword', *Tarry Flynn: a Play in Three Acts Based on the Novel by Patrick Kavanagh* (Loughcrew, Ireland: The Gallery Press, 2004), pp.100–01.

Fallon, P., *Tarry Flynn: a Play in Three Acts Based on the Novel by Patrick Kavanagh* (Loughcrew, Ireland: The Gallery Press, 2004).

Foster, J.W., 'The Geography of Irish Fiction', in Patrick Rafroidi and Maurice Harmon (eds), *The Irish Novel in Our Time* (Lille: Publications de L'Université de Lille III, 1975–76), pp.89–103.

Heaney, S., *The Place of Writing* (Atlanta: Scholars Press, 1989).

Kavanagh, P., *Tarry Flynn* (London: The Pilot Press Ltd., 1948).

Kavanagh, P., *Self-Portrait* (Dublin: The Dolmen Press, 1964).

Kavanagh, P., 'Introducing *The Great Hunger*', in Peter Kavanagh (ed.), *November Haggard: Uncollected Prose and Verse of Patrick Kavanagh* (New York: The Peter Kavanagh Hand Press, 1971), pp.15–16.

Kavanagh, P., *Selected Poems*, Antoinette Quinn (ed.) (Harmondsworth: Penguin Books, 1996).

Kavanagh, Peter, *Sacred Keeper: A Biography of Patrick Kavanagh* (Orono, Maine: The National Poetry Foundation, 1984).

O'Connor, P.J., *Patrick Kavanagh's Tarry Flynn: A Play in Two Acts* (Newark, Delaware: Proscenium Press, 1977).

NOTES

1. P. Fallon, 'An Afterword', in *Tarry Flynn: a Play in Three Acts Based on the Novel by Patrick Kavanagh* (Loughcrew, Ireland: The Gallery Press, 2004), pp.100–01.

2. Ibid., p.101.

3. Ibid.

4. Ibid.

5. Patrick Kavanagh, *Self-Portrait* (Dublin: The Dolmen Press, 1964), pp.7–8.

6. Quoted in Peter Kavanagh, *Sacred Keeper: a Biography of Patrick Kavanagh* (Orono, Maine: The National Poetry Foundation, 1984), p.249.

7. Quoted in Ibid., p.158.

8. Patrick Kavanagh, 'Introducing *The Great Hunger*', in *November Haggard: Uncollected Prose and Verse of Patrick Kavanagh*, ed. Peter Kavanagh (New York: The Peter Kavanagh Hand Press, 1971), p.15.

9. Patrick Kavanagh, 'The Great Hunger', in Antoinette Quinn (ed.), *Selected Poems*, (Harmondsworth: Penguin Books, 1996), p.22.

10. Kavanagh, 'Introducing *The Great Hunger*', p.15.

11. Ibid., p.15.

12. S. Heaney, *The Place of Writing* (Atlanta: Scholars Press, 1989), p.36.

13. Ibid., p.46.

14. Patrick Kavanagh letter to Peter Kavanagh, 18 August 1961, quoted in *Sacred Keeper*, p.339.

15. Patrick Kavanagh, *Sacred Keeper*, p.127.

16. The Bellman (Larry Morrow), 'Meet Patrick Kavanagh', in *Patrick Kavanagh: Man and Poet*, ed. Peter Kavanagh (Orono, Maine: The National Poetry Foundation, 1987), p.119.

17. Patrick Kavanagh, *Tarry Flynn* (London: The Pilot Press Ltd., 1948), p.195. The snippets of poetry attributed to Tarry in the novel may be the remaining evidence of Kavanagh's attempt to follow his brother Peter's advice and 'write it in verse'. As Peter Kavanagh explains in *Sacred Keeper*, p.128: 'He tried but except for a few verses gave up on the idea. Later he filleted out the theme entirely and published the work as it now stands'.

18. Ibid., p.123.

19. Patrick Kavanagh, *Tarry Flynn*, p.168.

20. Ibid., p.192.

21. Ibid., p.193.

22. Ibid., p.11.

23. Ibid., p.12.

24. Patrick Kavanagh, 'Inniskeen Road, July Evening', in *Selected Poems*, p.6.

25. See Fallon, *Tarry Flynn*, p.35.

26. Ibid., p.35.

27. Ibid., p.38.

28. Ibid., p.41.

29. Ibid., pp.60–1.

30. Peter Kavanagh, *Sacred Keeper*, p.174.

31. Patrick Kavanagh, *Tarry Flynn*, p.81.

32. P. Fallon, 'The Lost Field', in *News of the World: Selected and New Poems* (Loughcrew, Ireland: The Gallery Press, 1998), p.16.

33. Ibid., p.17.

34. P. Fallon, *Tarry Flynn*, p.96.

35. Ibid., p.96.

36. Ibid., p.97.

37. Ibid., p.11.

38. Patrick Kavanagh, 'Temptation in Harvest', in *Selected Poems*, p.77.

39. See P.J. O'Connor, *Patrick Kavanagh's Tarry Flynn: a Play in Two Acts* (Newark, Delaware: Proscenium Press, 1977).

40. J.W. Foster, 'The Geography of Irish Fiction', in Patrick Rafroidi and Maurice Harmon (eds), *The Irish Novel in Our Time* (Lille: Publications de L'Université de Lille III), p.90.

41. Ibid., p.90.

42. Ibid., p.94.

43. P. Fallon, 'Neighbours', in *News of the World*, p.40.

44. P. Fallon, 'An Afterword', in *Tarry Flynn*, p.101.

45. P. Fallon, 'Winter Work', in *News of the World*, p.51.

Fellow Feeling: or Mourning,
Metonymy, Masculinity

ED MADDEN

The formal qualities of this poetry require particular analytic strategies from the critic. It is very largely autobiographical and takes its claim to authenticity from that familiar covenant between reader and poet which tacitly agrees the immediacy and authority of such experience . . . But where the fictionality of the poetic speaker is routinely concealed, a responsible criticism must seek to recover the moment of his construction (it is almost always 'his'). If this work were to be read primarily as unmediated transcription of the experience of historical individuals, it would become impertinent to question the constitution of emotionally pivotal female figures – beloveds, wives, mothers, grandmothers – in it. My comments about these female figures, then, as about the central male ones, concern fictive beings whose status is virtual, not actual.[1]

In Peter Fallon's heartbreaking poetic sequence, 'A Part of Ourselves', an elegy for his son, John, who died soon after birth, there is one section that moves me deeply, in part because it is about the possibilities and impossibilities of emotional expression in the face of traumatic loss. First published in *Eye to Eye* (1992) and republished in *News of the World* (1993), this sequence includes seven lyric sections depicting the death and funeral of Fallon's newborn son, as well as the immediate emotional aftermath for Fallon and his wife. In the fifth section, Fallon writes:

> We broached the sorrow hoard
> of women, tales unmentioned in their marriages,
> unsaid to friends, to families.
> Fellow feeling loosed their tongues,
> about unwanted pregnancies, abortions, miscarriages . . . .[2]

The poem is about breaking silences and, in this stanza, un-doing the concatenation of the unmentioned-unsaid-unwanted, the three-fold negations of un-suggesting the strength of both cultural suppression and emotional repression. The women are able to give their losses expression because the speaker's 'Fellow feeling'[3] creates an intimacy, a connection, and there seems to be a kind of reciprocity, as if this connection also enables Fallon to express and understand grief in particular ways.

As Richard Russell eloquently demonstrates elsewhere, Fallon's poetry draws on the tradition of Patrick Kavanagh, and both Russell and Bryan Giemza trace Wendell Berry's influence on Fallon's work.[4] But if Russell and Giemza hear Kavanagh and Berry, I sense an additional pair of Irish and transatlantic voices in this stanza, voices that foreground for me an attention to form – and gender. 'Fellow feeling', after all, is not *fellow* (male) feeling; grief, like community, is gendered here. As Russell aptly remarks, the stories the women tell are an 'oral history' of local deaths,[5] an observation that suggests to me Eavan Boland's *The Journey* (1986), which appeared only six years before *Eye to Eye*. Boland's book specifically invokes 'The Oral Tradition' of women's lore about childbirth, and in the title poem, 'The Journey', Boland portrays what could be called a 'sorrow hoard / of women', a spectral world of women holding their dead children, a testament to unrecorded histories of infant and child mortality.[6] The other voice I hear in this stanza is Emily Dickinson.[7] Dickinson's oft-quoted poem about trauma begins, 'After great pain a formal feeling comes'.[8] Given the context of trauma and funeral, one must hear the ghost of 'formal feeling' in 'fellow feeling', especially as the section goes on to compare the mother's experience of loss to an amputation, her feeling of grief to an amputee's sensation of a phantom limb. The occluded ghost word *formal*, like the phantom limb, asks us to think about *form* – forms of language, forms of community, forms of loss, forms of grief, as well as the *formal* properties of poetry.[9]

What are the connections between *formal* feelings and *fellow* feelings? How do properties of form contribute to the articulation of feeling? In this essay I explore the relations of form and feeling in Fallon's poetry, focusing on three poems, the sequence 'A Part of Ourselves', 'A Fortune', and 'An Anniversary', which returns to the infant's death ten years later. On the one hand, I pay particular attention to issues of language, including prosody and figure. Fallon is a master of prosodic variation, and a poet given to strategic and careful use of figures of speech – the colloquial phrase, the poetic echo, the pun. Throughout I hope to demonstrate how formal elements of Fallon's short lyrics amplify and extend meaning. On the other hand, though, I want to keep in mind the issues this stanza raises about gender – about affective communities and the politics of affect, about gendered voices and gendered experiences of grief. Russell says Fallon's work as 'elegiac poet and farmer' is anchored in a 'domestic, masculine space',[10] but I want to begin to map the parameters of that masculine space, at least as it is expressed in these poems.[11] I can imagine the raised eyebrows of some readers: *We're finally seeing Fallon's work receive the critical attention it deserves, and you want to subject him to a feminist critique?*[12] I hope to illustrate in this essay the complex representation of gender Fallon offers, grounded in equally sophisticated formal poetic practices. As Fallon negotiates the silences and sounds of his rural world, he offers a moving and nuanced representation of what he means by 'fellow feeling', a complex negotiation of what is shared, in human experience, and what remains, because of the social construction of gender and sexuality, intractably different.

'THE SORROW HOARD / OF WOMEN'

I begin with the idea of 'the sorrow hoard / of women', as this seems to most clearly indicate the specificity of gender to the analysis of grief, as well as the forms it might take, delineated in the two figures of a shared albeit private *hoard* and the 'loosed' *tongues* motivated by fellow feeling – one a domain of memory, the other a figure for spoken language. Though both figures denote the silences of women, I would argue that this section of the poem draws on two gendered forms of social silence: the repressions associated with women's grief and infant mortality (as well as the repression of histories of infanticide and 'abortions') *and* the social repressions of men's emotions. In what follows, I will look at the gendered forms of mourning depicted in the poem, and their poetic *and* political contexts, turning to the 'loosed' tongues of the women and the connections – and ultimately disconnection – between the genders that the poem traces.

That the sorrow hoard is *socially* constructed, not natural (nor naturalised: this is not gender essentialism) is surely marked by the use of the first person plural – 'We broached the sorrow hoard'. The pronoun 'We', given its use elsewhere in the sequence, denotes the speaker *and his wife*, both excluded, for the moment, from this gendered knowledge. Further, the fact that Fallon locates the hoard in the domain of the 'unsaid' and 'unmentioned' indicates a social construction as well: these are *untold* stories of particular experience, not inaccessible ones. The inclusion of 'miscarriages' in Fallon's poem suggests a particularly fraught form of silence in Western culture, the lack of mourning rituals for miscarriages and stillbirths; such mourning tends to be personal and individual in nature rather than communal.[13] As I noted above, Russell's identification of oral history in these women's stories suggests a connection to Eavan Boland's 'The Oral Tradition', in *The Journey*, in which Boland connects oral tradition to women's lore about parturition. Like Fallon, Boland indicates the exclusion of these stories from representation: she only *overhears* the story of childbirth *after* the formal writing workshop has ended, and by the end of the poem, though she calls the tradition an 'archive', she admits that it is only accessible in 'innuendoes, hints, / outlines underneath / the surface'.[14] Later, in 'The Journey', she finds that the great spectral historical sorrow hoard of infant mortality is 'beyond speech, / beyond song, only not beyond love',[15] as if to suggest that emotional connection is the critical avenue to these stories.

If Western culture does not grant stillborn or miscarried children or infant deaths adequate rituals of mourning, 'A Part of Ourselves' is driven by and structured around rituals of mourning and acts of care, fundamental to them the shared knowledge of women and the 'fellow feeling' it relies upon and invokes at this turning point in the poetic sequence. If the dynamic seems primarily emotional, however, it is worth recalling that at the time of the poem's publication, this kind of knowledge – women's knowledge about parturition and infant mortality – had *political* implications, especially in Fallon's linking of infant mortality with both unwanted pregnancies and abortions. In 1983, the Eighth Amendment, a constitutional ban on abortion, passed in a divisive ballot referendum. In 1984, less than four months after the vote, Ann Lovett, a young girl who had concealed her pregnancy from her family and community, died after giving birth outdoors and alone in a grotto dedicated to the Virgin Mary. Three months later, an infant with stab wounds was found on the shore in Kerry, and a young woman accused of the murder admitted, instead, to giving birth in a field and burying the infant there when it died, a complex and difficult situation – and an appalling investigation on the part of the Gardaí – that was labeled the Kerry Babies case.[16]

Fallon alludes to this cultural history in earlier poems, such as 'If Luck Were Corn' and 'The Heartland', both published first in *The News and Weather* in 1987, the year after Boland's. *The Journey*, and both republished with 'A Part of Ourselves' in *News of the World* (1993). Fallon seems to combine the Lovett and Kerry stories in 'If Luck Were Corn', in which a girl conceals her pregnancy from her parents, and when the baby dies, she hides the body in the lake, where it is discovered by a boy fishing.[17] In 'The Heartland', 'the body of a baby girl' is found by a fisherman 'dumped in a blue pillowcase' in a local lake.[18] Fallon makes the historical context explicit in 'The Heartland', further connecting the Kerry incident to other forms of political discord and violence: 'The *Irish Times* reports the Kerry babies' / inquisition, another senseless slaughter near / the border'.[19] The comma after 'inquisition' lets the series of things reported blur into an appositive comment on the case. The *Times* reports two stories, one on the babies, the other on border violence; *or*, read as appositive rather than sequence, the Kerry Babies case itself is 'another senseless slaughter near'. The inclusion of the local baby found in a lake (a *near*by incident) only three stanzas later lets that alternate reading continue to resonate in the poem.

I have resisted reading these incidents in allegorical national terms, placing them, that is, in the 'list of Irish works linking miscarriage, stillbirth, and infant death with some kind of failure of the nation state, turning the suffering mother's body [or the child's] into a metaphor',[20] though Fallon's conjunction of the Kerry story with violence in the North might allow for such reading – as might his further comment in the poem that 'we never had to wait and wonder / if outside worlds might queer / this pastoral'.[21] Though Giemza interprets Fallon's *queered* pastoral as a rural space explicitly warped by the intrusion of political violence or news from the outside world, implicit here seems to be a sense of the queer as the non-reproductive, or even future-negating.[22] Dead children, or more specifically, infanticide, queers the stereotypically natural and reproductive space of the pastoral. If that is the case, however, 'If Luck Were Corn' undermines this easy reading, since a neighbour (that is, a *local* speaker, in possession of local knowledge) silences gossip by suggesting that these stories are always already part of the pastoral landscape:

but if you drained the ponds
in your own back yards
you'd find more than you bargained for.
You'd not let on,
but the like of that's gone on to yours
since the year of One.[23]

The Kerry Babies and Ann Lovett stories, rather than being seen as anomalous, were seen to be indicative of an unspoken and unrecorded history of crisis births and unwanted pregnancies, which Fallon seems to affirm here at the end of the poem.[24]

Clearly then, it is not a stretch to connect the 'sorrow hoard / of women' with a rich poetic and political context. If we return to 'A Part of Ourselves', this context adds an additional charge to the poem. Fallon continues,

Fellow feeling loosed their tongues,
about unwanted pregnancies, abortions, miscarriages,

as his remains, a fingerful of hair,
a photograph, his cold kiss called, 'Remember me',
and I stood with them at the lip
of graves. She cried from miles away,
'I miss my baby', as an amputee

laments a phantom limb.[25]

The speaker claims fellowship if not kinship with these women in their shared grief and their 'loosed' tongues of loss. Surely we hear the words 'lose' and 'lost' in the verb 'loosed' – as well as perhaps the implicit social judgment of 'loose' women. Yet if that rhyme of social disapprobation persists in the word choice, it does not persist in the speaker's stance. The phrase, 'I stood with them' could denote a political as well as emotional impulse, especially when the poem first appeared in 1992, the year that the 'X' case about abortion made its way through the Irish court system and as two referenda were being held in relation to the right to travel and the right to information regarding abortion. (Also, Paula Meehan's moving poem for Ann Lovett, 'The Statue of the Virgin at Granard Speaks', was published by Fallon's own press the year before, in *The Woman Who Was Marked by Winter* [1991].) Across the lyric, the slant rhymes of 'hoard', 'unsaid', and 'stood' chime the trajectory of this movement, from an unspoken domain of women to the speaker's shared grief and his subsequent or consequent intent to 'stand' with the women in their grief, a grief with political implications. Moreover, if the speaker stands with these women in support of abortion, a felony crime, then Fallon's fellow feeling here is also perhaps 'felon feeling' – the almost rhymes of 'fellow'/ 'feeling'/ 'Fallon' surely summoning the *felon*.

MOURNING, METONYMY, MASCULINITY

Their talk was a gesture,
an outstretched hand.[26]

The 'unsaid' stories of women mark an explicit form of gender silence in the poem. The other form of gender silence, implicit rather than explicit, is the silence of men, or more specifically, the repression of male expressions of emotion. Obviously, there are socially sanctioned events for the expression of male emotion, funerals being one, but Fallon's explicit representation of separate gendered spheres of grief and grieving must also bring to mind the silence of men, the social repression of men's emotions that may impugn or warp male expressions of grief. While some scholars of masculinity may argue that representations of 'men's emotional incompetence' are oversimplified or lacking in empirical data,[27] and while Irish culture (like Western cultures in general) may have changed to allow for more varied forms of male emotional expression, the idea that men do not express emotions (or have difficulty doing so) still obtains in Irish culture.

Traditional Irish masculinity relied on a configuration of genders that made men breadwinners and women 'carers' who did the emotional work of the family.[28] In the 2007 Irish-American film *Black Irish*, Brendan Gleeson as Desmond McKay tells his son, "'You can't have it both ways. Either you cry like a girl or you drink like a man'".[29] While this film may suggest a generational divide in the gendering of emotions, the decade Fallon published 'A Part of Ourselves' was one during which the difficulty of male emotions was seen to affect men of all ages. In 1998, soon after startling new statistics about young male suicide in Ireland were released and as a new 'Exploring Masculinities' curriculum was being launched in Irish schools (only a few months before the release of Fallon's selected poems), *Irish Times* writer Kathy Sheridan asked 'what toxic element in male conditioning' forces men to think they need to be strong and silent.[30] In a later report on the masculinities curriculum, a schoolboy remarked that "'fellows can't express their emotions as well as ladies, so it probably just bottles up inside them'".[31] Fallon's own poems sometimes offer portraits of silent men, or men unable to express emotions except through violence, against others or against themselves.[32] As I have argued elsewhere, at the end of the twentieth century, Irish and Irish-American texts not only 'emphasize a need for emotional expression that is disallowed if not disabled by traditional forms of masculinity', but also 'suggest that male emotional expression marks the limits of cultural intelligibility'.[33]

In the fifth section of 'A Part of Ourselves', the fact that the speaker 'stood with them at the lip / of graves' places them *all* at the border of articulation – the plural 'graves' suggesting that there are many stories to be told, for which Fallon's is only an echo, a marker, a metonym. Russell remarks that the enjambment from the first stanza to the second 'successfully enables John Fallon's death to be literally written into this communal outpouring of loss',[34] but one might equally emphasise that the child's death becomes part of an oral (not written) archive here, a history that is emphatically *not* communal but limited and constrained by gender – these are stories the women have not told their friends or family, or even their husbands. The enjambment instead allows these many 'unmentioned' and 'unsaid' stories from an oral archive to enter the world of print – if only in a gesture, in the metonymical gesture of '*as* his remains'.

I would emphasise the idea of the gesture, in part because there is an echo of Boland here. In Boland's 'The Oral Tradition', the overheard story is 'a gesture, / an outstretched hand'.[35] And in 'The Journey', Sappho emphasises that all those stories of loss that are beyond representation, outside story or song, are not 'beyond love'.[36] Gesture, as an attempt at emotional (re)connection and new or renewed understanding, grounds this section of the poem – especially as this moment of loss allows for the gesture toward the 'sorrow hoard' of losses that remain outside representation. I also have in mind the importance of the gesture in recent queer theory, in which the gesture is seen as an interruption in heteronormative time and culture. The gesture is 'laden with potentiality', 'not an end but an opening or horizon'.[37] If, as noted earlier, these unspoken histories of infant death 'queer this pastoral',[38] surely this poem suggests a different way of reading those stories. The gesture is synecdoche for a different politics.[39]

I would also emphasise, however, the metonymical structure of 'as his remains', though one might ask, is it metonymy or synecdoche? The answer depends on how 'fellow feeling' works. There is a rhetorical drama here that suggests and contests the gendered relations – between the grieving father and the sorrowful women – that this lyric attempts to install. Metonymy and synecdoche are related terms, both involving the rhetorical (and psychic) substitution of one thing for another; in fact synecdoche (the substitution of part for whole, or thing for class) is sometimes defined as a more specific form of metonymy (substitution by association or contiguity). However, I follow Harold Bloom here in seeing synecdoche as a figure of representation directed toward totality, 'however illusive', and metonymy as a trope that, in its substitutions of contiguity, disperses and fragments. Synecdoche, by substituting the fragment for the whole, aims to represent the whole; it is a trope, says Bloom, of restitution. Metonymy, on the other hand, by substituting one thing for another in contiguity, is a trope of displacement.[40] Figures of mourning can be either. In the poem, Fallon presents three specific objects of mourning: 'a fingerful of hair, / a photograph, his cold kiss'. The photograph, a likeness, is metonymical, but the hair is synecdochal, a part that would represent the whole. To remember is to re-member. Poignantly literal, the figure of the kiss could be either, or both, as well as a metaphor for death.

In the syntax of the poem, the women's stories are contiguous with the speaker's child's remains. Indeed, the conjunction *as* that begins the second stanza marks temporal connection (they are speaking at the same moment that his child's remains speak to him), but it surely also suggests that the women's voices are analogous to the voice of these remains: the women speak to him of their losses *as*, or *in the same manner as*, or even *by means of* these fetishised objects of personal loss. The child is metonymical for the hoard of sorrow, contiguous, associated. If 'Fellow feeling', however, connects the speaker to the women – he is one of them – then the child's death is *part of* the 'sorrow hoard'. Fellow feeling makes the metonymical into the synecdochal – in Bloom's terms, restituitive rather than dispersive. Fellow feeling would move metonymy into synecdoche, transform association into identification: my story isn't just associated with yours, it is one of yours, part of the lore. The small story stands in for the larger but previously gendered realm of human grief and human misery. Our griefs aren't simply related or similar, they are the same. Community formation and identification become in some (illusory or inadequate) way compensatory for personal loss. Indeed, this act of representation attempts to stop loss by locating loss here, metaleptically making this death stand in for all those earlier deaths.[41] Rather that dispersing and displacing loss across the landscape, fellow feeling would represent it, identify it, hold it against those dispersals by claiming this loss as *the* loss, this loss as the paradigmatic representation of all losses unspoken and unsaid. When the speaker 'stood with them at the lip / of graves', this is an act of identification that has psychic and rhetorical effects, as well as the political implications noted earlier.

That said, the poem immediately moves to undo all these articulations, connections, representations – moves, in fact, to disperse grief and reinstate gender difference. If the impulse of this lyric has been to connect with the emotional world of women through the articulation of their stories *as* his story, the effect is ultimately one of distance and disarticulation. Fallon writes, 'She cried from miles away, "I miss my baby", as an amputee / laments a phantom limb'. The use of 'as' here cannot be temporal. It is clearly figural: a simile. More importantly, this turn reinstates gender difference: the first-person plural of the 'we' (father and mother) in the first sentence is now dis-articulated into the speaker, the 'I' who 'stood with them', and a third-person 'she', who cried miles away. Over the course of the poetic sequence, the 'we' of the first three sections is disarticulated in the fourth, at the moment of the child's death, when 'they gave her sedatives' and when he 'sought and found the comfort of a friend'.[42] She takes communion (suggesting her turn to Christianity for consolation), while the speaker 'waited for the given end'.[43] So the use of 'we' at the beginning of the fifth sections is an attempt at healing the relationship in the face of this loss – by seeking the consolation of women's stories. Access to their sorrow not only enables the speaker's emotional expression, but also, it enables some form of reconciliation with his wife.

However, whether the standing-with of fellow feeling is effective or not as political or emotional strategy, the wife's cry returns to gender difference, figured here as geographical (and emotional) distance: 'miles away'. Linguist Charles Lock says 'metonymy is spatial', that it negotiates distance,[44] but the negotiations of gender difference and emotional expression of this lyric ultimately fail. It is as if the attempt to connect with women only makes apparent his disconnection from his wife. Emphasising the intractability of gender difference, the poem moves from figures of metonymy and synecdoche to metaphor – from tropes of substitution and association to what Bloom calls the figure of *perspective*, the trope that emphasises perspectival difference.[45] The speaker's mourning has been governed by metonymy, by association, objects that represent the child; his wife's mourning is governed by metaphor, a loss that feels like amputation. His focus has been the other, the fetishised parts of the child's body or things associated with the child. Her focus is an other that is *part of the self*, loss that feels like part of her own body. The metaphor – that the loss of a child is like the loss of a limb – refigures the articulation of fellow feeling as literal disarticulation, amputation.[46]

The disarticulation of the 'we' is coincident with the assertion of this disarticulating metaphor. Ironically, it is also this metaphor that strangely emphasises the synecdochal impulse – the substitution of part for whole – the title phrase that animates the entire poem: that the parents lost 'a part of ourselves'. Indeed, we might say that this metaphor of amputation foregrounds for us an awareness that the phrase we use so easily – a part of us, a part of myself – is, in fact, a *catechresis*, a metaphor so overused that we have forgotten its original intent (like a table's *leg*), so overused that we have forgotten how powerful that metaphor could be, that we have forgotten how literal the pain of loss can be.[47] The wife's statement here at the end of the fifth section reinvests the title with its metaphorical properties: to lose a child is to lose a part of oneself (or in this case, a *part* of the *whole* family). Or more precisely, her image reinvests the title's figure with physicality and feeling. The metaphor of an amputee's phantom pain gives *form* to that loss by imagining that loss as a missing limb.

As the poem moves on, in the sixth section, the speaker continues to mourn metonymically, associating his child's death with a tombstone from 1899, and with the sounds of the graveside (prayers, shovel), while his wife states emphatically a phrase now re-invested with meaning: 'We are leaving / a part of ourselves in that ground.'[48] She reclaims the first-person plural for them: 'We'. And we realise that the title of the poem is *her* assertion: thus the poet grants the importance of her grief, which is different albeit shared. Still, though, the speaker resists in some way the literal meaning that she has asserted earlier by giving her statement a kind of philosophical meaning in renaming 'a part of ourselves' (her voice) as 'The innocent part' (his voice).[49] Perhaps this is a pun, given the child's innocence, but also clearly a statement of experience's subversion of innocence, an attempt to inscribe moral or philosophical meaning on emotional or affective experience.

The poem concludes in a seventh and final lyric that emphasises the emotional impact while reenacting the moment of the child's death: 'He'll die again at Christmas every year.'[50] Tennyson surely haunts this line, with his use of Christmas as the annual reminder of familial loss in *In Memoriam*, as well as his own insistent mapping of cyclical or natural time against linear (human, mortal) time. I am also reminded of Tennyson's attempts to understand grief and mourning by imaging his loss through that of others – parents, fiancée, even queerly imagining himself as widower to his dear dead friend as wife. The two parents ('We') give their son a name and 'assert him', asserting further that 'he lived a lifetime'.[51] The emotional impulse here underlines the cultural silences around miscarriages and infant deaths. Fallon continues, 'Now certain sounds, / sights, smells are the shibboleth / of a season'.[52] If this phrasing continues the remaking of Christmas into a time of remembered loss, it also disarticulates the fellowship and community of the season, 'shibboleth' suggesting tribal difference and the communities of language and pronunciation invoked in Seamus Heaney's 'Broagh' in *Wintering Out*.[53] Connected with the earlier invocation of 'the sorrow hoard / of women', however, 'shibboleth' may also suggest community formation, a community marked and created through spoken word, in this case the articulation of previously untold stories.

In the poem's concluding lines, Fallon attempts to hold in balance the community of shared grief and the difference of gender, by returning to the moment of the child's death: 'In a hospital corridor/I held him in my arms. I held him tight./His mother and I, we held our breath–//and he held his'.[54] The poem thus concludes with the most heartbreaking figure of the poem, 'he held his [breath]', a pun that juxtaposes the shared emotions of the speaker and his wife with the death of the child. The pun may echo a short lyric of Wendell Berry's, 'The Cold Pane', which reads:

> Between the living world
> and the world of death
> is a clear, cold pane;
> a man who looks too close
> must fog it with his breath,
> or hold his breath too long.[55]

Though this poem may lie behind Fallon's use of the pun, however, the effect is very different. Berry's philosophical lyric is clever, almost humorous, in its employment not only of the pun of the held breath but also the homophonic pun of pane – pain. In Fallon's poem, the shift from figurative to literal is similar, but jarring rather than clever, made all the more so by the stanza break. As the parents figuratively hold their breath, hoping for a different outcome, the infant literally holds his, and he stops breathing. As with the wife's figure of phantom pain and amputation, which reinvests the catechretical 'part of ourselves' with physicality and feeling, this shift from the figural to the literal amplifies the sense of loss by using the pun to make it literal, and the falling note of the last line's iambic dimeter further marks the absence of breath, stopping short and thus erasing it: 'and he held his [breath]'.

'A FORTUNE'

Some readers of Fallon may resist my rhetorical reading of 'A Part of Ourselves' as, in some way, intrusive, even offensive, given the autobiography that grounds these poems. It was that sense that governed my prophylactic citation of Patricia Coughlan in the epigraph that begins this essay. As she notes, autobiographical poetry 'takes its claim to authenticity from that familiar covenant between reader and poet which tacitly agrees the immediacy and authority of such experience'.[56] I recognise a similar covenant with readers and even critics of Fallon.[57] To be attentive to figure is not to obviate the validity or power of the autobiographical. While I do not want to disavow the power of this agreement for readers (including myself), I do want to bracket it out for purposes of analysis – especially as I turn to 'A Fortune', a poem in which the construction of a gendered speaker is most clearly fictive and mediated, in part because of the use of second person, in part because of the revision of the poem's title.

'A Fortune' precedes 'A Part of Ourselves' in *News of the World*, and as Russell argues, it should be read as a prelude to the sequence.[58] I would argue further that it has direct resonances with the fifth section, in which the speaker 'broached the sorrow hoard / of women'. As originally published in *Eye for Eye*, the title of this poem was 'The World of Women',[59] an invocation of a gendered domain like the 'sorrow hoard'. The revision makes the connection even more apparent, if indirect, since the ironic 'Fortune' surely resonates with the implications of hidden or protected treasure in the word 'hoard'. Strangely, in the associative and perhaps unconscious connections between the two poems, the choice of the verb 'broached' seems equally revelatory. The central figure of 'A Fortune' is the grieving mother's breast, swollen with milk; to broach means to bring up a subject or to initiate a discussion, but it also means to break the surface (as the women's stories move into articulation?), or to tap or pierce in order to draw off liquid. And a broach is a pin worn by a woman, usually, above or at her breast. While the ideas of richness, gendered domains, and memory connect this poem to the 'sorrow hoard / of women', the associations of word choice circulate, awkwardly and uneasily, around the central figure of the woman's swollen breast.

The poem reads:

She whispers 'Stay'.
You lie by her side.
You touch the silk
bandages.
    Resist the will
to caress her breast.
It will fill
into a fortune of milk
for the baby who died
on Saturday.[60]

Read for the first time, the poem seems to open as seduction, but shifts, jarringly, on the enjambment of 'silk / bandages', silk transformed from the erotic (almost expected in the context of the first two lines) to the medical. As if to register the cognitive break this shift entails, the line itself is broken, echoing Fallon's comment at the beginning of 'A Part of Ourselves' that the death of the child is a 'a stammer, now a *broken* promise'.[61]

Further, the mode shifts at this broken line from narrative to imperative, as if the new context in which the man finds himself requires instruction in what to do, or perhaps, more importantly, what *not* to do: 'Resist the will / to caress her breast'. Narrative, after all, relies on cause and effect, on the naturalisation of generic expectation and narrative sequence. In the brief narrative that opens this lyric, a woman says 'Stay' and a man lies beside her, so the narrative expectation is that he will touch her sexually. In the context of the book (its rural male persona, its autobiographical elements), the use of 'you' invokes a male reader, but this structural gendering only obscures the real effects of second person here, which is not to create intimacy or identification, but actually to allow the speaker to distance himself from the scene, to displace the trauma away from the 'I'. This is clear if one imagines the other possibilities: 'You whisper "Stay" / I lie by your side', or 'She whispers "Stay". / He lies by her side'. The first person feels artificial in its intimacy, if projected through the poem, and neither first nor third person would allow for the felt urgency of the imperative: resist what you want to do, what, in fact, feels natural.

The nine-line poem is structured in concentric rhymes. The first line rhymes with the last, the second with the penultimate, and so on: 'stay/Saturday', 'side/died', 'silk/milk', 'will/fill'. If the break in the poem suggests quatrain and sestet (that is, if we try to read the broken line as two lines), it is rhyme that heals the rift, the rhyme pattern clearly suggesting a nine-line poem even as it registers the broken line as *break* (not an indented line). That is, sound compensates. The fifth or middle line has no matching line: 'breast' has no echoing end-rhyme, ironically emphasising that the breast filling with milk will not be nursed, will not find its natural complement. Further, this line about that which should not be touched includes an internal rhyme that emphasises touching, caress – breast, and worse, 'breast' pulls together the vowel sound of carESS and the consonant of resiST, as if to emphasise the impulse that lies, thwarted, at the heart of this poem.[62]

The break on the fourth line that disrupts the poem's mirrored rhyme structure also disrupts the dimeter rhythm of the opening lines, the dactyl of 'bandages' followed by a pause, a caesura ensured by both period and the mid-line break. 'Resist the will' seems to reinstate the dimeter pattern, but instead the seventh and eighth lines – 'into a fortune of milk / for the baby who died' – want to swell into trimeter. As Eamon Grennan remarks elsewhere, Fallon's 'metrical fluency' includes a tendency to subvert or 'unbalance' rhythmic patterns, 'usually by lengthening the line – turning it towards the rhythm of speech', as he does here.[63] The language resists the rhythmic template here; although the preceding dimeter beat forces one to hear those lines as dimeter, it is as if the flow of language itself enacts the natural excess (milk, syllables) curtailed by the artificial (or unnatural) strictures of the rhythm – appropriate to a poem about a life cut short. The last line, 'on Saturday', tells us that the infant died within the past week, the final dactyl not only echoing the falling note of 'bandages' at the poem's break, but also, in its concision, foregrounding both the brevity of the child's life and the recentness of his death.

ANNIVERSARIES, OR SPACE AND TIME

As if home were a place
and not a time . . . .[64]

Some of the figures that structure the gendered forms of feeling in the poems based in the infant death of John Fallon continue to circulate in Fallon's work, as if to affirm their affective value – as if to affirm, that is, not only their centrality to his poetic, but also the persistence of the trauma they represent. In 'Less Ado', for example, Fallon recycles the pun of the held breath. With a friend in the hospital, he watches a perfectly still lake for the ripple, 'a breath of wind // made visible', which is inevitable in the living world. He writes, 'You count your blessings. / The evening beats its low tattoo. / You hold your breath. You breathe / again'. At the heart of the poem, almost literally, is an awareness of his own mortality: 'Now time's what you've / less of'.[65]

The charged word *hoard* returns in 'A Flowering', where it seems a condensation of themes, denoting something outside or resistant to representation, but also a richness, something cherished in memory. Elegiac and ecological, a poem celebrating an unnamed and usually unseen animal, the poem is about the pine marten, a rare and protected Irish mammal, described as 'not on the maps' and nothing recorded; since it is known to the speaker only through heraldry, the speaker wonders even 'Were they real at all'? Until he saw a pair in the wild, a moment he describes as 'a richness // I've hoarded'.[66] The poem is still marked by loss and absence, though, as the poet describes one found dead on the road, another known only through tracks in morning frost.[67]

The most obvious traces of the persistence of a fundamental trauma, the loss of a child, are in the poems 'A Will', in which he says to 'my son, my future', 'I would have my loves outlive me,'[68] and 'Another Anniversary'. In the latter poem, Fallon writes:

> You turn
> hearing the joy
> of football
> in the yard.
> You yearn
> for the footfall
> of the lost,
> the scarred.[69]

Though divided into alternating monometer and dimeter lines, the first stanza feels like a formal trimeter quatrain: 'You turn hearing the joy / of football in the yard. / You yearn for that footfall / of the lost, the scarred'. Read this way, however, the prosody would push the symbolically rich rhymes of 'turn'/'yearn' and 'football'/'footfall' into interior rhymes. But the form as Fallon has published the poem foregrounds the two end words that, significantly, don't rhyme: 'joy' and 'lost', as if to emphasise that the 'joy' is impossible to rhyme (to find again) because of what (or who) is 'lost'. Like the 'sorrow hoard', 'the lost, the scarred' includes the dead child within a larger domain of trauma and loss. Again note Fallon's infrequent use of second person; as in 'A Fortune', rather than inviting the reader to identify with the speaker, the effect is one of distance, an emotional distancing that echoes the temporal distancing of the poem. (Could the 'you' also be the mother in this poem? Perhaps.)

The poem continues:

> Again, again
> and again
> you feel the sten-
> gun attack
> of that 'What if?'
> and that 'What then?'
> Well, then
> he'd be a boy
>
> who's ten.[70]

Fallon begins the second stanza by inverting the monometer-dimeter pattern, and the breaking of 'sten-gun' suggests the artificial constriction of the rhyme and rhythm. Sten guns were British submachine guns, perhaps best known from use in the Second World War – but also used during the IRA Border Campaign (1956–1962), after the IRA had re-armed themselves through raids on British bases in Northern Ireland. While the rhyme requires both the gun and its syllabic breaking, the choice of this particular gun adds a national charge to the questions of 'What if?' and 'What then?' – a resonance Fallon doesn't explore, but an echo of his tendency in earlier poems to 'queer' the pastoral by including not only news from the outside but poetic figures charged with national or political content.[71]

At the two questions, however, the rhythm changes, as if to affirm that the counterfactual conditional is a different narrative, a different pattern. After these two lines of repeated (like a machine gun) iambic dimeter questions, the form varies further. The poem returns to a monometer-dimeter couplet – 'Well, then, /

he'd be a boy' – as if to suggest a return to the opening narrative pattern, but an alternate version of the opening in which the dead boy lives on. The strong iambic does not allow a conversational pause on 'Well', forcing an understated and almost offhand reading of these lines and their counterfactual conclusion: *well then, if that happened, then this would be true.* However, as the poem drops, with another stanza break, into the clipped iamb of 'who's ten', we surely sense the echo of the stanza pattern of 'A Part of Ourselves', which included a similar drop into an often shorter final line. At the same time, the rhyme insists on an ironic form of closure, as if we hear a dimeter quatrain: 'of that "What if?" / and that "What then?"/ Well, then he'd be / a boy who's ten'. Or perhaps even a tetrameter couplet (one iamb short of the traditional heroic couplet). Such a restructuring would hide what is so apparent in the printed version: the echo of 'joy' in the first stanza (where it has no rhyme) with 'boy' here at the end, making clear that it can only be echoed in the counterfactual fiction.

'Ten', however, is the word that condenses, rhythmically and emotionally, the trauma and the yearning of this poem. Obviously, with the addendum of the date, 2000, below the poem, the number confirms the meaning of the title, the boy now dead ten years. The word also chimes against 'sten' and 'again' and 'then' – especially the double 'then', which concludes the counterfactual if-then statement and which contrasts with the actual and the now. Moreover, as Debra Fried notes, rhymes on cardinal numbers carry a potent charge. Such a rhyme seems 'an inevitable confirmation of sense', with a 'surprising yet inevitable punch-line effect like a good pun'.[72] Ironically, the rhyme also toys with a common Irish pronunciation of the *th-* sound as a hard *t* – a shibboleth, we might say. If 'then' may sound like 'ten', given the tendency of some Irish speakers to pronounce *th-* as a dental plosive, then 'ten' also sounds like 'then' – and the boy of ten is really the boy who is 'then', the boy who remains in the past.

These poems recycle figures from the elegiac poems and demonstrate the relations of form to structures of feeling, but they do not obviously address gender, so I want to conclude, briefly, with a poem that does. Fallon returns to gendered forms of feeling and the central figure of the breast in the 1998 poem, 'Happy. Loving Women', which seems compensatory when read in relation to 'A Fortune' and to the elegiac sequence it precedes. Beginning with his own childhood, the speaker describes a life spent in the care of women. 'From Osnabrück to Lennoxbrook', Fallon writes, 'I grew up in the care of loving women. / Loughcrew'.[73] This statement is literally the center, the heart, of the poem, a hinge that moves him from his childhood elsewhere to his family home in Loughcrew, the poem's pivot being 'the care of loving women'. But this middle stanza is an odd stanza. The two preceding and the two following stanzas all use hard rhymes for the second and fourth lines: 'well/spell', 'ball/wall', 'overhear/ear', 'harden/garden'.[74] This stanza continues, 'A maple in late May/blazes Japan', rhyming 'women' with 'Japan', a rhyme that is more forced than slant.[75] The artificiality of the rhyme, like the artificiality of the Japanese maple in Loughcrew, as well as the geographic movements of migration (of the self and the transplanted maple, both relocated to the childhood home), all suggest strategies of force: an unnatural attempt to construct a natural home, literal or psychic, but grounded in structures of gender, 'the care of loving women'.

The very end of the poem returns to the breast, icon of both broken family and broken relation in 'A Fortune':

> And once, just recently, I brushed
> against her breast and I felt it harden.
> The woman of the fields
> has strayed into the garden.[76]

The movement is casual – 'brushed' and 'strayed' are casual verbs, verbs that suggest this recovery is unintentional, even natural, albeit transformative. The moment is Edenic, not simply a turn from work to pleasure, but a return to *the* garden. If the breast inevitably functions as the primary figure of women's (maternal) care, then the breast the speaker was not allowed to touch in 'A Fortune' recovers its sexual *and* maternal value in this poem. Against the artificiality of the poem's center, this last stanza claims a natural Eden of gender, the naturalness reinforced by the rhyme 'harden'/'garden'. Against a world of loss, the speaker insists on his happiness, 'loving women'. Against the earlier invoked 'sorrow hoard / of women', the poem reinstalls a compensatory world of women's care writ large – 'the care of loving women' written across time (personal history) and space (the geographies of migration and transplant). Tellingly, the title allows 'Loving' to function as a pun, either a description of the women (these are happy, loving women), or a gerund for the speaker (he is happy, loving women), making clear the centrality of female care to his sense of a safe world, his own happiness.

REFERENCES

Allen, F., 'Review of Peter Fallon, *News of the World: Selected and New Poems* (1998)', *Metre*, 5 (Autumn/Winter 1998), pp.116–118.

Berry, W., *A Part* (San Francisco, California: North Point Press, 1980).

Berry, W., *Collected Poems: 1957–1982* (San Francisco, California: North Point Press, 1985).

Black Irish., Film. Dir. B. Gann. Anywhere Road Entertainment and Creanspeak Productions, 2007.

Bloom, H., *A Map of Misreading* (Oxford: Oxford University Press, 1975).

Boland, E., *The Journey and Other Poems* (Dublin: Arlen House, 1986; Manchester: Carcanet Press, 1987).

Connolly, L. and T. O'Toole, *Documenting Irish Feminisms: The Second Wave* (Dublin: Woodfield Press, 2005).

Coughlan, P., '"Bog Queens": The Representation of Women in the Poetry of John Montague and Seamus Heaney', in Toni O'Brien Johnson and David Cairns (eds), *Gender and Irish Writing* (Philadelphia: Open University Press, 1991), pp.88–111.

Culler, J., 'The Call of the Phoneme: Introduction', in Culler (ed.), *On Puns: The Foundation of Letters* (New York: Basil Blackwell, 2005), pp.1–16.

Cullingford, E.B., 'Seamus and Sinéad: from "Limbo" to *Saturday Night Live* by way of *Hush-A-Bye Baby*', *Colby Quarterly*, 30, 1 (March 1994), pp.43–62.

Dickinson, E., *The Complete Poems of Emily Dickinson*, in T.H. Johnson (ed.) (Boston: Little, Brown, and Company, 1960).

Edelman, L., *No Future: Queer Theory and the Death Drive* (Durham, North Carolina: Duke University Press, 2004).

Fallon, P., *The News and Weather* (Dublin: The Gallery Press, 1987).

Fallon, P., *Eye to Eye* (Loughcrew, Ireland: The Gallery Press, 1992).

Fallon, P., *News of the World: Selected Poems* (Winston-Salem, North Carolina: Wake Forest University Press, 1993).

Fallon, P., **News of the World: Selected and New Poems** (Loughcrew, Ireland: The Gallery Press, 1998).

Fallon, P., *The Company of Horses* (Loughcrew, Ireland: The Gallery Press, 2007).

Ferguson, H., 'Men and Masculinities in Late-modern Ireland', in B. Pease and K. Pringle (eds), *A Man's World? Changing Men's Practices in a Globalized World* (London: Zed Books, 2001), pp.118–134.

Ferriter, D., *Occasions of Sin: Sex & Society in Modern Ireland* (London: Profile Books, 2009).

Fried, D., 'Rhyme Puns', in J. Culler (ed.), *On Puns: The Foundation of Letters* (New York: Basil Blackwell, 2005), pp.83–99.

Galasinski, D, *Men and the Language of Emotions* (Houndmills, UK: Palgrave Macmillan, 2004).

Gleeson, J., P. Conboy and A. Walsh, *The Piloting of 'Exploring Masculinities' (1997–1998): Context, Implementation, and Issues Arising: Report of External Evaluation* (Dublin: Stationery Office, 2004).

Grennan, E., 'Sing a Hymn to Works and Days: Review of *The Georgics of Virgil*, trans. Peter Fallon', *Metre*, 17 (Spring 2005), pp.116–120.

Heaney, S., *Wintering Out* (London: Faber, 1972).

Kelleher, M., '*The Field Day Anthology* and Irish Women's Literary Studies', *Irish Review*, 30 (2003), pp.82–94.

Kenny, C., *Moments That Changed Us* (Dublin: Gill & Macmillan, 2005).

Lock, C., 'Debts and Displacements: on Metaphor and Metonymy', *Acta Linguistica Hafniensia: International Journal of Linguistics*, 29, 1 (1997), pp.321–337.

Madden, E., 'Exploring Masculinity: Proximity, Intimacy, and *Chicken*', in C. Magennis and R. Mullen (eds), *Irish Masculinities: Reflections on Literature and Culture* (Dublin: Irish Academic Press, 2011), pp.77–88.

Madden, E., '"Gently, not gay": Proximity, Sexuality, and Irish Masculinity at the End of the Twentieth Century', *Canadian Journal of Irish Studies*, 36, 1 (Spring 2012), pp.69–87.

McKimm, M, 'Review of Gerard Smyth, *The Mirror Tent*; Matthew Sweeney, *Black Moon*; Peter Fallon, *The Company of Horses*; and Frank McGuinness, *Dulse*', *The Warwick Review*, 2, 1 (2008), pp.83-91.

Muñoz, J.E., *Cruising Utopia: The Then and There of Queer Futurity* (New York: New York University Press, 2009).

Orenstein, P., 'Mourning My Miscarriage', *New York Times Magazine*, 21 April 2002. Online at http://www.nytimes.com/2002/04/21/magazine/mourning-my-miscarriage.html (accessed 1 December 2012).

Russell, R.R., 'Loss and Recovery in Peter Fallon's Pastoral Elegies', *Colby Quarterly*, 37, 4 (December 2001), pp.343–356.

Sheridan, K., 'New Laddism Blamed for Big Boys Behaving Badly', *Irish Times*, 10 January 1998, p.11.

Stafford, W., *Traveling through the Dark* (New York: Harper and Row, 1951).

Sullivan, M., 'The Treachery of Wetness: Irish Studies, Seamus Heaney and the Politics of Parturition', *Irish Studies Review*, 13, 4 (2005), pp.451–468.

Trotter, M., 'Personal Correspondence', 5 November 2012.

NOTES

1. P. Coughlan, '"Bog Queens": The Representation of Women in the Poetry of John Montague and Seamus Heaney', in Toni O'Brien Johnson and David Cairns (eds), *Gender and Irish Writing* (Philadelphia: Open University Press, 1991), pp.91–2.

2. P. Fallon, *News of the World* (Winston-Salem, North Carolina: Wake Forest University Press, 1993), p.74. I quote from the 1993 U.S. publication. 'A Part of Ourselves' was originally published in *Eye to Eye* (Loughcrew, Ireland: The Gallery Press, 1992), pp.54–60, and republished in Ireland in *News of the World: Selected and New Poems* (The Gallery Press, 1998), pp.74–7.

3. Ibid.

4. See R.R. Russell, 'Loss and Recovery in Peter Fallon's Pastoral Elegies', *Colby Quarterly*, 37, 4 (December 2001) and Giemza in this volume. Although I diverge from and extend Russell's interpretation, his essay deeply influenced my own reading of Fallon. I am grateful to both Russell and Giemza for their insights and suggestions.

5. R. R. Russell, 'Loss and Recovery in Peter Fallon's Pastoral Elegies', p.352.

6. See E. Boland, *The Journey and Other Poems* (Manchester: Carcanet, 1987), pp.14–16, 39–42.

7. R.R. Russell, 'Loss and Recovery in Peter Fallon's Pastoral Elegies', p.353, notes Fallon's 'Dickinsonian use of the dash' for emphasis.

8. E. Dickinson, *The Complete Poems of Emily Dickinson* in T.H. Johnson (ed.), (Boston: Little, Brown, and Company, 1960), p.162.

9. As Jonathan Culler suggests, a 'similarity of sound and grammatical structure' may '[pass] into or [give] rise to semantic relationships', a principle that will return in the formal readings of this essay. See Culler, 'The Call of the Phoneme: Introduction', in Culler (ed.), *On Puns: The Foundation of Letters* (New York: Basil Blackwell, 2005), p.9.

10. See R.R Russell, 'Loss and Recovery in Peter Fallon's Pastoral Elegies', p.343.

11. A fuller analysis of masculinity in Fallon's poetry would have to contend with the many rural character narratives he develops, as well as the violent male midwifery of his sheep poems ('Caesarean', or 'Fostering', in which he takes on the role of 'Isaac's wife') and the gendered representations of space in poems such as 'The Witches Corner'.

12. I have in mind here Moynagh Sullivan's account of feminist critiques of Seamus Heaney. Citing Margaret Kelleher's 2003 analysis of the reception of Patricia Coughlan's groundbreaking 1991 essay, '"Bog Queens": The Representation of Women in the Poetry of John Montague and Seamus Heaney', Sullivan says that despite Coughlan's 'sophisticated interlinking of politics and formalism', a 'spurious distinction between political readings concerned with ideology and formalist readings concerned with aesthetic values' has persisted in Irish studies. Worse, 'Feminist readings of Heaney, as *political* readings, have been understood in the main body of Irish Studies, if not as bad form and somehow anti-Irish, certainly as missing the point and as quite unrelated to the proper business of reading Heaney as a *poet*'. See Sullivan, 'The

Treachery of Wetness: Irish Studies, Seamus Heaney, and the Politics of Parturition', *Irish Studies Review*, 13, 4 (2005), p.452. As cited in Sullivan, see also M. Kelleher, 'The Field Day Anthology and Irish Women's Literary Studies', *Irish Review*, 30 (2003), p.84.

13. See, for example, Peggy Orenstein's 'Mourning My Miscarriage', *New York Times Magazine*, 21 April 2002, online at http://www.nytimes.com/2002/04/21/magazine/mourning-my-miscarriage.html (accessed 1 December 2012). Orenstein begins by noting that there is 'little acknowledgment in Western culture of miscarriage, no ritual to cleanse the grief'.

14. See E. Boland, 'The Oral Tradition,' *The Journey and Other Poems* (Manchester: Carcanet Press, 1987), pp.14–16. Though it may be only coincidence, I would note here the formal similarities of Boland's and Fallon's poems as well. As Fergus Allen noted in 'Review of Peter Fallon, *News of the World: Selected and New Poems* (1998)', *Metre*, 5 (Autumn/Winter 1998), p.177, 'Fallon's preferred form is the stanza of four, five or six irregular lines, in which the second or third rhymes with the last'. The seven sections of 'A Part of Ourselves' all use two five-line stanzas that replicate Allen's description of Fallon's preferred form (the second line rhymed by the fifth), followed by a single line of varying length – almost an echo of Gerard Manley Hopkins's curtal sonnet form. Boland's 'The Oral Tradition', *The Journey and Other Poems*, p.16, similarly uses five-line stanzas, irregularly rhymed, but frequently in the last third of the poem rhyming second and fifth lines.

15. E. Boland, 'The Journey', in *The Journey and Other Poems*, p.41.

16. See L. Connolly and T. O'Toole, *Documenting Irish Feminisms: The Second Wave* (Dublin: Woodfield Press, 2005), pp.65, 111–113.

17. See P. Fallon, *News of the World*, pp.44–5. See also Fallon, *The News and Weather* (Dublin: The Gallery Press, 1987), pp.26–7.

18. See P. Fallon, *News of the World*, p.43 and *The News and Weather*, p.25. The references to fishermen finding the infants also echo Seamus Heaney's poem 'Limbo' from *Wintering Out* (London: Faber, 1972), p.70, a poem drawn into this cultural context (Kerry Babies, women's reproductive rights) by its inclusion in Margaret Harkin's film *Hush-A-Bye Baby* (1990). For a useful discussion of this context, see E. Cullingford, 'Seamus and Sinéad: from "Limbo" to *Saturday Night Live* by way of *Hush-A-Bye Baby*', *Colby Quarterly*, 30, 1 (March 1994), pp.43–62

19. P. Fallon, *News of the World*, pp.42–3; see also Fallon, *The News and Weather*, pp.24–5.

20. The phrasing comes from Irish theatre historian Mary Trotter, 'Personal Correspondence', 5 November 2012.

21. See P. Fallon, *News of the World*, p.43; see also P. Fallon, *The News and Weather*, p.24.

22. See L. Edelman, *No Future: Queer Theory and the Death Drive* (Durham, North Carolina: Duke University Press, 2004).

23. See P. Fallon, *News of the World*, p.45.

24. L. Connolly and T. O'Toole write, 'The death of Ann Lovett stands as a testimony to the many thousands of Irish women who experienced and concealed "crisis" pregnancies in twentieth century Ireland' (p.65). Journalist Colum Kenny would later write of Lovett, 'Nobody suggested that what had happened in Co. Longford was unique', asking, 'What kind of society drives women to such extremes?'. See C. Kenny, *The Moments That Changed Us* (Dublin: Gill & Macmillan, 2005), p.43. As Diarmaid Ferriter notes, quoting Colm Tóibín, when Gay Byrne devoted three radio shows to letters from listeners responding to the Lovett case, it resulted in 'the most relentless assault which has ever been presented to a mass audience on the accepted version of reality in this country', as respondents told of concealed births, primitive abortions, domestic violence and incest. See D. Ferriter, *Occasions of Sin: Sex & Society in Modern Ireland* (London: Profile Books, 2009), pp.524–5. Cullingford, 'Seamus and Sinéad', p.51, notes further, quoting Irish historian Angela Bourke, that infanticide may have been common in Ireland.

25. See P. Fallon, *News of the World*, p.74.

26. See E. Boland, 'The Oral Tradition', in *The Journey and Other Poems*, p.14.

27. See, for example, D. Galasinski, *Men and the Language of Emotions* (Houndmills, UK: Palgrave Macmillan, 2004), pp.12–18.

28. See H. Ferguson, 'Men and Masculinities in Late-modern Ireland', in B. Pease and K. Pringle (eds), *A Man's World? Changing Men's Practices in a Globalized World* (London: Zed Books, 2001), pp.120–121.

29. See *Black Irish*, dir. B. Gann (Anywhere Road Entertainment and Creanspeak Productions, 2007).

30. See K. Sheridan, 'New Laddism Blamed for Big Boys Behaving Badly', *Irish Times*, 10 January, 1998, p.11.

31. See J. Gleeson, P. Conboy, and A. Walsh, *The Piloting of 'Exploring Masculinities' (1997–1998): Context, Implementation, and Issues Arising: Report of External Evaluation* (Dublin: Stationery Office, 2004), p.73. For a discussion of this curriculum in relation to evolving understandings of masculinity, see E. Madden, 'Exploring Masculinity: Proximity, Intimacy, and *Chicken*', in C. Magennis and R. Mullen (eds), *Irish Masculinities: Reflections on Literature and Culture* (Dublin: Irish Academic Press, 2011), pp.77–88.

32. See, for example, P. Fallon 'Brothers', in which 'He said little / or nothing, nothing we heard', in *News of the World*, pp.52–3, or 'Carnaross 2', and 'Big', ibid pp.24, 66–7.

33. See E. Madden, '"Gently, not gay": Proximity, Sexuality, and Irish Masculinity at the End of the Twentieth Century', *Canadian Journal of Irish Studies*, 36, 1 (Spring 2012), pp.69–87.

34. See R.R. Russell, 'Loss and Recovery in Peter Fallon's Pastoral Elegies', p.352.

35. E. Boland, *The Journey*, p.14.

36. Ibid., p.41.

37. See J.E. Muñoz, *Cruising Utopia: The Then and There of Queer Futurity* (New York: New York University Press, 2009), p.91.

38. See P. Fallon, 'The Heartland', *News of the World*, p.43.

39. See J.E. Muñoz, *Cruising Utopia: The Then and There of Queer Futurity*. Reading gestures in queer performance, Muñoz argues, 'Gestures transmit ephemeral knowledge of lost queer histories and possibilities within a phobic majoritarian public culture' (pp.66–7). Drawing on Giorgio Agamben, Muñoz further characterises the gestural as a means without prescribed ends, a 'temporal interruption' or 'a temporality that sidesteps straight time's heteronormative bent' (pp.90–1). I recognise that I am appropriating queer theory here for feminist politics, but I think the impulse – like the reading of the gesture – allows for different potential readings. As Muñoz uses this idea to revise Lee Edelman's anti-relational and anti-utopian politics in *No Future*, so I imagine the possibility of this to revise the 'queered' pastoral in Fallon.

40. See H. Bloom, *A Map of Misreading* (Oxford: Oxford University Press, 1975), pp.94–5, 98–9. Bloom follows Kenneth Burke, who links metonymy with reduction, synecdoche with representation, and metaphor with perspective.

41. H. Bloom, ibid., p.95, specifically links metalepsis to synecdoche: 'As tropes of restitution or representation, synecdoche enlarges from part to whole; hyperbole heightens; metalepsis overcomes temporality by a substitution of earliness for lateness'.

42. See P. Fallon, *News of the World*, p.73.

43. Ibid.

44. C. Lock further connects metonymy to Freudian displacement, synecdoche to condensation. See Lock, 'Debts and Displacements: on Metaphor and Metonymy', *Acta Linguistica Hafniensia: International Journal of Linguistics*, 29, 1 (1997), pp.333–4.

45. See Bloom, *A Map of Misreading*, p.94.

46. R.R. Russell, 'Loss and Recovery in Peter Fallon's Pastoral Elegies', p.352, points out that the image of amputation echoes the opening section of the poem, in which the speaker and his wife are 'not forearmed' – and further notes a motif of severed limbs in *Eye to Eye*. See especially the poem 'A Handful of Air' in *Eye to Eye*, pp.30–31.

47. On catechresis and metonymy, see C. Lock, 'Debts and Displacements', p.334.

48. See P. Fallon, *News of the World*, p.75.

49. Ibid.

50. Ibid., p.76.

51. Ibid.

52. Ibid.

53. S. Heaney, 'Broagh', *Wintering Out* (London: Faber, 1972), p.27.

54. See P. Fallon, *News of the World*, p.76.

55. See W. Berry, *Collected Poems: 1957–1982* (San Francisco, California: North Point Press, 1985), p.201. The poem was originally published in *A Part* (San Francisco, California: North Point Press, 1980).

56. See P. Coughlan, '"Bog Queens": The Representation of Women in the Poetry of John Montague and Seamus Heaney', pp.91–2.

57. In Russell's own groundbreaking essay on Fallon – one of the first to take seriously the poetry of Fallon – he repeatedly turns to the autobiographical and the authentic as a grounding strategy. In his reading of the pastoral, for example he, says Fallon invested this 'moribund' and conventional form with new life, in part by his use of an 'intensely lived, realistic setting populated by contemporary farmers he knows personally', in part by granting the form 'legitimacy by his [own] profession of sheep farming'. See R.R Russell, 'Loss and Recovery in Peter Fallon's Pastoral Elegies', p348.

58. See R.R Russell, 'Loss and Recovery', pp.350–351.

59. See P. Fallon, *Eye to Eye*, p.53.

60. See P. Fallon, *News of the World*, p.69.

61. See Ibid., p.70; my emphasis.

62. In the echo chamber of this tiny poem, I wonder if I hear William Stafford's 'Traveling through the Dark', in *Traveling through the Dark* (New York: Harper and Row, 1951), p.11, in which the speaker touches the side of a dead deer, feeling in its body the never-to-be-born fawn; the poem is similarly centered on a moment of hesitation about what to do.

63. See E. Grennan, 'Sing a Hymn to Works and Days: Review of *The Georgics of Virgil*, trans. Peter Fallon', *Metre*, 17 (spring 2005), p.118. Similarly, Michael McKimm says that in many of the poems in the later volume, *The Company of Horses*, Fallon uses 'an intricate yet unforced rhyme scheme, often irregularly changing the scheme's order

to achieve rhythms and intonations of natural speech'. See M. McKimm, 'Review of Gerard Smyth, *The Mirror Tent*; Matthew Sweeney, *Black Moon*; Peter Fallon, *The Company of Horses*; and Frank McGuinness, *Dulse*', *The Warwick Review* 2, 1 (2008), p.88.

64. P. Fallon, 'The A.G.M.', in *Eye to Eye*, p.21, or 'The AGM', in *News of the World: Selected and New Poems*, (1998), p.50.

65. P. Fallon, *The Company of Horses* (Loughcrew, Ireland: The Gallery Press, 2007), p.56.

66. Ibid., p.22.

67. Further confirming Giemza's tracing of the influence of Wendell Berry on Fallon's work, this poem seems a version of Berry's 'To the Unseeable Animal', *Collected Poems: 1957–1982*, pp.140–141. Fallon reverses Berry's attempt to preserve the animal's mystery by keeping it in darkness, instead imagining a 'denizen / of dusk' that might 'flower, now and then again, // in light' (*The Company of Horses*, p.23). The poem also offers a demythologising counterpoint to Ted Hughes's animal poems, especially 'Pike'.

68. P. Fallon, *The Company of Horses*, pp.54–5.

69. Ibid., p.51.

70. Ibid.

71. Similarly, in 'My Care', the news of border violence persists in pastoral figures, the 'riot / of kindling' and 'the soft explosions' of a household fire. See P. Fallon, *News of the World* (1993), p.41.

72. See D. Fried, 'Rhyme Puns', in J. Culler (ed.), *On Puns: The Foundation of Letters* (New York: Basil Blackwell, 2005), pp.97–8.

73. See P. Fallon, *News of the World: Selected and New Poems* (1998), p.131.

74. Ibid.

75. Ibid.

76. Ibid.

Part III

Fallon and the Natural World

All That Lasts: Peter Fallon's Loughcrew

SHAUN O'CONNELL

In midsummer of 1985 I first came to North County Meath, to Loughcrew, to Peter Fallon's Garden Lodge, to talk about poets and Ireland. I came admiring Peter's poetry of place: 'Think of all that lasts. Think of the land. / The things you could do with a field.'[1] Peter, more than any other Irish poet since Patrick Kavanagh, connected to his community, for Peter worked the land and tended to animals with his neighbors, from sheep-shearing to common pasturing, while overseeing The Gallery Press, Ireland's principal publisher of poetry, and composing his own body of work. (Kavanagh, though, abandoned his 'important place' in Inniskeen, County Monaghan, for Dublin, while Fallon left Dublin to live at Loughcrew.) I came to witness his fusion of poetry and place, but he showed me more than I imagined.

After a bus trip from Dublin, along the Navan Road, I met Peter in Kells. The poet, shod in long rubber boots, handed an extra pair to me, then drove to a cattle and farm equipment auction. Peter had an easy way with the locals – ruddy, craggy men, many wearing black coats and caps, carrying long sticks, smoking and talking conspiratorily, watched warily by cows. We walked the farm, deep in mud and cow shit, but Peter bought nothing. He was there, it seemed, mainly to make contact with fellow cattle and sheep farmers. He nodded, had an easy word with this or that man, moving with the same grace he brought to his Dublin literary world, to his Deerfield Academy classes, to his poetry readings at home and abroad. Clearly Peter was a man who knew who he was and where he was.

At Loughcrew, outside Oldcastle, Peter lived in a former gardener's lodge, a two-story stone structure, looking a bit like a fortress gingerbread house, the only extant evidence of what once was the Loughcrew estate, some 180,000 acres appropriated more than 350 years ago from Catholics by the Naper family in reward for their service to Oliver Cromwell in his brutal domination of Ireland. Now only one building stands and one poet remains in possession.

The lush Meath land surrounding Peter's Garden Lodge is serene but never still. Clouds float shadows across the rolling hills, over copses of trees and open fields, past wandering cows and sheep, over patches of land in all shades of green – all arranged with a painterly eye. Sudden showers blur and soften the impressionistic landscape. Peter's passion for the place was evident. 'This did not just happen', he said, in admiration of the big house family that planned and sculpted the topography and for the laborers who shaped its design. He too was about his own design: to combine poetry and publishing in his pastoral demesne.

> I came on a place and had to stay
> that I might find my feet, repair
> the mark of human hand, and repossess
> a corner of my country.[2]

A high wall, stone and mortar, separates his Garden Lodge from the road to Oldcastle. That wall extends for a dozen kilometers around the former garden; an inner wall separates four acres of grass, where sheep grazed on my first visit. In the morning the sheep's plaintive bleats wake you. From the second-story guest room, through the heavy dawn mist, while your eyes were clearing, you could see them drift around their walled-in demesne in groups that appear like shifting clouds.

Though lorries whipped past beyond the wall, from inside the Garden Lodge the outside world seemed far away. Fittingly, its front door opened not toward the road but inward, toward the enclosed pastoral space of Peter's 'care'. Leaving his car along the road, huddled against the wall, we entered his holdings through a narrow gate, making our way past a flock of chickens which fluttered over to be fed, flightless ducks who squawked, a ruminative cow and a friendly old goat. Despite his array of non-human dependents, Peter then lived as simply as Thoreau: a wood-burning stove, a modest kitchen with ancient appliances, a small study, no television, not even a phone, though Dubliners could reach him through an elaborate system of message pass-alongs. But he would not long remain alone for, as he granted on my first visit, 'There has been some talk in town of my marrying'.

Peter showed me his millennium-old souterrain, a network of tunnels which branch off so that pursuers would be confused and trapped, while those on the run could find their way to an enlarged inner chamber to wait out the attack. Above ground, his walled-in acres also hold the remains of an elaborate garden which, a century ago, supplied daily flowers and out-of-season fruits to the now dismantled big house. These buried images of pre-Celtic, hidden Ireland and faded Ascendancy rule concentrate in his significant place.

We walked to the nearby church of Oliver Plunkett's family. Plunkett, Archbishop of Armagh, charged with high treason, was executed in 1681, his family's lands confiscated. Around his untended grave Peter, in a small memorial gesture, sometimes brought his goat to graze, tidying up the grass.

The best part of that sunny, breezy afternoon came when we hiked through fields and up a steep hill to the Loughcrew passage tomb on top, or 'mountain of the hag'. From Loughcrew Hill we gazed down on the undulant Boyne Valley, site of ancient burial tombs and decisive military battles; then north to the hill of Slane, where Patrick lit the flame of Christianity in 432; finally east to the hills of Tara, former seat of Celtic High Kings and site of Daniel O'Connell's political rallies in the early nineteenth century. Atop serene Loughcrew Hill, patrolled by cows and sheep, a large earth mound encases a megalithic tomb, perhaps 5,000 years old. Inside the tomb or cairn are large rocks carved with mysterious swirls and designs, means by which ancient peoples communicated with the spirit world, emblems by which we can still feel their living presence while running our fingers over their hard surfaces as we would tomb engravings. Here, I thought, was the center of Ireland. Here was a landscape and a vision, as Scott Fitzgerald might put it, commensurate with our capacity for wonder.

Now, three decades on, all seems changed, but not utterly. Despite Ireland's enduring troubles and economic turmoil, much of value remains. Over the years, Peter has made many changes – alterations in the spirit of preservation. He did marry and he and his wife Jean moved The Gallery Press from Dublin to a house along the road to Oldcastle, not far from their lodge. The sheep, along with the fowl and eventually the goat, were sent off to neighbors' fields as the Fallons' 'care' shifted to their two fine children, Adam and Alice. The wall along the road now has an opening, so cars can enter. The lodge has a beautiful addition – large windows, upstairs and down, overlook their holdings – and a new door opens out into the wider world, balancing the old door which still opens inward.

So, too, has Peter, while enriching his 'small holdings' at Loughcrew, added to his impressive body of work, particularly in his aptly-titled collection *News of the World: Selected and New Poems*, and his brilliant translation of Virgil's *Georgics*, that two-thousand-year-old poem which celebrates and combines the pastoral and the poetic. The Gallery Press has been twice honored, on its twenty-fifth and fortieth anniversaries, by ceremonies held at the Abbey Theater, crowded occasions which drew an array of celebrities, from President Mary Robinson in 1995 to Seamus Heaney and nearly every other significant Irish poet in 2010. Peter joked to the Abbey full house in 2010 that the fiftieth anniversary celebration of The Gallery Press in 2020 would be held in Croke Park, but at the end of the day The Gallery Press's consolidation of Ireland's poetic voices will mean more to Ireland than any World Cup football match.

'All I ever wanted was / to make a safe house in the midlands', Peter wrote in 'My Care', but he has made much more.[3] He has moved the center of Irish poetry to Loughcrew, between the Dublin and Belfast literary centers; he has shaped an exemplary and coherent life combining poetry with his living cares; he has extended and expanded our sense of what it means to be an Irish poet while still thinking 'it exquisite / to stand in the yard, my feet on the ground, / in cowshit and horseshit and sheepshit', as he wrote in 'Winter Work'.[4] Peter Fallon is a well grounded man, holding dominion over these once flowering fields, these subterranean tunnels and ancient burial tombs, at ease in his dear, perpetual place.

REFERENCES

Fallon, P., *News of the World: Selected and New Poems* (Loughcrew, Ireland: The Gallery Press, 1998).

NOTES

1. P. Fallon, 'The Lost Field', *News of the World: Selected and New Poems* (Loughcrew, Ireland: The Gallery Press, 1998), pp.16–17.

2. P. Fallon, 'The Heartland', in ibid., pp.52–3.

3. P. Fallon, 'My Care', in ibid., p.60.

4. P. Fallon, 'Winter Work', in ibid., p.51.

Nature's News: The Place(s) of Peter Fallon's Poetry

RICHARD RANKIN RUSSELL

There is currently an upsurge of criticism that concerns itself with Irish literature and the environment, a natural marriage that has taken too long to declare itself, although it has long been present in the literature. For example, in 2009, Pat Boran gave a lecture to the Yeats Winter School in Sligo entitled 'Nine-and-Fifty Swans: Glimpses of Nature in Recent Irish Poetry', in which he analysed the nature poetry of Yeats, Kavanagh, Seamus Heaney, Michael Longley, Francis Harvey, Vona Groarke and others. Drawing on Moya Cannon's introduction to Harvey's 2007 *Collected Poems*, Boran holds that Harvey's 'hallmark "vividness and lucidity". . . is the same kind of very literal focus that distinguishes Longley's finest work', observing further that 'This idea that precision itself might be the link between the work of the naturalist and that of the poet is one that can be found centuries ago in the wonderful marginalia of the illuminated manuscript tradition . . . '.[1] Boran memorably argues in closing that 'A good poet is always a kind of gardener or curator, on his knees in the garden of language, tending the orchard of images, filling the basket of form'.[2] The very next year, in 2010, Christine Cusick published her edited collection of essays, *Out of the Earth: Ecocritical Readings of Irish Texts*, which covers writers ranging from Lady Morgan and William Carleton in the nineteenth century to Synge, Richard Murphy, Paula Meehan, and other authors in the twentieth century and beyond. In his introduction to the volume, John Elder notes that literature of the environment 'can remind us that particularity is the escape-hatch out of stultifying notions of history, culture and the land, and an opening to our shared humanity with ancestors in the Paleolithic and kindred beyond the seas'.[3] Finally, in 2011, James McElroy sounds a similar theme of particularity to that raised by Boran and Elder when he opens his wide-ranging survey of ecocriticism and Irish poetry by citing Kuno Meyer's claim in *Selections from Ancient Irish Poetry* that 'an intense love of nature "in its tiniest phenomena as in its grandest, was given to no people so early and so fully as the Celt"'.[4] Despite seemingly affirming the exaggeration of Meyer's claim – haven't all early peoples evinced such a love of nature? – McElroy's article helpfully plumbs the long-standing tradition of the strand of Irish poetry that focuses on nature in all its teeming intimacy from medieval lyrics through the contemporary poetry of Longley, Medbh McGuckian, Cannon, and others, in the process showing the necessity of continued critical forays into this living tradition.

Peter Fallon has become one of the contemporary Irish poets most identified with a particular place – his area of Loughcrew, in northern County Meath, where he ran a sheep farm for years and still lives. Seamus Heaney still writes about his upbringing in rural County Derry; Michael Longley about the townland of Carrigskeewaun in western County Mayo; Eavan Boland about her suburb of Dundrum, north of Dublin; but none of them actually live in these places full-time anymore or at all (in Heaney's case). And certainly none of them have worked the land in adulthood like Fallon has until very recently. Fallon has often been linked to Robert Frost and certainly the similarities are there – the spare language, the wry angles of observation, the appreciation of good land and neighbors – but as Fallon told me recently, he has found Frost finally too detached from the land and its rhythms because he was never a farmer. He specifically invoked Frost in discussing his own poem, 'Caesarean', about a ewe (pronounced 'yoe' in Fallon's part of Ireland) he helped kill in order to help deliver her babies. But when they opened the ewe up, they found premature twins, 'Too young to live'[5] who shortly thereafter die. The speaker and his friend James realise, 'We had done what we could. Now there / were other things to do. We said nothing for a while.'[6] By burying themselves in their work, attending to other births, the two men are able to help other ewes, while silently mourning the death of those twin lambs. As an example of Frost's relative disconnection from farming life, Fallon cited what he called the unrealistic moment in Frost's famous poem, 'Out, Out', when the boy's hand is cut off and work is not stopped. Work went on that night for the two men in Fallon's poem, but he argued to me and my literature class that surely farm people would stop for something as important as the loss of a boy's hand, whereas he and his friend were sobered by the lambs' death but in the absence of an injury to a human, were helping 1300 ewes with over 100 births a night and had to move on with their work.[7]

I cite this remark of Fallon's to suggest how he himself realises that he is that rare thing in a rapidly urbanising Ireland – a practicing poet who writes lovingly and realistically of one specific area that until very recently, he was an intimate part of through animal husbandry. Irish poetry has become increasingly globalised in the last quarter century, so much so that Fallon and Derek Mahon, writing in their introduction to the *Penguin Book of Contemporary Irish Poetry* in 1990, remark that 'These poets are tied less to particular places – or parishes – than ever before . . . . You might say these writers *commute*'.[8] If many contemporary Irish poets evince an uncertainty about the location of their home, Peter Fallon seems securely rooted in his home ground, although he has had a series of places in which he has successfully chosen to dwell. My emphasis on choice is purposeful: As Eamon Grennan has noted about Fallon's Loughcrew in a fine essay on his poetry through *News of the World*, Fallon's selected poems (published in America in 1993 and in Ireland, in an expanded edition with new poems in 1998), 'one of this place's most important features . . . is the fact of its being a *chosen* place, a place deliberately selected to be commensurate with a life'.[9]

Fallon was actually born in then-West Germany in 1951 and then moved with his family to Meath in February, 1957. As he has noted, his 'home life centred on my uncle's farm in Carnaross' once back in Meath.[10] He has recalled approvingly that 'the day we arrived to stay permanently in Ireland, he [my Uncle Peter] took this then five-year-old boy by the hand and had me "help" him with a lambing. On that February afternoon he put before me what has turned out to be a crucial, sustaining part of my life'.[11] Fallon then attended Trinity College, Dublin, in the early 1970s. Although he enjoyed university life in Dublin, he 'was gravitating from Dublin back to the countryside', having 'happened on an old house in Loughcrew, in North Meath, a hen's race from my home place'. There, 'I re-entered a world of farming, first helping with a neighbour's flock and subsequently (and on a smaller scale) with sheep and cattle of my own. I learned, or remembered, the language which surrounded me when I was a boy. I knew again a vocabulary and idiom belonging to the way of life in a local community'.[12] Fallon suggests here how he learned to speak both an academic language of the university but that the more important language he relearned was the language of a local, rural community. It was not until 1988 that he moved The Gallery Press, founded in February, 1970, to Meath. The many years he has spent as an adult in this area of Meath have enabled him to develop an intimate relationship with a place removed from the frenetic pace of contemporary Dublin.[13]

Fallon's radical commitment to rural life was signaled in the title of his 1987 volume, *The News and Weather*, which, as he told Jerry Lincecum in a 1990 interview, purposely suggested that the events of rural life were just as newsworthy as national or international ones: 'A few years ago, I published a book called *The News and Weather* and though this [title] would normally connote national events or international affairs, I wanted it particularly to try to record the things I was hearing, the kind of overheard, overseen, familiar series of incidents and events and emotions in a community'.[14] Maurice Harmon's essay in the present volume privileges this sense of locally-attuned poetry as 'news'. Fallon's emphasis on recording daily rural experience within community as expressed in this interview has become a hallmark of his poetry. Although he has written poems from solitary points of view, he prefers to evoke his role within the community of Loughcrew. Fallon has gradually written himself into the fabric of his community and his environmental poetry represents a stunning achievement in contemporary writing perhaps surpassed only by his friend and leading voice in American agrarian writing, Wendell Berry.

If Berry has bulked large as an exemplar for Fallon in more recent years, Patrick Kavanagh was a crucial influence for him earlier in his career[15] and he has written a three-act play called *Tarry Flynn* (2004) based on Kavanagh's novel of the same name, an adaptation explored by Thomas O'Grady in his essay in the present collection. Fallon has recalled that 'It was a way of re-reading a novel, first published in 1948, by a poet whose works had continued to weave their spells since I read them closely for the first time when I was an undergraduate . . . more than twenty years earlier'.[16] When he was writing the play, he wondered if it would still speak to the concerns of newly wealthy, more secular, contemporary Ireland in the early twentieth century just as Kavanagh's novel captured rural Ireland in the late 1940s. But he quickly realised that 'Kavanagh's vision, and version of a life are founded in enduring verities'.[17]

It has become a commonplace for Irish writers to invoke Kavanagh's insistence on writing about local culture generally, expressed both in his poem 'Epic' and in his essay, 'The Parish and the Universe', but Fallon seems especially to value Kavanagh because of his emphasis on a local landscape close to Fallon's townland in County Meath. As he told Lincecum about the elder poet, Kavanagh 'did take the landscape of his stony gray soil of County Monaghan, a little bit north of where I live, and he recognised that to know a field in that place could be a lifetime's activity; he said to a generation, by his example and his utterances, "It's alright; trust what you know and that should be the meat and matter of what you're writing".[18] Fallon goes on to quote from Kavanagh's 'Epic' later in this interview, just as he and Mahon cite that poem and 'The Parish and the Universe' in their introduction to the *Penguin Book of Contemporary Irish Poetry*. Using an agricultural term, Fallon and Mahon note that 'Epic' 'gave single-handed permission for Irish poets to trust and cultivate their native ground and experience'.[19] Fallon's emphasis above in his choice of *The News and Weather* to signify the importance of local events recalls Kavanagh's closing remark in 'The Parish and the Universe' about how he and other Irish emigrants to London rush to buy the local Irish papers: 'Lonely on Highgate Hill outside St. Joseph's Church I rushed to buy my Dundalk Democrat, and reading it I was back in my native fields. . . . So it is for these reasons that I return to the local newspapers. Who has died? Who has sold his farm?'.[20]

Linking Fallon to Kavanagh and Berry enables us to better understand his interest in and attachment to place through locating him on a map of twentieth-century writers concerned with the environment, but what term is appropriate for Fallon's poetry about the natural world? Is he pastoral or anti-pastoral, as for example, Jonathan Allison has argued Kavanagh was in two successive stages of his career?[21] Is he agrarian, as Berry has styled himself but with an important disclaimer of not being racist, as many of the Nashville Fugitives, and later Agrarians were?[22] Is he georgic, as his recent translation of Virgil's classic suggests? The difficulty inherent in 'labeling' Fallon correctly in terms of his relationship to his environment may spring from the fairly amorphous meaning of the growing field of ecocriticism itself. One of the pioneers in the field, Lawrence Buell, has argued convincingly that the 'environmental turn in literary studies is best understood . . . less as a monolith than as a concourse of discrepant practices', going on to cite Cheryl Glotfelty's 1996 definition of ecocriticsm – "the study of the relationship between literature and the physical environment" – as 'candid rather than evasive'.[23]

One way to approach the matter is through understanding the dual ways in which we apprehend landscape. Patrick J. Duffy has argued that landscape is produced both 'materially and metaphorically: materially, in the sense that the landscape is a legacy of past economic and social order; and metaphorically in the sense that it produces meanings which vary over time as different "readings" or constructions are put on it'.[24] Fallon's Loughcrew functions in both of these ways; for instance, he has discussed the materiality of his landscape in interviews and in poems like 'The Speaking Stones' He has pointed out the historical and cultural layers of the Loughcrew landscape and of his own farm and house:

> The hills in Loughcrew are crammed with the cemetery of prehistoric graves. . . . Then the house where I live. . . . is a part of an old estate; this was a Cromwellian estate and much of it is in ruins, but some of it is intact for two to three hundred years, certainly. [In the] landscape of the immediate area of the house, it is possible to go into a *sutterain*, or underground corbelled passage that opens into a chamber, from between 8 and 1000 years AD. Move from that to this *mott* or bailey that is beyond the garden wall from a couple of hundred years afterwards and [it is possible] in a matter of minutes, literally, to take a kind of step through several thousand years. I have no wish to live in the past, but sometimes I find ghosts inhabiting my presence.[25]

Fallon's home in County Meath, his literal house, functions as a 'concentration of intimacy in the refuge', as Gaston Bachelard argues about the house in general.[26] Interestingly, Fallon conflates both his natural landscape and his artificial house through something like a spectrally-inspired memory. His poetry often articulates the different readings of this landscape through his insistence on the oral tradition such as *dinnsheanchas*, or Irish place-lore, as, for example in his poem 'The Rag-tree, Boherard', which concludes by the speaker noting the community had 'heard tell of the way / it simply took up roots and walked'[27] or in 'The Speaking Stones'.[28] He thus recognises Loughcrew's historically and geographically grounded materiality even as he records and contributes to particular folkloric readings of its terrain.

In an important essay on the environment in Thomas Hardy's work, Richard Kerridge delineates two distinct responses to the natural world: 'The unalienated lover of nature inhabits; the alienated lover of nature gazes. The first is a native, deeply embedded in a stable ecosystem; the second is a Romantic, a tourist, a newcomer, and a reader'.[29] But what to do with a writer like Fallon, born abroad and thus alienated from a local Irish landscape, who then inhabits that landscape much of his childhood and adolescence; spends several years in Dublin; returns to live in Loughcrew by 1975; but later makes long visits to Ballynahinch, County

Galway, a locale that features prominently in his latest poetry? He simultaneously inhabits and gazes upon his Meath landscape and more recently, his borrowed Connemara landscape. Embedded in those changing ecosystems, he nonetheless constantly seeks new environments in which to immerse himself, most particularly, that around Deerfield Academy in western Massachusetts, where he has lived for a year twice now in his career, in 1976–77 and 1996–97.[30] Fallon's dwellings in a series of places in flux accords well with a dynamic sense of place itself. In his essay for this collection, Derek Mahon similarly points out how Fallon engages with his living landscape. As Edward Casey has argued, 'A place is more an *event* than *thing* to be assimilated to known categories' and further, that '[a]s an event, it is unique, idiolocal'.[31] One of Fallon's most sympathetic and penetrating critics, the American poet-farmer Wendell Berry argues, 'To be committed to the news of so local and personal world is to be committed to change, and by 1998, the year of the [Irish] publication of *News of the World: Selected and New Poems*, Mr. Fallon had proved himself a poet quick and alert, turning like a good weather vane to meet the changes and the shifting requirements of the world as it presented itself to him and as he found it'.[32] Even the acronym formed from the first part of the title, *NOW*, suggests the urgency and immediacy of Fallon's belief in poetry as breaking news with its reports of local weather conditions and other tidings of natural development. His work consistently displays a conscious awareness of this dynamism inherent in unique environments.

Moreover, Fallon's emplaced poetry suggests the moral dimension of environmental commitment. In his discussion of Fallon's 'The Lost Field', Eamon Grennan has argued that that poem's 'tone contains something of that moral energy to be found in the response to any clearly understood vocation'.[33] And Fallon himself has implicitly recognised this aspect of his environmental writing by noting the moral underpinning of influential earlier authors. For example, in his reflections on his translation of Virgil's *Georgics*, he suggests, 'the crowning achievement of *The Georgics* is that – and herein lies the moral power of the poem – Virgil has infused his descriptions of a way of life with prescriptions for a way to live'.[34] He concludes these remarks by arguing that 'Virgil's is an ecological art. Although he knew the tears in things, he painted the picture of happiness the moral life may bring'.[35] Fallon similarly believes that a close connection to a local environment with both the suffering and happiness that such a life brings is inherently moral if we respect the community of flora and fauna that we inhabit.

Such a belief underpins a significant strand of environmental literary criticism. For example, David Jacobson argues that 'place has a distinctly moral element, containing as it does notions of belonging, of one's rightful place in the world, locating individuals and people geographically and historically and orienting them in the cosmos'.[36] More important, Wendell Berry, 'the most wise and thoughtful man I know' according to Fallon,[37] has long argued for a profound moral dimension of belonging to place. Although Berry's Christian worldview differs from Fallon's own relative agnosticism, Berry's religious reading of the environment has important correspondences with Fallon's own more secular attitude toward it. For instance, in 'Christianity and the Survival of Creation', Berry argues, 'If we think of ourselves as living souls, immortal creatures, living in the midst of a Creation that is mostly mysterious, and if we see that everything we make or do cannot help but have an everlasting significance for ourselves, for others, and for the world, then we see why some religious teachers have understood work as a form of prayer'.[38] In this regard, Fallon's embrace of hard, dirty manual farm work in poems such as 'Winter Work' becomes a sort of ecstatic prayer: 'I think it exquisite / to stand in the yard, my feet on the ground, / in cowshit and horseshit and sheepshit'.[39] Such an attitude accords with Grennan's suggestion that in its use of a phrase about a shed being founded on a rock, Fallon's poem 'The Old Masters' displays 'some secular reverence toward this chosen place and all its elements'.[40]

I have argued previously that Berry's 'pastoral elegies' subvert aspects of this subgenre such as nostalgia and abstractions of rural inhabitants by their rejection of 'nostalgia and the bucolic ideal' in favor of 'an intensely lived, realistic setting populated by contemporary farmers he knows personally'.[41] Perhaps the main quality of Fallon's pastoral elegies is his portrayal of his often 'intense sense of loss in the midst of the pastoral plenum that surrounds him as a kind of secondary irony and sustenance'.[42] Such a view is even evidenced in an expansive sense by his lovely lyrical sequence, 'A Part of Ourselves', dedicated to the memory of his baby John Fallon, who lived from 7 December to 8 December 1990. While by no means an environmental poem, the title of the epilogic poem to the sequence, 'A Human Harvest', and the opening lines suggest that the metaphor of harvest is appropriate for the arrival of a new baby in the Fallon family: 'Our wishes quicken into flesh / and yield a human harvest'.[43] Harvest in its varying connotations becomes a motif in Fallon's poetry after 'A Human Harvest'. For example, the more straightforwardly environmental poem, 'Harvest in Spring', a later poem featured in the third section of the 1998 Irish edition of News of the World, entitled 'The Heart's Home', celebrates a different kind of harvest, the maple syrup that is 'March and April's / nectar, sweet yield / of swamp- and sugar-maples'.[44]

This celebration of nature's profusion and abundance occurs repeatedly in other Fallon poems that often use the catalog device as a way of naming, 'collecting', and displaying natural wonders such as trees and flowers that the poet has gazed upon often. They prove the truth of his statement that 'In poetry, the payment, or act, of attention is basic and crucial. Ways of seeing: ways of saying'.[45] 'A Shiver', from 'The Deerfield Series: Strength of Heart', for example, welcomes 'everywhere / the miracle of trees–', following that dash with seven quatrains listing trees, the seventh one concluding with a chiasmus and a paratactic clause that attempts to gather all other unnamed trees into this catalog: 'birches and maples, / maples and birches, / and all the other lovely trees / shiver in a human breeze'.[46] The slightly sinister quality of that last phrase implies how easily our movements disturb the natural world and calls to mind Gerard Manley Hopkins's 'Binsey Poplars', a poem that features the destructive action of woodcutters who hewed down a lovely grove of those trees in north Oxford, England. Hopkins is an important literary and environmental figure for Fallon: both the American and Irish editions of *News of the World: Selected and New Poems* feature an epigraph from Hopkins's 'Inversnaid': 'Long live the trees . . . ', a line that is incorporated into 'The Heart's Home'.[47] 'A Shiver' reminds us all how quickly the particularity of nature, epitomised by Hopkins's notion of inscape, can be erased and not easily replaced. And the remarkable title poem from 'The Heart's Home' performs another linguistic celebration of the natural world, singing the praises of wildflowers, trees, even weeds and suggesting that the imagined place populated by such natural denizens will be a space of healing and peace:

> Let it be a healing place,
> where the heart releases care.
>
> Long live the weeds
> and, yes, long live the wilderness.
> A clump of thistledown flies
> down besides a pair of butterflies.
> Peace settles
> there, among couch and docks and nettles,
> convolvulus, and bittercress.[48]

The last stanza, in which the speaker welcomes his love into this place 'where refuge clings like mistletoe',[49] again reminds us that Fallon's poems of nature often seamlessly stitch animal, plant, and human life together into a patchwork quilt of difference and profundity that suggests how we all might live together in harmony.

Fallon's extremely modified pastorals, however, suggest the inadequacy of using the term, at least as Oona Frawley does in the conclusion of her *Irish Pastoral*. Despite arguing that Eavan Boland (in her evocation of her suburban Dundrum), Seamus Heaney, (in his rejection of nostalgia and observation of rural violence), and other writers have significantly reinterpreted pastoral 'in recent decades', Frawley finally argues that 'Irish authors have almost continually looked to landscape as a site of stability and continuous identity . . .', seemingly undermining her own attempts to broaden the definition of pastoral as multivalent.[50]

Another way of evaluating Fallon's environmental writing and one that would not have to be hedged about with the caveats that Frawley gives for the pastoral mode generally throughout her often substantial study would be thinking of it as a contemporary example of 'georgic', a tradition that he consciously writes himself into with his many poems about his Meath sheep farm and with his acclaimed recent translation of Virgil's *Georgics*, as the essays in this volume by Justin Quinn and Joseph Heininger attest.[51] In this practice, too, Fallon is linked to Berry's Christianity because the *Georgics* share 'with the Bible an emphasis on the relationship of agricultural productivity and ritual observance, although the Roman obsession with astrology and augury differentiates it from the practices represented in the Old Testament'.[52] Greg Garrard views Berry as 'The foremost proponent of georgic today', and he notes that 'his practical vision can probably be shared by non-Christians, although they would have to look elsewhere for philosophical justifications'.[53] 'Fostering' (originally published in Fallon's 1983 volume, *Winter Work*), his lovely poetic recasting of the Jacob and Esau story from the Old Testament in the context of tricking an ewe into believing an orphaned lamb is hers through dressing the lamb in her dead lamb's skin, is one of the only Fallon georgics to directly employ scriptural language, whereas Berry's georgics often use such narratives and terms.

But Fallon's georgics do share with Berry's georgic poetry, essays, and fiction a preference for a shorn, unadorned prose and a corresponding directness in communicating their meanings. For example, Fallon writes in 'The Lost Field', a poem dedicated to Berry and his wife Tanya, 'Think of all that lasts. Think of land. / The things you could do with a field. / Plough, pasture, or re-claim. The stones / you'd pick, the house you'd build'.[54] The repetition of 'think' and the alliteration of 'think' and 'things' along with 'Plough', 'pasture', and 'pick' does not make this spare language too literary; rather, these devices emphasise its homespun quality, recalling the persistent rhythms of talk in rural areas. Fallon has suggested that this is a poem that moves from 'longing to belonging'[55] and it enacts a significant moment in his poetry – when he moves back 'home from Dublin / to take my place'.[56] When he concludes by vowing, 'I'm out to find that field, to make it mine', he simultaneously pays homage to Berry's Kentucky georgic and begins articulating his own commitment to a native place where he will take up the life of farming and write about that farming.[57]

Fallon's acclaimed translation, *The Georgics of Virgil*, not only confirms him as the leading practitioner of georgic poetry in Ireland, but also, 'Its concentration on the working of the land casts a retrospective colouring over many Irish poems that have preceded it: Heaney's early work, Kavanagh's *The Great Hunger*, Yeats's peasant poems, Allingham's "Lawrence Bloomfield in Ireland", even Samuel Ferguson's "Inheritor and Economist" and "Lament for Thomas Davis"'.[58] As Peter Denman holds, 'Having the *Georgics* to hand means that those Irish poems of the land can be repositioned in relation to a European classical tradition of rural poetry'.[59] Thus, Fallon's translation brings the poetry of rural Ireland written during the last two centuries out of a purely nationalist context and into a wider European conversation with classical georgic poets like Virgil. Furthermore, Fallon himself has called our attention to how particular scenes resonate with two rural classics of the English poetic tradition: '[the] series of *tableaux* which would not be out of place in "The Deserted Village" or the *Lyrical Ballads*: the farmer and his wife at her loom in firelight (1.291–296), the women carding wool by sputtering candlelight (1.390ff.), the sense of domestic order and the householder's children waiting for a show of his affection (2.523ff) and, throughout, the congeniality of social and sporting gatherings'.[60]

His translation widens its compass, then, by fully entering the spirit of a specific place, 'into what is concentrated there like a fully saturated color', and in so doing, as Edward Casey has articulated about the process of getting into place, he achieves an expansiveness that enables his spirit of place to 'Mov[e] out, entering not just the area lying before and around me but entering myself and others as its witnesses or occupants . . . sweep[ing] the binarism of Self and Other . . . into the embracing folds, the literal im-plications, of implacement'.[61]

It achieves this creation of community by virtue of its particular turns of phrase, which both attend to local soil and farming conditions, and to the vernacular tongue of County Meath, Ireland,[62] while recalling a common literary heritage to

English speakers everywhere in hearkening back to Wordsworth, Goldsmith, and even Chaucer. Consider a cluster of lines from early in Fallon's translation:

> Come the sweet o' the year, when streams begin to melt
>> and tumble down the hoary hills
> and clods to crumble underneath the current of west
>> winds,
> it's time again to put the bull before the deep-pointed
>> plow to pull his weight
> and have the share glisten, burnished by the broken sod.
> There's the crop, which twice has felt a touch of snow and
>> twice of frosty weather,
> That is a beggared farmer's prayer come true.
> That's the one to fill his sheds until they're fit to burst.[63]

To this ear, such lines redolently recall the memorable opening lines of Chaucer's 'General Prologue' to his *Canterbury Tales* without being overly derivative:

> When in April the sweet showers fall
> And pierce the drought of March to the root, and all
> The veins are bathed in liquor of such power
> As brings about the engendering of the flower,
> When also Zephyrus with his sweet breath
> Exhales an air in every grove and heath
> Upon the tender shoots, and the young sun
> His half-course in the sign of the *Ram* has run . . . . [64]

The use of parataxis, the invocation of spring, the urge to journey – not on pilgrimage to Canterbury, but into the field – all lead us into the weather of the poem and its natural rhythms. The lines propel us along much as the bull pulls along the 'deep-pointed / plow'.

After Fallon gave up sheep farming in recent years, he has increasingly written of another place – Ballynahinch in the Connemara area of western Ireland, a rock-strewn environment very different from the relatively lush townland of Loughcrew.

In my review of *The Company of Horses*, Fallon's latest volume of poetry, I have pointed out the 'the way in which his verbs assume a more central role than they do in much of the earlier poetry',[65] signifying both his joy and wonder at nature and his realisation of his own limited time on earth. The verbal urgency of such poems as 'Go' also suggests Fallon's desire to communicate with others the pressing matter of worldwide environmental problems through his immersion in the depopulated landscape in and around Ballynahinch.

Many of these new poems first appeared in *Ballynahinch Postcards* (2007), a collection with a title suggesting that these are poetic dispatches sent out from a new place, an updating, as it were, of Fallon's sense that the happenings of rural places, first signified by the titles of *The News and Weather* and *The News of the World*, are worthy of our attention. The term 'postcards' further connotes brief missives from a tourist sent back to those who await his arrival at home. But this environment has proven to be a lasting place of retreat for Fallon, enabling him to complete much recent work. In his 'Acknowledgments' at the end of this chapbook, Fallon notes that his sojourns to Ballynahinch Castle itself, 'a place I've loved since I stumbled on it one wet and weather night in the summer of 1977', and Hilary's House nearby, 'have been an excitement and a sustenance. These sojourns . . . . helped me complete my translation *The Georgics of Virgil* (2004) and many of the poems in my forthcoming *The Company of Horses* (2007), as well as all of the glances and glimpses in this edition'.[66] Terming these poems 'glances and glimpses' call to mind a signal quality of short fiction, but it also suggests that they are lyric snapshots, verbal pictures sent out with affection for a particular place to a beloved readership.

Many of the short lyrics in this collection achieve their poetic power by virtue of their compression and particularity. For example, the second two, untitled lyric sections of 'Chatelaine' are only fourteen and twenty syllables, respectively. This second lyric runs simply, 'Sunset on the river, / gold frame around // a single cloud'.[67] In these three lines, this lyric becomes a verbal postcard to the reader, framing the single cloud with the golden sunset. The third lyric is more alive with natural motion: 'Still lake and river ripple– // the antics of an otter / possessed the whole morning'.[68] The agency and power of the lone otter is sufficient to impart movement to what seems at first to be another postcard scene; in his 'antics', the otter lifts this lyric out of the circumscribed, static bounds of the promised tableau of a typical postcard and ripples the lines themselves with his possession of them. This last lyric continues to reverberate in a later lyric, 'One World', in which we are told, 'Nearly two days after / the tsunami // an extra ripple where the river bumps against the sea.'[69] The otter's disturbance of the 'Still lake and river' in the earlier lyric seem at least as momentous, as newsworthy, as the 'extra ripple' caused by the tsunamic halfway around the world in the later poem, suggesting again how Fallon succeeds in bringing the news of nature, whether seeming inconsequential movements or life-changing ones, to us in these terse lyrics.

These brief poems bring us nearly full-circle to the opening concerns of this essay, particularly Pat Boran's claim about the continuity of particularity in Irish nature poetry from the medieval manuscripts to the present. Fallon's *Ballynahinch Postcards* echo in our minds because of their indebtedness to the Irish medieval lyric and the Japanese haiku tradition in their precise, pared-down lines. Seamus Heaney has remarked upon the 'unique cleanliness of line' in 'Early Irish nature poems', in which 'The tang and clarity of a pristine world full of woods and water and birdsong seems to be present in the words. Little jabs of delight in the elemental are communicated by them in a note that is hard to describe. Perhaps Wordsworth's phrase "surprised by joy" comes near to catching the way some of them combine suddenness and richness . . . ' as does the ancient lyric "The Blackbird of Belfast Lough"'.[70] As Heaney further observes, 'In its precision and suggestiveness, this art has been compared with the art of the Japanese haiku. Basho's frog plopping into its pool in seventeenth-century Japan makes no more durable or exact music than Belfast's blackbird clearing its throat over the lough almost a thousand years earlier'.[71] To return to Fallon's last two lyrics from 'Chatelaine' quoted above, both employ the three lines of the typical Japanese *haiku*, and the lyric about the sunset stays within the traditional seventeen-syllable limit set by the haiku convention, while the one about the otter is only twenty syllables. Thus, these lovely Fallon lyrics – and many other from *Ballynahinch Postcards* – both hearken back to the ancient Irish lyric and link up with the *haiku* in their concision and precision, both grounding the poems in an ancient, seemingly immemorial landscape and simultaneously widening their geographic compass into the Asian nation of Japan.

The concluding poem in *Postcards*, 'A Brighter Blue (Postscript)' is the longest of these poems, but shares with them their glorying in the natural world in Hopkinsesque tones. Some of these short lyrics are not even titled, which practice sets them up as brief interludes between the slightly longer, titled poems. All these lyrics accord with Fallon's belief of the 'news' that nature and rural communities give us if we observe carefully. For example, in 'A Visiting', the speaker tells us of his 'reward' for observing nature all day: 'a hare / and hawk, a waterhen and heron', and in 'Late', the speaker is greeted with a view of the mountain Ben Lettery 'Two days after / my return' (Fallon's emphasis).[72] Fallon's borrowed landscape of Connemara is more aquatic than Loughcrew: he vows, for example, in 'Devotions', 'I must take more time / to learn from rivers', and a number of these poems are about the nearby sea as well.[73] Taken together, Fallon's adopted terrain expands the compass and coverage of his environmental poetry.

The blackbird on the cover of *Ballynahinch Postcards* signifies his ability to flit between places important to him, yet the bird is also pictured as firmly perched on a tree limb. This dual symbol conveys an apposite picture of him and his dynamic, yet grounded relationship to his different environments in Meath, Dublin, and Ballynahinch as he celebrated the fortieth anniversary of Gallery Press in 2010 and as he entered his sixties in 2011. In this sense, his posture accords with what Edward Casey has argued is the continual work of emplacing ourselves: 'Getting back into place, the homecoming that matters most, is an ongoing task that calls for continual journeying between and among places'.[74] While theorist Marc Augé has claimed that 'non-places are the real measure of our time' as we shuttle through transitory, generic spaces such as offices and airports,[75] Peter Fallon's marked ability to inhabit real, lived spaces distinguishes his poetry and his worldview from Augé's finally vacuous concept of 'supermodernity' and its adherents, suggesting the continuing appeal of the natural world for humans and indeed, our obligation to take care of it. As the interaction of Irish studies and environmental literary criticism develops, successful engagements will likely focus on the dynamism of place and humans' moral relationship to it, just as I hope this analysis of the places of Fallon's poetry has.

REFERENCES

Allison, J., 'Kavanagh and Antipastoral', in M. Campbell (ed.), *The Cambridge Companion to Contemporary Irish Poetry* (Cambridge: Cambridge University Press, 2003), pp.42–58.

Augé, M., *Non-Places: Introduction to an Anthropology of Supermodernity*, trans. John Howe (London, Verso, 1995).

Bachelard, G., *The Poetics of Space* (Boston: Beacon, 1994).

Berry, W., 'Still Standing', *The Oxford American*, 25 (January/February 1999), pp.64–9.

Berry, W., 'Christianity and the Survival of Creation', in Norman Wirzba (ed. and introd.), *The Art of the Commonplace: The Agrarian Essays of Wendell Berry* (Washington, D.C.: Shoemaker and Hoard, 2002), pp.305–20.

Berry, W., 'Foreword', *Airs and Angels* by Peter Fallon (Carrollton, OH: Press on Scroll Road, 2007), pp.ix–xv.

Boran, P., 'Nine-and-Fifty Swans: Glimpses of Nature in Recent Irish Poetry', in P. Boran (ed.), *Flowing, Still: Irish Poets on Irish Poetry* (Dublin: Dedalus Press, 2009), pp.146–61.

Buell, L., *The Future of Environmental Criticism: Environmental Crisis and Literary Imagination* (Malden, Massachusetts: Blackwell, 2000).

Casey, E., *Getting Back into Place: Toward a Renewed Understanding of the Place-World* (Bloomington: Indiana University Press, 1993).

Casey, E., 'How to Get from Space to Place in a Fairly Short Stretch of Time: Phenomenological Prolegomena', in S. Feld and K. H. Basso (eds), *Senses of Place* (Santa Fe: School of American Research Press, 1996), pp.13–52.

Chaucer, G., *The Canterbury Tales*, trans. Neville Coghill (London: Penguin, 2003).

Denman, P., 'Realms of Light', *The Poetry Ireland Review*, 81 (2004), pp.76–9.

Duffy, P.J., *Exploring the History and Heritage of Irish Landscapes* (Dublin: Four Courts Press, 2007).

Elder, J., 'Introduction', in Christine Cusick (ed.), *Out of the Earth: Ecocritical Readings of Irish Texts* (Cork: Cork University Press, 2010), pp.1–4.

Fallon, P., 'Interview with Jerry Lincecum', Austin College, Sherman, Texas, 11 October 1990. Audiotape.

Fallon, P., 'Peter Fallon and The Gallery Press: An Interview with Peter Denman', *The Poetry Ireland Review*, 34 (Spring 1992), pp.32–7.

Fallon, P., *News of the World: Selected Poems* (Winston-Salem, North Carolina: Wake Forest University Press, 1993).

Fallon, P., *News of the World: Selected and New Poems* (Loughcrew, Ireland: The Gallery Press, 1998).

Fallon, P., 'Afterwords', *The Georgics of Virgil*, trans. Fallon (Loughcrew, Ireland: The Gallery Press, 2004), pp.120–27.

Fallon, P., 'An Afterword'. *Tarry Flynn: A Play in Three Acts Based on the Novel by Patrick Kavanagh* (Loughcrew, Ireland: The Gallery Press, 2004), pp.100–01.

Fallon, P., *The Georgics of Virgil* (Loughcrew, Ireland: The Gallery Press, 2004).

Fallon, P., *Ballynahinch Postcards* (Aghabollogue, Ireland: Occasional Press, 2007).

Fallon, P., *The Company of Horses* (Loughcrew, Ireland: The Gallery Press, 2007).

Fallon, P., 'Attention, Please?' *Introduction to Ten Pint Ted and Other Stories and Poems: 2009 Fish Anthology* (Cork: Cork University Press, 2009), n.p.

Fallon, P., 'Class Discussion', in Richard Rankin Russell's English 3351 class at Baylor University, Waco, Texas, 26 March 2009.

Fallon, P., 'Poetry Reading at Beall Poetry Festival', Baylor University, Waco, Texas, 26 March 2009.

Fallon, P. and D. Mahon, 'Introduction', in Fallon and Mahon (eds), *The Penguin Book of Contemporary Irish Poetry* (New York: Penguin, 1990), pp.xvi–xxii.

Frawley, O., *Irish Pastoral: Nostalgia in Twentieth-Century Irish Literature* (Dublin: Irish Academic Press, 2005).

Garrard, G., *Ecocriticism* (New York: Routledge, 2004).

Grennan, E., 'Chosen Home: The Poetry of Peter Fallon', *Éire-Ireland*, 29, 2 (Summer 1994), pp.173–87.

Heaney, S., 'The God in the Tree: Early Irish Nature Poetry', in *Preoccupations: Selected Prose, 1968–1978* (London: Faber, 1980), pp.181–9.

Jacobson, D., *Place and Belonging in America* (Baltimore: Johns Hopkins University Press, 2002).

Kavanagh, P., 'The Parish and the Universe', in *Collected Pruse* (London: Macgibbon and Kee, 1967), pp.281–3.

Kerridge, R., 'Ecological Hardy' in K. Ambruster and K.R. Wallace (eds), *Beyond Nature Writing: Expanding the Boundaries of Ecocriticism* (Charlottesville: University of Virginia Press, 2001), pp.126–42.

McElroy, J., 'Ecocriticism and Irish Poetry: A Preliminary Outline', *Estudios Irlandeses*, 6 (2011), pp.54–69.

O'Donoghue, B., '"Bulls and Bees": Review of Peter Fallon, *The Georgics of Virgil*', *The Times Literary Supplement*, 10 December 2004, p.28.

O'Neill, M., '"Couch and Docks and Nettles": Review of Peter Fallon, *News of the World*', *The Times Literary Supplement*, 10 September 1999, p.23.

Riordan, M., '"Naturally Matter-of-Fact": Review of Peter Fallon, *Winter Work*; Eamon Grennan, *Wildly for Days*; Seamus Deane, *History Lessons*; Aidan Carl Mathews, *Minding Ruth*; Robert Johnstone, *Breakfast in a Bright Room*', *The Times Literary Supplement*, 15 March 1985, p.294.

Russell, R.R., 'Loss and Recovery in Peter Fallon's Pastoral Elegies', *Colby Quarterly*, 37, 4 (December 2001), pp.343–56.

Russell, R.R., 'Peter Fallon', in Jay Parini (ed.), *British Writers, Supplement XII* (New York: Scribner, 2006), pp.101–16.

Russell, R.R., 'Peter Fallon. *The Company of Horses*', *New Hibernia Review*, 12, 2 (Summer 2008), pp.154–6.

NOTES

1. P. Boran, 'Nine-and-Fifty Swans: Glimpses of Nature in Recent Irish Poetry', in Pat Boran (ed.), *Flowing, Still: Irish Poets on Irish Poetry* (Dublin: Dedalus Press, 2009), p.149.

2. Ibid., p.161.

3. J. Elder, 'Introduction', in Christine Cusick (ed.), *Out of the Earth: Ecocritical Readings of Irish Texts* (Cork: Cork University Press, 2010), p.4.

4. J. McElroy, 'Ecocriticism and Irish Poetry: A Preliminary Outline', *Estudios Irlandeses*, 6 (2011), qtd. p.54.

5. P. Fallon, *News of the World: Selected and New Poems* (Loughcrew, Ireland: The Gallery Press, 1998), p.38. Further references to *News of the World* are to this edition, not to the 1993 American edition, unless otherwise noted.

6. Ibid., p.39.

7. P. Fallon, 'Class Discussion', in Richard Rankin Russell's English 3351 class at Baylor University, Waco, Texas, 26 March 2009.

8. P. Fallon and D. Mahon, 'Introduction', in Fallon and Mahon (eds), *The Penguin Book of Contemporary Irish Poetry* (New York: Penguin, 1990), pp.xx, xxi.

9. E. Grennan, 'Chosen Home: The Poetry of Peter Fallon', *Éire-Ireland*, 29, 2 (Summer 1994), p.173.

10. P. Fallon, 'Afterwords', *The Georgics of Virgil*, trans. Fallon (Loughcrew, Ireland: The Gallery Press, 2004), p.123.

11. P. Fallon, 'An Afterword', in *Tarry Flynn: A Play in Three Acts Based on the Novel by Patrick Kavanagh* (Loughcrew, Ireland: The Gallery Press, 2004), p.123.

12. Ibid.

13. He has even stated, 'Peter Fallon and the Gallery Press: An Interview with Peter Denman', *The Poetry Ireland Review*, 34 (Spring 1992), that 'I don't believe in the necessity of Dublin. I never subscribed to the notion of everything working from the city. I do go to Dublin regularly. But you need to get away from it, to have some other life, and I don't think I'd be able to have that in Dublin' (p.37).

14. P. Fallon, 'Interview with Jerry Lincecum', Austin College, Sherman, Texas, 11 October 1990. Audiotape.

15. See Maurice Riordan's largely appreciative review of Fallon's 1983 volume, *Winter Work*, '"Naturally Matter-of-Fact": Review of Peter Fallon, *Winter Work*; Eamon Grennan, *Wildly for Days*; Seamus Deane, *History Lessons*; Aidan Carl Mathews, *Minding Ruth*; Robert Johnstone, *Breakfast in a Bright Room*', *The Times Literary Supplement*, 15 March 1985, p.294. Riordan suggests in his analysis of the concluding couplet of Fallon's 'Fostering' – 'and he was Esau's brother and I Isaac's wife / working kind betrayals in a field blessed for life' (*News of the World*, 41) – that 'The shift to the mythic and the sacred . . . owes something to the example of Patrick Kavanagh; but Fallon's concentration and craft are evident in the choice of "raiment" to lift the

description just enough to allow the biblical allusion' to the story of Esau, Jacob, and Isaac in Genesis 27. See also Michael O'Neill, '"Couch and Docks and Nettles": Review of Peter Fallon, *News of the World*', *The Times Literary Supplement*, 10 September 1999, p.23, who observes that 'An influence on this poem ['Winter Work'] and Fallon's practice more generally is [Patrick] Maguire's creator, Patrick Kavanagh, who, in "Iniskeen Road: July Evening", boasts, yet curses, that he is "king / Of banks and stones and every blooming thing"' (23).

16. P. Fallon, 'An Afterword', p.100.

17. Ibid., p.101.

18. P. Fallon, 'Interview with Jerry Lincecum'.

19. P. Fallon and D. Mahon, 'Introduction', p.xvii.

20. P. Kavanagh, 'The Parish and the Universe', in *Collected Pruse* (London: Macgibbon and Kee, 1967), p.283.

21. See J. Allison, 'Kavanagh and Antipastoral', in M. Campbell (ed.), *The Cambridge Companion to Contemporary Irish Poetry* (Cambridge: Cambridge University Press, 2003), pp.42–58.

22. See W. Berry, 'Still Standing', *The Oxford American*, 25 (January/February, 1999), pp.64–9.

23. L. Buell, *The Future of Environmental Criticism: Environmental Crisis and Literary Imagination* (Malden, Massachusetts: Blackwell, 2000), p.11.

24. Duffy, P.J., *Exploring the History and Heritage of Irish Landscapes* (Dublin: Four Courts Press, 2007), p.15.

25. P. Fallon, 'Interview with Lincecum'.

26. G. Bachelard, *The Poetics of Space* (Boston: Beacon, 1994), p.37.

27. P. Fallon, *News of the World*, p.25.

28. P. Fallon, *The Speaking Stones* (Loughcrew, Ireland: The Gallery Press, 1978), p.39.

29. R. Kerridge, 'Ecological Hardy', in K. Ambruster and K.R. Wallace (eds), *Beyond Nature Writing: Expanding the Boundaries of Ecocriticism* (Charlottesville: University of Virginia Press, 2001), p.134.

30. See my essay, 'Peter Fallon', in Jay Parini (ed.), *British Writers, Supplement XII* (New York: Scribner, 2006), pp.113–14, for an analysis of 'The Deerfield Series: Strength of Heart', Fallon's long sequence about the history of that area of Massachusetts, including colonial American encounters with local Native Americans. See also Joyce Peseroff's essay in the current collection, 'Some Notes on Peter Fallon's *The Deerfield Series: Strength of Heart*'.

31. E. Casey, 'How to Get from Space to Place in a Fairly Short Stretch of Time: Phenomenological Prolegomena', in S. Feld and K.H. Basso (eds), *Senses of Place* (Santa Fe: School of American Research Press, 1996), p.26.

32. W. Berry, 'Foreword' to *Airs and Angels* by Peter Fallon (Carrollton, Ohio: Press on Scroll Road, 2007), p.ix.

33. E. Grennan, 'Chosen Home: The Poetry of Peter Fallon', p.174.

34. P. Fallon, 'Afterwords', *The Georgics of Virgil*, p.123.

35. Ibid., p.127.

36. D. Jacobson, *Place and Belonging in America* (Baltimore: Johns Hopkins University Press, 2002), p.5.

37. P. Fallon, 'Afterwords', *The Georgics of Virgil*, p.124.

38. W. Berry, 'Christianity and the Survival of Creation', in Norman Wirzba (ed. and introd.), *The Art of the Commonplace: The Agrarian Essays of Wendell Berry* (Washington, D.C.: Shoemaker and Hoard, 2002), p.316.

39. P. Fallon, *News of the World*, p.51. In his 'Poetry Reading at Beall Poetry Festival', Baylor University, Waco, Texas, 26 March 2009, Fallon recalls Berry's first words to him when he met the older writer for the first time at his Kentucky farm. As he milked one of his cows, Berry looked up, saying approvingly, 'She's a splashy shitter'. Fallon then stated that was the moment he knew that he and Berry would get along well. Drawing on this memory of Berry's statement, Fallon observes about starlings in 'A Refrain' from *The Company of Horses* (Loughcrew, Ireland: Gallery Press, 2007), p.26, that 'each of them's / a splashy shitter . . . .'

40. E. Grennan, 'Chosen Home: The Poetry of Peter Fallon', p.177.

41. R.R. Russell, 'Peter Fallon's Pastoral Elegies', p.348.

42. Ibid., p.349.

43. P. Fallon, *News of the World*, p.78.

44. Ibid., p.130.

45. P. Fallon, 'Attention, Please?', *Introduction to Ten Pint Ted and Other Stories and Poems: 2009 Fish Anthology* (Cork: Cork University Press, 2009), n.p.

46. P. Fallon, *News of the World*, pp.104, 105.

47. Inside front cover of *News of the World: Selected and New Poems* (Winston-Salem, NC: Wake Forest University Press, 1993; Loughcrew: Gallery Press, 1998). 'The Heart's Home' is published only in the Gallery edition of *News of the World*, p.133.

48. P. Fallon, *News of the World*, p.133.

49. Ibid., p.134.

50. O. Frawley, *Irish Pastoral: Nostalgia in Twentieth-Century Irish Literature* (Dublin: Irish Academic Press, 2005), pp.157, 158.

51. I do not have the space to discuss fully the political aspects of Fallon's translation but find it puzzling that in his 'Afterwords', p.126, he criticizes 'George W. Bush rushing to war' in Iraq as an example of *The Georgics'* topical relevance, but points out neither Iraqi dictator Saddam Hussein's devastating draining of the swamps of the Marsh Arabs ('Ma'dan') during his tyrannical regime, nor the many murders Hussein committed.

52. G. Gerrard, *Ecocriticism*, p.109.

53. Ibid., p.114.

54. P. Fallon, *News of the World*, p.16.

55. P. Fallon, 'Class Discussion'.

56. P. Fallon, *News of the World*, p.16.

57. Ibid., p.17.

58. P. Denman, 'Realms of Light', *The Poetry Ireland Review*, 81 (2004), p.77.

59. Ibid., p.77.

60. P. Fallon, 'Afterwords', p.126.

61. E. Casey, *Getting Back into Place: Toward a Renewed Understanding of the Place-World* (Bloomington: Indiana University Press, 1993), p.314.

62. See B. O'Donoghue, '"Bulls and Bees": Review of Peter Fallon, *The Georgics of Virgil*', *The Times Literary Supplement*, 10 December 2004, p.28, where he points out that 'The translator attains vividness and exuberance by a vernacular freedom, often from the rural Irish: "jizz them up", "take a running jump", "a thing of nothing", "grabbed a hold of him . . . ", "a sup of water", "weak with the hunger"'.

63. P. Fallon, *The Georgics of Virgil*, p.15.

64. G. Chaucer, *The Canterbury Tales*, trans. Neville Coghill (London: Penguin, 2003), p.3.

65. R.R. Russell, 'Peter Fallon. *The Company of Horses*', *New Hibernia Review*, 12, 2 (Summer 2008), p.154.

66. P. Fallon, *Ballynahinch Postcards* (Aghabollogue, Ireland: Occasional Press, 2007), n.p.

67. Ibid.

68. Ibid.

69. Ibid.

70. S. Heaney, 'The God in the Tree: Early Irish Nature Poetry', in *Preoccupations: Selected Prose, 1968–1978* (London: Faber, 1980), p.181.

71. Ibid.

72. P. Fallon, *Ballynahinch Postcards*.

73. Ibid.

74. E. Casey, *Getting Back into Place*, p.314.

75. M. Augé, *Non-Places: Introduction to an Anthropology of Supermodernity*, trans. John Howe (London, Verso, 1995), p.78.

The Obscenities and
Audiences of Peter Fallon

JUSTIN QUINN

I

A question arises in several of Peter Fallon's finest early poems: who speaks? Since he writes lyric poetry, one expects that it is the poet, but often the poet's voice is suppressed in order to allow access to other people. But not just any other people, and not just particular other people: rather a community, loosely defined by the area of Oldcastle, in County Meath, where Fallon has lived, published and farmed for over two decades. It is rarely one individual, but rather a collective voice which, while containing dissenting opinions, makes them harmonise. It is an old tension, going back at least to Wordsworth who at once tried to express the spontaneous overflow of his own emotion while calibrating, or tempering, his lines with folk wisdom and old poetic forms. Fallon, however, implicitly rejects the Romantic idea that nature is best appreciated by lone wanderers with large imaginations and little to do: Fallon has lots to do, and wittily and frequently reminds his readers of the pure, literal 'shittiness' of farm work.[1] Moreover, he stresses the way in which a community can be wiser than one person.

Another English poet whose example is instructive is Edward Thomas: Fallon strikes similar notes in similar forms. Thomas was drawn to the ways in which the landscape accrues human meaning over generations so that ultimately it becomes impossible to separate the two without destroying both. He listens carefully to the way particular communities imprint themselves on their places, making his songs less expressions of himself than allowing those communities to sing through his forms. Thomas also likes to fudge his answers to the question 'Who speaks?', for instance, most beautifully in 'Aspens' or 'The Penny Whistle'.[2] Vagueness can be a poetic boon as well as a fault, here allowing Thomas to be exact on other matters, more particularly the way we are woven seamlessly into the songs and seasons of the natural world.

There is a further similar strand: if a poem like Fallon's 'Silver Fir' or 'Proprietary' were stitched into Thomas's *Collected*, it would not be egregious. These two are examples of a new note of attention to the natural world which is found in *The Company of Horses* (2007). In this essay I will argue that in the first part of Fallon's career he makes his poems by letting the collective voice of his community speak, and in *The Company of Horses* he abandons this device, returning to lyric subjectivity uninterrupted by the voices around him, in order to address the theme of cohabitation with the flora and fauna of County Meath. But this lyric subjectivity is no longer something as debased as self-expression; or if it is self-expression then it expresses a self that has been enlarged and profitably complicated by the suppression of mere egotism in the earlier work.

II

Richard Rankin Russell has written of the ways in which community plays an important role in Fallon's poetry. While I don't argue with the general outlines of that interpretation, I do challenge the details; and through such a challenge I wish to come to a new characterisation of how the voice of the community works in Fallon's poems. Through a comparison with Wendell Berry, Russell asserts the connection with the community of Meath:

> Berry's approval of Fallon's 'voices' is telling. Just as Berry has masterfully incorporated the rural dialect of his part of the American South into his fiction and poetry, Fallon has skillfully integrated Irish words and phrases into his poetry: in both cases the poet's relationship to the land and to his rural neighbors is reinforced. For example, in the poem 'Winter Work', Fallon uses the Irish word *meitheal* in line thirteen. In his notes to *News of the World: Selected Poems*, he glosses the word as 'a co-operative work force. I remember especially the congregations of friends and neighbours to help with the threshing. And I've learned since then of Amish barn-raising or "frolics" and, in New England, of sewing and quilting bees'. In the context of the poem, the word ties his individual life as a farmer together with those of his neighbors: 'I warm to winter work, its rituals / and routines . . . alone / or going out to work with neighbours, a *meitheal* still'.[3]

I quote this passage at length because I wish to use this word *meitheal* to prise open the issue of Fallon's diction. The choices governing poetic diction entail questions of audience: if not, firstly, the question who is speaking, then rather the question who is being spoken to. (By answering the latter question, the former is ultimately answered, as we shall see.) For Fallon hopes his poetry will speak to and for two audiences: the first is local, that of his community in Meath; and the second is international, to be found as far afield as Kentucky, Yorkshire, Massachusetts, Dublin, Texas, or wherever those who praise him happen to live.

'Meitheal' is at once the sign of at-homeness and alienation. Irish is the first official language of the Republic of Ireland, and yet it is also a language that very few people speak in the country. There is an area in Meath consisting of two villages that is officially recognised as Irish-speaking, but it is not in the vicinity of Oldcastle. Such words are now more likely to be found labelling state-funded agencies and services in a tokenistic gesture – FAS, Luas, Raidió Teilifís Éireann. Luas means 'speed' and refers to Dublin's light rail system, but do not try to buy a ticket through Irish if you're in a rush. However, *meitheal* clearly has a personal resonance for Fallon, and it is not used, as Irish words are often used by other poets, in an opportunistic nationalist manner. There is a similar ambiguity in the declaration mid-way through the poem 'My Care', which contrasts the violence of the world with the cosy, fireside position of the speaker. But the contrast is not clear-cut: 'All I ever wanted was / to make a safe house in the midlands'.[4] Coming after talk of terrorist activities in Northern Ireland, the term 'safe house' is richly ambivalent.

In the same way the Irish word simultaneously asserts belonging and displacement; the word has to be glossed for Irish and non-Irish readers alike, and although I have no experience of Fallon's particular community in Oldcastle, I hazard a guess that it would be the height of pretentiousness to use such a word in general company; certainly, this would be true in many other parts of Ireland, both urban and rural. The word has thus been reduced to a mere personal sacredness, which is the realm of the lyric poem. Here we are at the heart (a favourite Fallon word) of the enabling tension in the early poetry: he has left Dublin to join a community; essential to that is a suppression of individuality and adoption of the voice of the collective. But behind him, in the urban expanses, he has left friends who 'hibernate // in dreams and fear'.[5] One of them writes of her wrecked life from Rathgar in Dublin, and what is remarkable here is the word 'write': that the friend's information arrives in Fallon's country home in a letter serves to distance Dublin – not in a phone call, not in a visit (it was about an hour and half by car from Rathgar to Oldcastle at that time). Fallon pushes the city away in order to assert his connection with his community:

> I warm to winter work, its rituals
> and routines, and find – indoors
> and out – a deal of pleasure, alone
> or going out to work with neighbours,
>
> a *meitheal* still. All I approve persists,
> is here, at home. I think it exquisite
> to stand in the yard, my feet on the ground,
> in cowshit and horseshit and sheepshit.[6]

The very action of pushing the city away then becomes definitive for the country home: the main feature of the community depicted in the poem, and elsewhere, is that it is *not* the city. The first two quatrains, which refer to friends atomised as suffering individuals in urban space, frames the assertion of the last two quatrains quoted here. There is also a degree of smugness in the approval of the first line of the second quatrain. The achievement of the early poems is to portray a community that would criticise that complacent egotism: Fallon's fellow farmers would make short work of a blow-in from Dublin who 'approved' of them. I will deal in detail with Fallon's portrayal of the people that surround him in Meath, but for now it would be wrong to go further without remarking on the excellence of the rhyme 'exquisite / sheepshit'. Here, in small, is a pattern of the larger themes of the poem, and Fallon's career in general: 'I think it exquisite' is the language of the urbane connoisseur, perhaps savouring a good vintage or a well-humidified cigar. It shifts from the register of the preceding line, with all the complications of *meitheal*. Then, in the second-last line of the poem, talk of the poet's 'feet on the ground' shifts the tone again, this time towards cliché. Then the poem fires its shot, like a flare angled back illuminating the terrain that has been traversed. Whereas '*meitheal*' was a rather abstract way to refer to the community, with the 'cowshit and horseshit and sheepshit', the actual language of the place and of the community come shoving into the poem itself. He has withheld this diction from himself and the reader in order to make the reward all the more surprising and glorious. This is the central moment of many of his poems: when he lets the lightly edited voices of the community into the poem.

It might seem to follow from 'Winter Work' that Fallon thinks that suffering occurs only in cities, whereas country life is idyllic. But he knows that the countryside also has huge suffering, and what he attends to (and this is what, by implication, the city lacks) is the community that deals with this pain. For instance, 'Carnaross 2' is about a suicide who was also possibly a paedophile. The story is told in the first person plural and is idiomatic, although it eschews the condescension of dialect. The speaker tells how the man's brother comes to the house to ask to use the phone and 'We overheard, as was the way, / quiet talk.'[7] The man then comes back to them:

> Then she said
> I'm sorry for your trouble
> and told him to sit down.
> She said she'd wet the tea.[8]

This poem has none of the play of registers to be found in 'Winter Work'; rather, it achieves its effect by keeping its diction and delivery very close to that of the idiom of the community, clinched by that wetting of the tea. The poem itself is a kind of collective 'quiet talk' in the background of terrible, dramatic events, which has no room for highfalutin phrases, unless they are spoken by the priest. The poem then continues to gather the signs of the man's decline:

> First it was a withered calf.
> Then this and that. One thing
> led to another. Soon
> he wouldn't bother his head
> to read *The Celt*.
> The bad word on the wind
> weighed heavily on him.
>
> And maybe he did touch the little girls,
> and maybe he didn't.
>
> But he went into the bog wood.
> The rope was found missing
> when his brother went to milk.[9]

There are only the tiniest poetic flourishes here beyond the community idiom ('The bad word on the wind') but even that might be admissible in conversation.

Fallon forensically holds up the vacuity of the explanations, not in the hostile fashion of, say, the state pathologist, but in sympathy. (There is also humour in the idea that not reading *The Anglo-Celt* is a symptom of suicidal tendencies.)

There is also a striking moral ambiguity in the two lines about paedophilia. The line break suggests moral apathy, implying that the speaker doesn't care if he did, but the line after that ('and maybe he didn't'), brings complexity to reductive moral truth. The lines are pitched to outrage people who are outraged by paedophilia – the editorialists, the crusading politicians, the dinner-party demagogues (in times past, one would have added priests to the list) – by flirting with the idea that the rural community doesn't care about it, unlike the supposedly sophisticated urban population. The lines are indeed shocking: surely it's important to find out if he did or not. But the speaker knows this, and settles the matter in the following lines by narrating how he committed suicide. What's the point in getting to the bottom of it, if the man's hanging from a tree? Justice arguably has been served. But having raised the suspicion of apathy, the poem cannot not fully and finally exclude it: after all, if the community knew about this man's paedophile activities *before* he committed suicide, why was nothing done? The question pertains not only to 'Carnaross 2', but to Ireland in general in the twentieth century.

'If Luck Were Corn' deals obliquely with another difficult issue: teenage pregnancy and infanticide. There is not one instance of that stalwart of lyric expression, the word 'I', in the entire poem; rather, once again, the community speaks and Fallon follows the contours of its talk rather than concentrating on the awful events themselves.

> She thought she'd hide the swaddling clothes,
> lay the body in the lough,
> and carry on. Who'd know?
> There wouldn't be a word about it.
> No one would be a bit the wiser.[10]

Who speaks here? It possibly reports what went on in the girl's mind, but that reporting is perhaps taking place over a shop- or bar-counter. Unfortunately for the girl, there were many 'words about it', in part the poem itself.

> Flesh of her flesh, bone of her bone–
> her brother found the body.

Fishing. He didn't know. He told the guards.
The rest you know yourselves. The rest
was in the papers. An inquest. Enquiries.
The question of charges.[11]

The 'yourselves' here suggests that the poem speaks to a larger group, or reports conversation to a larger group: it is, thus, public speech, and in the poem this becomes published speech. But it deliberately avoids sounding like official speech: the poem's speaker does not want a grand-standing tone (either to express outrage or his own sympathy for the girl), rather Fallon pitches it to catch exactly the semi-public occasion of a group of people who have casually met to discuss recent events.

There was one week's talk
on Herbstreet's step,
the usual sympathy:
she was only a child herself,
and wasn't that a cross to bear;
and the common savagery:
boys will be boys . . . and girls will be mothers,
she has cried the laugh she had last year.[12]

What the poem ultimately pays tribute to is not the suffering of the girl or the collective judgement of the town, rather, in its final verse, to a single individual (not the speaker) who challenges the townspeople: 'if you drained the ponds / in your back yards / you'd find more than you bargained for'.[13] The morals of any community are never just crowd-sourced; they occasionally also depend on outliers who challenge the drift towards complacency. Fallon does not abrogate such a role to himself and neither does he conclude with a description at how he felt about the whole thing. The poem then is about the process of moral adjustment that takes place in personal interactions in the community. The individual can repair the community's judgement, and likewise, on other occasions, collective judgement correctly overrides the scruples or mawkishness of a single person. This is the imaginative work that the poem carries out.

Even that most personal grief, the death of one's child, is given a communal dimension in 'A Part of Ourselves'. The subtitle reads: 'In memory of John Fallon,

born 7 December, died 8 December 1990', and it is not until the tenth line do we
encounter the word 'we', thus identifying the parents as speakers. Up to this the
lines shimmer and slide without an owner:

> Forewarned but not forearmed–
> no, not for this.
> A word first whispered months ago
> and longed for longer tripped on the tongue,
> a stammer, now a broken promise.
>
> Averted eyes. Uncertain talk
> of a certain strange condition.
> The scanned screen slips out of focus,
> a lunar scene, granite shapes, shifting.
> We bent the weight of attrition
>
> knowing it might have been worse.[14]

Who whispered the word? Who stammers? Who broke the promise? Whose eyes
were averted? Whose talk was uncertain? Because of the subtitle the reader can
answer such questions fairly accurately, but Fallon relishes the delay of clarity,
making the talk float without an owner or agency. It is a device, admittedly, but it
is a device that reveals much about his aesthetic procedures in the early poetry,
as he lets the talk unowned by any individual, but rather of the collective, into
poem after poem.

In the fifth section, Fallon recounts how the loss releases other people's stories:

> We broached the sorrow hoard
> of women, tales unmentioned in their marriages,
> unsaid to friends, to families.
> Fellow feeling loosed their tongues
> about unwanted pregnancies, abortions, miscarriages . . . .[15]

This part places the parents' loss against similar losses of their neighbours;
the following part finds such loss in preceding inhabitants of the same place
(the poet remembers a child's grave in Loughcrew dated 1899). Paying such a
terrible price, Fallon is given more knowledge of his place. Russell remarks that

"'A Part of Ourselves', while composed of many lamentations, is ultimately a long praise poem that writes the dead baby into the memory of the living. In this second function of the elegy, Fallon's poem also displays an allegiance to Berry's agrarian concept of communal preservation.[16] But there is a tension between such communal preservation and poetry as Fallon writes (and publishes it): the question is whether Fallon is writing about his community or for his community. The options are not mutually exclusive, but as with the word *'meitheal'* above, which clearly has a personal meaning for Fallon, but a more questionable public meaning, so too does 'A Part of Ourselves' raise questions about its first audience. Poetry, in the general European tradition, easily accommodates personal lament, but the more difficult issue is what it would mean to perform 'A Part of Ourselves' for Fallon's own community – in a local hall, perhaps, or a school room in the evening. As writing and reading groups permeate Ireland, with their cognates in group therapy and organisations like Alcoholics Anonymous, it is less unusual now for such a personal loss to be expressed publicly outside the occasion of a funeral mass. The questions of audience eddy unanswered up to the end of *News of the World: Selected and New Poems* (1998).

III

The Company of Horses was published in 2007, fifteen years after Fallon's last stand-alone collection; in the meantime he published some new poetry in his selected poems of 1998. He also published a translation of Virgil's *Georgics* in 2004 to wide acclaim. The poems that I have looked at above all originate in the earlier period, and *The Company of Horses* uses the community neither as theme nor poetic method in the way that I have described above. Neither is the book a return to the egotism that Fallon worked hard to repress in poems like 'The Heartland' and 'My Care'. But the lyric subject does come to the fore, and wields the first person pronoun as never before. Vegetation and animals are encountered by the speaker of the poems, not as he stands as detached observer, but rather through stories of work and hunting. Murder is one particularly intense way, among many, of knowing another being. The world is revealed through its instrumentality, not by unmoving contemplation of essence.

Before considering some poems from this collection, I would like to return briefly to *The Georgics*. Much like the word *'meitheal'* above, the Latin author is both at home in Fallon's chosen landscape and alien. He is at home in it in two ways. First, through language. Latin has been a language of Ireland since the

Middle Ages, albeit functional in limited circles. It took on greater currency when mass was openly celebrated through it, and this state of affairs persisted until Vatican II in the early 1960s. Thus, while the language was not obviously used for daily communication, it was nevertheless associated with the sacral space of the church, whose rituals punctuated the lives of all its congregation. It was widely taught in schools and indeed is still taught in Glenstal Abbey, where Fallon attended as a boarder. In the afterword to his translation, Fallon remarks that 'at boarding school, I started Latin. At the time I was first introduced to passages from *The Georgics* my home life centred on my uncle's farm in Carnaross. I could not have guessed that my everyday experiences of land work and livestock and my read-about encounters with these subjects would ever coalesce'.[17]

The second sense is indicated in the quotation: Virgil's poem is about agriculture and mixes lyrical description with practical advice. The lesson of the Latin poem is that the work that Fallon has been engaged upon in Meath, which he obliquely figured as being in opposition to the metropolitan centre – with its putative standards of sophistication and culture – fully engages with the European literary tradition, namely through one of its founders. One does not have to scrape the mud off one's boots before coming into the parlour of European literature; rather, the more cowshit, horseshit and sheepshit the better. This is the kind of fact that most readers of literature *know*, but it is quite something else to put it into practice in the course of a life dedicated to writing poetry. It takes time, as well as many extra-poetical realisations.

There is an important sense then that Fallon's translation of Virgil was as much a return to his community as were his early notations of semi-public utterance in poems like 'If Luck Were Corn' and 'Carnaross 2'. And yet it is a clear extension of his imaginative landscape. For instance, Fallon's 'The Deerfield Series', a sequence of poems set in and around a private school in Massachusetts, occupied an anomalous position in his oeuvre up to this point. There were many continuities with the earlier lyrics in style and theme, but they could not balance the geographical dislocation. Biographical vagary had not yet been transformed into imaginative necessity. The bridging device was his translation of Virgil.

Thus, it is not until one of the final poems of *The Company of Horses* that this anomaly is made whole. 'Depending on Water' begins with demonstrative emphasis:

There, just there
where the river bends,
a string that isn't there
suspends

a shoal of shad.
Our light craft lends
itself to water and bears
us as the world intends–

that is, deliberately.[18]

Deictic utterance depends on context, on this occasion, place. The speaker is insistent that we see what he sees, and yet we do not occupy the same space or time, and this goes to the centre of the paradox of such a local art as Fallon's: the work is concerned with a community in the Irish midlands, but as publication it circulates in an international literary space (viz., the plaudits from prominent American and English poets on Fallon's various books), read by people who cannot see what he means when he shouts: 'There, just there'. Fallon knows and plays with this, especially in the third line's reference to something that, in fact, 'isn't there'. We are born by our light craft – poetry, a boat – not as we intend, but as the world does; biographical vagary by another name. The poem then mentions the Deerfield river and a lake in Ireland, presumably near Loughcrew. Deerfield is thus one particular elsewhere plucked out of the multiple elsewheres of the world (elsewhere meaning here not Loughcrew). But no longer do we have the contrast of Loughcrew and world. The poem concludes:

For all their loss there's
something in the years that mends.
We've thought and talked about
the need for what transcends

belovèd places
much as their grace commends
them to us – for nothing ends
with family, and friends.[19]

If Fallon depended on the land for his imaginative work in the early books, here he learns to depend on water: the book glides easily over different geographies (but never globetrots). There is a poem set on the Orkneys, another on the Blaskets, a sequence in Ballynahinch, and a couple of versions of Ovid. Here he finds a poetic that comfortably straddles two disparate places on either side of the Atlantic. In 1995 Seamus Heaney commented that Fallon's 'journeyings have been as important as his sense of belonging in Meath, and have helped his vision both to widen and focus'.[20] I argue however, that this change didn't occur until *The Company of Horses* (2007), and the manifesto is 'Depending on Water'.

The comfort of this evolution, however, is not satisfactory. The finest poems in the book are laconic, disciplined, and lapidary, continuing the mode of earlier poems like 'An Easter Prayer' and 'Spring Song'. Many favour a short line, dense alliteration and rhyme; and the shorter the line the more pronounced the rhyme. The rhymes are meant to be noticed, and are employed not for decoration, but like rivets to hold the argument together. They are also loosely deployed – in some poems there are only two lines that rhyme, for instance, 'Proprietary', which I give in full:

> Who owns, he wonders,
> as he passes,
> these holdings, sites
> and old demesnes?
>
> And hears the verdict
> of the wind–
> trees and brambles,
> weeds and grasses.[21]

In the earlier poem 'The Lost Field', he declares: 'I'm out to find that field, to make it mine.'[22] Russell comments on this decision: 'Fallon is reaffirming his desire to find and stake claim to the lost field that has evaded his family's reach for so long. On a more metaphoric level, the field represents the poetic arena Fallon hopes to find and negotiate through his own poetry, much of which centers upon the physical landscape of his sheep farm.'[23] But in the later poem a different owner asserts title. The poem only lightly reveals itself as slightly rhymed in its last line, as 'grasses' picks up 'passes' of the second, but the effect is strong, first, because the lines are so short, and second, because it is a feminine rhyme. Also, there is the pleasing idea of the wind's verdict being an echo. There is also an intense use of assonance throughout, which in so small a compass thickens the phonetic mix. What this effects is hard to say, although we know it is integral to the poem (particularly the [oΩ] sound in the first verse). Certainly the clipped sound of 'verdict' in the second versé brings to an end the sibilants and repeated vowel sound of the first verse, only to have the former return in the poem's last word. In such a short poem the phonetic effects are half the argument.

Another poem that is similar in this respect is 'Crane', which I give here in full:

We watch him
watching us.
Then he picks his way

in slow-
motion through
the minefield of the shore.

Now he unfolds
the parcel of himself
and starts to gather up

the vast contraption of his wings
and crank himself
aloft.

Press ups
and downward pressing
on the bed of air

transform his slack
machinery, grey matter
to a miracle of flight:

hunched heap,
long loper,
sack of shite.[24]

The assonances and obvious alliterations of the last verse are complemented by the repeated plosive; the internal and end rhymes ('slack'/'sack', 'flight'/'shite') also intensify the effect. But one immediately wants to object to a poem that solves the puzzle of the bird much like a quadratic equation and ends up with the result that it is a 'sack of shite'. It insults the animal it would seem to set out to praise. The *OED* helpfully tells us that 'shit-sack' goes back to at least the eighteenth century; and 'shite' is the Old English form that preceded 'shit'. This, then, is an old, solid insult, that draws purely on the resources of Old English and is still current ('sack of shite' is particularly popular with an adjectival participle: the first page in Google refers to a prominent American politician as a 'lying sack of shite'); a Latinate 'container of excrement' doesn't do the job. An explosion of shit at the end of a poem is an effect that we have encountered before in Fallon, but although he is clearly drawn to its shock effect (obscenity invading the elevated lyric diction of the preceding poem – e.g., 'miracle of flight', 'bed of air'), he is not going for the cheap laugh: when we stay with the line, we realise that the crane, like every other animal, has inside it a 'sack of shite', and the entire somatic envelope can be considered as a carrier of excrement. Fallon insists on the scatological as integral to our sense of nature, just as in another poem, 'Fair Game', he insists on violence as a way of coming to know a bird. Reviewing the collection, Colin Graham remarked, 'Fallon avoids giving the animals in his poems human traits or his humans animal traits, and instead leaves open the ways in which we should understand ourselves in the world'.[25] 'Crane' is a prime example of such an opening and it forcefully transgresses the tawdry reverences of eco-kitsch, sharpening our perception in its course.

The poem also tells us that perception, in nature, is a two-way street. The opening makes it clear that human beings are not detached observers of the natural world: 'We watch him / watching us.' The voice of the collective is still here, but it is turned outward to the natural world. This is the signal difference between Fallon's early work and *The Company of Horses*: the collective is no longer at the centre of the poem's imaginative work, rather it has become the vehicle to view the world. ('Fair Game' mentioned above also uses the first person plural.) Elsewhere he uses the intermediary 'you', which is primarily understood as the second person singular, but has overtones of the plural also. 'Silver Fir' is a good example of this turn. What is constant is a lack of interest in the revelations and emotional shifts that might be going on in the lyric speaker (whether singular or plural): obviously the poems deal with emotion, but the self does not step forth as ultimate emotional guarantor of the poems (in hackneyed use in other poets of the type: 'And then I realised . . . '; 'And then I remembered . . . '). These poems no longer aim to reveal something about the self, or the community, but rather what lies beyond, or indeed what they live with: the birds and the horses of the title poem.

'The Company of Horses' is one of the finest in the book. It employs the second person singular, and the verbs towards the end drift into the imperative. The poem describes the horses when they are away from the company of humans, and how they are then transformed by it, as the owner whispers his '*Ohs* and *Whoa*, / *Oh the boy* and *Oh the girl*,'[26] in the horse's ear. In a manoeuvre unusual for Fallon, the conclusion of the poem lifts both man and horse to the level of mythology. Poets who mythologise have had a hard time of it in the last few decades, but Fallon gets away with this beautifully, in a poem about the way that horses and humans live and work together. The farm and its rhythms are the barely visible framework for the poem, so this is clearly the same space of the earlier poems. Yet here Fallon is unconcerned about the gossip in Oldcastle (viz., the talk on Herbstreet in 'If Luck Were Corn'): he honours horses independently of human beings, but ends by celebrating the bond forged by having spent large parts of their lives together. It is an enlargement of the earlier idea of community, and it is an enlargement of Fallon's imaginative domain.

REFERENCES

Fallon, P., *News of the World: Selected and New Poems* (Loughcrew, Ireland: The Gallery Press, 1998).

Fallon, P., 'Afterwords', *The Georgics of Virgil*, trans. Fallon (Loughcrew, Ireland: The Gallery Press, 2004), pp.120–27.

Fallon, P., *The Georgics of Virgil*, trans. Fallon (Loughcrew, Ireland: The Gallery Press, 2004).

Fallon, P., *The Company of Horses* (Loughcrew, Ireland: The Gallery Press, 2007).

Graham, C., 'Where Nature and Humans Meet, Rev. of *The Company of Horses*', *Irish Times*, 1 December 2007, p.16.

Heaney, S., 'Tributes to Peter Fallon: 25 Years of Gallery Press', *Irish Literary Supplement*, 14, 2 (Fall 1995), p.6.

Russell, R.R., 'Loss and Recovery in Peter Fallon's Pastoral Elegies', *Colby Quarterly*, 37, 4 (December 2001), pp.343–356.

Thomas, E., *The Annotated Collected Poems*, ed. E. Longley (Highgreen, UK: Bloodaxe, 2008).

NOTES

1. For instance, see P. Fallon 'Winter Work', in *Winter Work* (Loughcrew, Ireland: The Gallery Press, 1983), p.48; 'Country Music' and 'Dung' in *The News and Weather* (Loughcrew, Ireland: The Gallery Press, 1987), p.28, 18; and 'A Refrain' in *The Company of Horses* (Loughcrew, Ireland: The Gallery Press, 2007), pp.26–7.

2. E. Thomas, *The Annotated Collected Poems*, ed. E. Longley (Highgreen, UK: Bloodaxe, 2008), pp.97, 50.

3. R.R. Russell, 'Loss and Recovery in Peter Fallon's Pastoral Elegies', *Colby Quarterly*, 37, 4 (December 2001), p.347. I have removed Russell's in-text references lest they be confused for those of this essay.

4. P. Fallon, *News of the World: Selected and New Poems* (Loughcrew, Ireland: The Gallery Press, 1998), p.60. Subsequently only the first quotation from each poem is referenced.

5. See P. Fallon, *News of the World*, p.51.

6. Ibid.

7. P. Fallon, *The News and Weather*, p.17.

8. Ibid.

9. Ibid.

10. Ibid., p.26.

11. Ibid.

12. Ibid., p.27.

13. Ibid.

14. P. Fallon, *Eye to Eye* (Loughcrew, Ireland: The Gallery Press, 1992), p.54.

15. Ibid., p.58.

16. R. R Russell, 'Loss and Recovery', p.12.

17. P. Fallon, 'Afterwords', *The Georgics of Virgil*, trans. Fallon (Loughcrew, Ireland: The Gallery Press, 2004), p.123.

18. P. Fallon, *The Company of Horses*, p.52.

19. Ibid., p.53.

20. S. Heaney, 'Tributes to Peter Fallon: 25 Years of Gallery Press', *Irish Literary Supplement*, 14, 2 (Fall 1995), p.6.

21. P. Fallon, *The Company of Horses*, p.40.

22. P. Fallon, *News of the World*, p.17.

23. R. R.Russell, 'Loss and Recovery', p.345.

24. P. Fallon, *The Company of Horses*, p.28.

25. C. Graham, 'Where Nature and Humans Meet, Rev. of *The Company of Horses*', *Irish Times*, 1 December 2007.

26. Ibid., p.19.

Peter Fallon's *Georgics*:

Praises, Lessons and Lamentations in Virgil's 'studies of the arts of peace'

JOSEPH HEININGER

Peter Fallon's translation of the *Georgics* of Virgil has been widely and justly praised. First published in 2004 by The Gallery Press, Fallon's translation was revised and republished in 2006 in an Oxford World's Classics edition, with an introduction and notes by Elaine Fantham.[1] The translation has been praised by reviewers such as Eamon Grennan, Seamus Heaney, Bernard O'Donoghue, and others. As the 2004 Poetry Books Society citation states, readers are both 'earthed and engrossed' when they read Fallon's careful remaking of Virgil's 'poem of the earth', as Michael Putnam has designated the *Georgics*.[2]

In his review of Peter Fallon's translation in the *Irish Times*, Seamus Heaney addresses the practical and political virtues which characterise Virgil's *Georgics* for both Roman and contemporary readers. As Iain Twiddy acknowledges in 'Pastoral and Aftermath: Seamus Heaney', Heaney's review of Fallon's translation pointedly remarks on the *Georgics'* didactic correctness and thoroughness and its post-bellum timeliness: the poem was written 'in or around 29 BC, two years after Octavian's victory at Actium, the decisive battle of the civil war'.[3] Twiddy elaborates, confirming this point about the significance of the post-war placement of the *Georgics*: 'According to Heaney, the poem was "Virgil's dream of how his hurt country might start to heal"'.[4] That Heaney should make this public claim for the artistic equilibrium and moral correctness of the *Georgics* is not surprising, given that he has powerfully articulated the idea of the 'redress of poetry' as an imaginative space in which the fixed ideas and dominant prejudices of an age can be questioned by putting them under poetry's aesthetic and moral microscope. Within the cultural and political atmosphere following the Ulster peace accords as well as during the search in Irish life and letters after the 1994 ceasefire to find ways in which 'his hurt country might start to heal', Peter Fallon's version of the *Georgics* may also be read as an example of an Irish poet and farmer's attempt to 'sing in time of war the arts of peace'; In other words, as Fallon himself has said of his work of translation, 'Ultimately, the translator's aim should be to honor the original. I learned along the way I also harboured hopes that I might inscribe the biography of one place in another age'.[5] This authorial comment seems to point directly to Fallon's effort as a translator to transpose the matter and the spirit of Virgil's after-Actium song of the arts of peace into a post-1994 Irish imaginative and cultural context, all without violating the spirit of the Latin original. We shall see in examining several specific aspects of Fallon's translation – his masterful use of consonance, assonance, and alliteration, his energetic, flavorful diction and suggestive, precise imagery, and his occasional use of iambic pentameter or trochaic meters to vivify his lines – just how his individual phrases and lines combine to make an expert reworking of Virgil's Latin into a contemporary English rendering of 'Virgil's dream of how his hurt country might start to heal'.[6]

Two other literary and philosophical contexts suggest themselves as necessary for a full articulation of the work of the *Georgics*. First, as the Virgil scholar Christine Perkell points out, the poem 'does deal with such topics as the planting of grain and the care of vines, livestock, and bees'. But because 'it deals with much else as well, touching on a variety of issues critical to contemporary Rome . . . it has, therefore, long been recognised that the poem is not truly an agricultural manual, for which purpose it would, in fact, be both incomplete and inaccurate, but a meditation on urgent political and moral questions'.[7] In other words, the *Georgics* makes a targeted effort to contribute to Roman civic life, aiming its poetry toward the education of the wise and prudential countryman as distinct from the wayward or corrupt townsman, and thus participates in the literary imagination's ethical project of building a more just public discourse and a more equitable society. It participates in the greater project of what the philosopher Martha Nussbaum has conceptualised as literature's contribution to 'poetic justice', in which the poem 'has the potential to make a distinctive contribution to our public life'.[8] Secondly, as Louis L. Martz has observed in discussing Milton's

Paradise Regain'd, the poetic style of that late poem is not epic or ambitious in the style of *Paradise Lost*, in which Milton asks the Heavenly Muse to aid his 'adventrous Song / That with no middle flight intends to soar / Above th' Aonian Mount'.[9] Rather, as Martz contends, in *Paradise Regain'd*, Milton 'chooses to make a middle flight in the georgic style, which Virgil himself may be said to define at the outset of his second book': Not that I could ever hope to feature all things in my verses– / not even if I had a hundred mouths, as many ways of speech, / and a voice as strong as iron.[10] The most significant resemblance, as Martz indicates, is that both *Paradise Regain'd* and the *Georgics* 'share a common ethical theme: the praise of the temperate, disciplined, frugal life, as opposed to the grandeur, luxury, and vice of empires'.[11]

Such clear indications of political and social contextualisation for the *Georgics* open useful interpretive ways before us. Perkell and Martz's emphasis on the poem's investigation of moral questions and the praise of the temperate and frugal life therein allows readers of Fallon's translation to see his version of Virgil's poem as addressed to two kinds of 'countrymen': the wise farmer, the 'countryman [who] cleaves earth with his crooked plough'[12], and the sensible and careful citizen, a philosophically-minded man who searches for instruction in how to lead a temperate, disciplined, and frugal life. Because of the dual, overlapping audiences the poet imagines for the *Georgics,* and the memorable passages it features, we shall see that the *Georgics* is both a pastoral poem devoted to seasonal activities on the land, including wise husbandry of animals, careful cultivation of vines, proper beekeeping, and other natural instruction, and a peacetime poem that asserts as its governing themes Nussbaum's outward engagement with political and civic justice and Martz's inward stance inclined toward philosophical meditation. As its traditional themes of managing a satisfactory country life emerge in Book I, we see that the *Georgics* is first a pastoral poem of a practical and didactic kind: the poem's four books contain many passages that elaborate upon correct performance of seasonal agricultural practices, care of domestic animals, proper methods of arboreal cultivation, and the arts of successful beekeeping. In addition, the sections of the poem in which Virgil invites the reader to consider the social and political implications of the countryman's leading his temperate, ordered life in peacetime rather than in wartime can be seen as the poet's meditative engagement with what Perkell has characterised as the poem's urgent moral questions.

From the time of John Dryden's influential poetic translation of Virgil in 1697 through David Ferry's impressive 2005 translation of Virgil into American-accented

English, the *Georgics* have supplied a specifically pastoral and didactic vision of harmonious country living for the farmer as long as he wisely minds the signs of weather and provides for abundance as well as for potential scarcity.[13] What is noticeably different about Peter Fallon's version, as both Heaney and Twiddy suggest, is that Fallon emphasises the view that the poet's pastoral, georgic lessons to the countryman throughout the four books are actually 'studies of the arts of peace' (the phrase occurs at the close of the poem, at Book Four, 564) undertaken in response to the recent war (Octavian's victory at Actium in 31 BC). Thus the main lines of Heaney's review of Fallon's version direct contemporary readers to a fruitful engagement with the major themes of this ancient work. Readers will find that in their poetic and moral integrity and their sequential lessons on the prudence and attractiveness of that peacetime vision, Fallon's *Georgics* do enliven an 'alternative [imaginative] space to war'.[14] By attending to the poem's 'alternative space to war', Heaney has done readers of Fallon's translation a significant service by redirecting our attention to the salient and memorable parts of this poem addressing 'the arts of peace'. For example, in Books One and Two, the *Georgics* address the propitious moments in springtime in which to harness the ox to the ploughshare. Furthermore, in passages I shall soon consider, Virgil sings of what one might call the use and care of the ploughshare rather than the sword, although the sword does not entirely vanish from consideration.

Early in Book One, after the invocation and request for the blessings of Liber (Bacchus) and Ceres, Virgil instructs the farmer to begin his plowing 'in the sweet of the year':

> Come the sweet o' the year, when streams begin to melt and
>> tumble down the hoary hills
> and clods to crumble underneath the current of west winds,
>> it's time again to put the bull before the deep-pointed plough to
>> pull his weight
> and have the share glisten, burnished by the broken sod.[15]

Then, after urging caution to the countryman in choosing which lands to work ('And yet before we take our implements to unfamiliar territory / we must work to ascertain its changing weather and winds' moods, / to learn the ways and habits of that locality– / what's bound to flourish there, and what to fail),'[16] Virgil begins to instruct his reader quite spiritedly in the arts of springtime ploughing:

And so onward!
From the sun's first tender touch, run your mighty teams
through fertile fields, tossing sods about
for baking heat to break them down to dust.
But if you've not got high-yielding soil you will do well
to rake it with a shallow sock by the shine of that time's
    brightest star,
to ensure either that weeds won't block the way for wholesome
    crops
or that a bare sandy plot retains whatever moisture's there.
  Take turns to let the land lie fallow after it's been harvested,
let fields left to themselves recuperate and renew themselves
    with firmer footing
or, with a switch of season, set down, say, tawny emmer or
    einkorn,
where once you'd gathered an outpour of pulses
with their rustling pods, or drawn spindly vetch
and bitter lupins' brittle stalks and susurrating stems.
For it's a fact and true, a crop of flax will parch a place,
as will wild oats, as will a sprawl of poppies doused in their
    forgetfulness.[17]

In this passage, we can hear the voice of the Roman poet instructing the countryman with expert care about spring ploughing and the correct way to leave land fallow after harvest. In the first three lines, we also become aware of some of the repetitive, consonance-shaped, alliterative and pleasant-sounding qualities of Fallon's translation, with its alliterative consonance of the 't' sound ('first tender touch'); to its repetition ('sun's', 'run', and 'dust') throughout these three lines of the short 'u' vowel sound; to its nearly Anglo-Saxon pairings of two alliterative consonants, 'b' and 'd', sounded close together in the third line ('baking' and 'break'; 'down to dust'): 'From the sun's first tender touch, run your mighty teams / through fertile fields, tossing sods about / for baking heat to break them down to dust'.[18] The last lines of this passage are also quite rich in consonance, metrical regularity, and alliteration, and show Fallon's talents for employing a particularly lively and precise diction and imagery in his poetic language:

> Take turns to let the land lie fallow after it's been harvested,
> let fields left to themselves recuperate and renew themselves
>   with firmer footing
> or, with a switch of season, set down, say, tawny emmer or
>   einkorn,
> where once you'd gathered an outpour of pulses
> with their rustling pods, or drawn spindly vetch
> and bitter lupins' brittle stalks and susurrating stems.
> For it's a fact and true, a crop of flax will parch a place,
> As will wild oats, as will a sprawl of poppies doused in their
>   forgetfulness.[19]

The opening line provides a veritable cascade of liquid sounds with 'let the land lie fallow', and the next lines mix more of these liquids ('let fields left to themselves') with the strongly alliterative consonants in 'recuperate and renew themselves', 'with firmer footing', and 'with a switch of season'. In fact, the consistent use of consonance and assonance, and of alliterative repetition either stretching over several unrhymed lines or sometimes concentrated and balanced on either side of a caesura in the Anglo-Saxon style, are notable hallmarks of Peter Fallon's style as a translator. I want to emphasise the point that although the translated lines do not have end-rhymes, it is through no failing of the translator's eye or ear. Rather, he accomplishes the knitting together of Virgil's images and ideas with his expert use of the devices of repetition I have singled out above, and constructs many passages full of the sonic pleasures of regular metrical beats: 'and bitter lupins' brittle stalks and susurrating stems. // For it's a fact and true, a crop of flax will parch a place, / As will wild oats, as will a sprawl of poppies doused in their forgetfulness'.[20] Here we enjoy the panoply of repetitions, 'b's' and 's's' giving way to 'p's' and the assonance of the short 'a' vowel sound that weaves its way through most of the second line, ending in the third line with the wonderful, acoustically pleasing phrase 'as will a sprawl of poppies doused in their forgetfulness'. The combination of a Keatsian overabundance suggested by the visual phrase a 'sprawl of poppies' with the intense sensation of smell registered by the verb 'doused' adds special power to the poet's warning to the farmer: the poppies no less than the wild oats will indeed 'parch a place' that should then be left fallow for a year.

Although the above passages celebrate with memorably strong language the richness of the farmer's cultivated land as well as his care of his fallow land, Book One of the *Georgics* ends by taking a turn away from the peaceful arts of cultivation toward a more sober, even pessimistic mood of reflection on the countryman's activities as he turns the soil with his plough and finds the buried implements of war. Virgil writes, in Fallon's vigorously idiomatic translation:

> Nothing surer than the time will come when, in those fields,
> A farmer ploughing will unearth
> rough and rusted javelins and hear his heavy hoe
> echo on the sides of empty helmets and stare in open-eyed
>   amazement
> at the bones of heroes he's just happened on.
>   . . . .More than enough, and long ago, we paid in
>   blood
> For the lies Laomedon told at Troy. Long, long ago since
>   heaven's royal estate
> begrudged you first your place among us, Caesar,
> grumbling of your empathies with the cares of men and the
>   victories they earn.
> For right and wrong are mixed up here, there's so much warring
>   everywhere,
> evil has so many faces, and there is no regard for the labours
> of the plough. Bereft of farmers, fields have run to a riot of
>   weeds.
> Scythes and sickles have been hammered into weapons of war.
> Look here, the east is up in arms; look there, hostilities in
>   Germany.
> Neighbouring cities renege on what they pledged and launch
>   attacks–
> the whole world's at loggerheads, a blasphemous battle,
> as when, right from the ready, steady, go, chariots quicken on a
>   track
> until the driver hasn't a hope of holding the reins and he's
>   carried away
> by a team that pays heed to nothing, wildly away and no control.[21]

As Book One concludes, these lines represent Virgil's dire warning about the extent of political and agricultural misrule and the consequent upheavals and devastations of war, and Fallon catches the notes of prophetic severity and lamentation in Virgil's imagery when he uses the alliterative phrases 'Bereft of farmers, fields have run to a riot of weeds. / Scythes and sickles have been hammered into weapons of war'.[22] The themes of the total wrongheadedness and widespread destruction of war are enunciated by images of anarchy and civil disorder. These ideas strongly mark the last lines of Book One as Fallon renders them: 'the whole world's at loggerheads, a blasphemous battle, / as when, right from the ready, steady, go, chariots quicken on a track / until the driver hasn't a hope of holding the reins and he's carried away / by a team that pays heed to nothing, wildly away and no control'.[23] The image of the wild, uncontrolled team is a powerful example of a world gone anarchically wrong, and its darkness is mitigated only by the poet's change of thematic direction in the opening of Book Two. Here Virgil announces a more sanguine exploration of Bacchus's patronage of the vine and a primer on the propagation of trees.

In Book Two, as Fallon adapts Virgil's language into what Ted Hughes described as his 'snappy and weighty' vernacular (back cover of *News of the World*, American and Irish editions), a major theme of the *Georgics* emerges: the poet's praise of careful husbandry in the observance of agricultural practices. Moreover, in a section giving advice on seasonal planting, Virgil inserts a beautiful passage of almost thirty lines devoted to the arrival of spring. This passage provides a song of praise for the season of birth and growth. Fallon's gifts of exact language make the Virgilian text come alive: the reader hears the verses celebrating the earth's renewed fecundity, the joyful noises of growth, the flowering of seasonal fruits, and the generally Edenic 'dawning' of nature in this passage praising spring.

> Pay no heed to anyone, however well he's versed in plant
>   production,
> who tells you to begin to plough rock-solid land while north
>   winds still
> bare their teeth. When winter seals the countryside
> broadcast corn can't get a foothold in the soil.
> It's spring's first flush that's best for sowing vines,
> when that bright bird returns, the bane of lanky snakes,
> or, if not then, the first cold snap of autumn, before the sun's
> fiery steeds have touched on winter, although in truth, the
>   summer's gone already.
> Spring it is, spring that's good to the core of the wood, to the

> leaves of groves,
> spring that reawakens soil and coaxes seeds to fruitfulness.
> It's then almighty father, Air, marries the earth
> and penetrates her with prolific showers, and, their bodies joined
> as one, unbridles life's potential.[24]

In classical literature, the marriage of earth and sky is known as the *hieros gamos*, or 'sacred marriage'.[25] Both Lucretius and Homer represent this primal marriage, and in this passage in Book Two, Virgil puts forth a praise song of the season's great awakenings. I want to direct attention to Fallon's choice of verbs and the rhyming or metrically pleasing phrases that give vitality and movement to this passage: 'Spring it is, spring that's good to the core of the wood, to the leaves of groves, / spring that reawakens soil and coaxes seeds to fruitfulness'.[26] The many rhyming and near-rhyming repetitions of the 'o' sound throughout these lines are remarkable, especially in 'good to the core of the wood', and the assonance and consonance created by the phrase 'leaves of groves' is pleasing to the ear. Throughout this passage, Fallon's verbs are active: 'reawakens', 'coaxes'. Virgil concludes this passage with his representation of the *hieros gamos*, and, in honoring this representation, Fallon chooses a series of verbs suggesting conjugal union and sexual intercourse ('marries', 'penetrates', 'joined', and 'unbridles'), and repeats the plosive sound of the 'p' in the most sexual of the images, 'penetrates her with prolific showers': 'It's then almighty father, Air, marries the earth / and penetrates her with prolific showers, and, their bodies joined as one, unbridles life's potential'.[27]

There is considerably more to Virgil's song of spring in Book Two; it is a *locus classicus* of the *Georgics* to discover the extent of the Latin poet's song of praise to the season. The well-chosen, active verbs in Fallon's translation ('reverberate', 'let down', 'infuses', 'fear', 'scour', 'prompt') give an excellent sense of the energy which characterises spring's activities:

> The woodlands off the beaten track reverberate with singing
> birds
> and, right on time, cattle come into their season –
> the countryside stands to deliver – and in the warmth of western
> breezes
> the plains let down their very breasts; a gentle wash infuses
> everything

and new growth ventures to believe it's safe beneath the young,
still unfamiliar sun, and vine shoots fear no southern gales
nor roaring northerlies that scour rain clouds from the sky;
rather, they prompt their buds to boldness and leaves to colour
    everywhere . . . .[28]

The spring passage concludes with a comparison between spring and Eden, invoking the fruits and fecundity of paradise and the world's creation. It reads:

        . . . . That days were not that different at the dawning
of the world I can easily believe, nor proceeded differently.
Then it was spring, all basked in spring,
and winter's winds bit their tongue–
all this when livestock first unclosed their eyes
and man, begot of rocks, first held up his head,
with creatures loosed to roam woodscape and stars to ramble
    skies.[29]

Here images of 'the dawning of the world' and recollections of the creatures of a paradisal kingdom abound, always aided by Fallon's poetic choices of appropriate verbs, rhyming vowel patterns, and alliterative joinings of consonants: 'basked in spring', 'winter's winds', 'begot of rocks', and the wonderful multiplicity of consonant and vowel sounds in 'loosed to roam woodscape and stars to ramble skies'. The next lines pose a philosophical and horticultural question, combining the two realms into one theme: the paired human quests for mental and physical harmony in the face of disruptive forces. In a lively auditory recuperation of the Anglo-Saxon and Latin origins of these words, Fallon's version directs us to see spring's 'tender growth' as it tries to 'survive vicissitudes', which is itself a phrase featuring a sonic triad with its repeated 'v's', 's's', and 'i's': 'Indeed, how could such tender growth survive vicissitudes / if there were not between the cold and warmth a spell of dreamlike quiet, / when heaven's kindness brought its gift of ease'?[30] Not only do these lines suggest that 'dreamlike quiet' is a necessary soil for strong and lasting growth, but also the invocation or naming of 'heaven's kindness' and 'gift of ease' suggests a divine beneficence, a blessing. Although this passage is obviously not explicitly Christian or Biblical in the way a Miltonic allusion is, its allusive echoes remind readers of these established poetic tropes and place the Virgilian appeal to peace and ease within the imaginative ambit of readers who know the iconography of Milton's paradise. This rhetorical question also properly ends the grand celebration of growth and sexual renewal in the spring passage; in the next lines, a different matter and a more pragmatic tone emerge in which the poet offers advice about spring planting: 'What's more, whenever you set down your slips / don't forget to land them well, / or dig in around them bits of pervious stone and broken shells.'[31]

Next, in a passage radiant with the love of arboreal creatures, I will examine Fallon's version of Book Two's commentary on the beauties and practical uses of trees, beginning with the olive and the apple and extending to pitch pines and later, cypresses, boxwoods, oaks, and elms. The cultivation and praise of trees begins with the sturdy olive:

> On the other hand, the olive thrives almost by neglect,
> needing no encounter with hooked hoe or sickle blade
> once it's found its feet in fields and faced the winds (and faced
>   them down).
> The earth itself, once it's been broken open, provides sufficient
>   moisture
> for growing plants to yield rich harvests in the ploughshare's
>   wake.
> That's the way you'll cultivate the best of olives – choice of
>   Peace.
>   Just as apples, as soon as they have sensed a surge of
>   strength
> along their trunks, stretch quickly for the stars all on their own–
> they need no helping hand from us.
> And all the while wild woodlands teem with fruits,
> and the preserves of birds blaze with blood-red berries.[32]

When the poet's attention turns to apples, Fallon's translation highlights the alliterative consonance of the 's' and 'r' sounds, as well as the 'h' sound in 'helping hand', all of which pleases the reader's ear with rhythmic repetition, as in the beautifully crafted passage cited above. Given Fallon's attentiveness to the Irish woodlands and cultivated landscapes in his own poetry from his first collections through 2007's The Company of Horses, his notable care in adapting the forest images and themes of Virgil's poem is evident. At the conclusion of Virgil's observations on olives and apples, Fallon's eye attends to the surfaces of trees and his ear to the rhythms, rhymes, and stresses of spoken English, and together they enliven a distinctively beautiful pair of Virgil's lines: 'And all the while wild woodlands teem with fruits, / and the preserves of birds blaze with blood-red berries'.[33] The strong active verbs Fallon chooses here are exactly right: 'teem' and 'blaze' show, respectively, the vital surge of activity and the visual force of the 'blood-red' color in the trees' leaves and berries. The consonantal alliteration of 'w's' and 't's' in the first line, and especially the plosive 'p' matched with the three initial 'b's' in the second line, as well as the pleasing internal rhyme of 'preserves' and 'birds', are all features of Fallon's auditory skills as a poet. As a further measure of Fallon's distinctive strength as a translator, these lines feature both iambic and trochaic stresses, with more iambic meter in the first line ('wild woodlands teem with fruits') and trochaic meter in the second ('the preserves of birds blaze with blood-red berries'). In rendering these lines into vivid English, Fallon has demonstrated what an accomplished poet's eye and ear can do, given the right material. The combination of the two metrical schemes in succeeding lines and the visually arresting imagery of the woods, birds, and berries is reminiscent of Shakespeare (in *As You Like It* and *A Midsummer Night's Dream*, for example, and also of Wordsworth, in the first, exploratory books of *The Prelude*).

Unlike the lamentation over the destructiveness of war and the reversion toward savagery that comes with turning ploughshares into swords that together mark the conclusion of Book One, Virgil ends Book Two of the *Georgics* with a positive image of the countryman sturdily at work behind his plough. Fallon's language expertly portrays the vigor and economy of such a life:

> A countryman cleaves earth with his crooked plough. Such is
> the labour
> of his life. So he sustains his native land and those who follow
> in his footsteps; so he supports a team of oxen and keeps cattle
> in good order.
> All go and no let up – so that the seasons teem with fruit,
> fields fill up with bullocks, and big arms of barley stand in
> stooks.
> They've overflowed the furrows, they'll burst the barns.
>   . . . – and in such ways the autumn serves
> its bounty,
> while up on open ground the vintage basks on boulders and
> ripens in the sun's caress.[34]

Great alliterative skill knits together the first three lines of this passage, with parallelism, elegant consonance, near-rhyme, and rhyme all combining to make these lines an example of wrought language yielding effective poetry. These poetic techniques also mark the lines that follow 'All go and no let up': 'so that the seasons teem with fruit, / fields fill up with bullocks, and big arms of barley stand in stooks. / They've overflowed the furrows, they'll burst the barns . . .'35

At the outset, the reader can hear the rhyming long 'e' sound which unites 'seasons' with 'teem', and can also note several instances of the alliterative initial 'f' sound, as well as 'b' and 'st'. These all occur in the lines, 'fields fill up with bullocks, and big arms of barley stand in stooks'. While those consonantal alliterations I have mentioned play throughout these lines, Fallon also demonstrates his skill in using internal rhymes and near-rhymes, modulating the 'u' vowel sound from 'fruit' to 'fill up' to 'bullocks' to 'furrows' and finally to 'burst'.

These optimistic observations and reassuring images of the countryman at work 'cleav[ing] earth' with his 'crooked plough' conclude Book Two of the *Georgics*. There are no sobering notes of war and war's alarms, including the farmer's hoe echoing on the sides of 'empty helmets', such as marked the conclusion of Book One.

In Book Three, just after encountering the famous lines avowing that 'the best days of our lives are first to fly', the reader finds an interesting treatise on various kinds of animal husbandry, especially the selection, care, and breeding of horses. I will concentrate on these sections of Book Three because the particular flavor of Fallon's love of horses comes through in these lines and because, in Virgil's estimation, horses deserve the title of the noblest of domesticated animals:

> Poor creatures that we are, the best days of our lives
> are first to fly; along come sickness, sorrows and the sores
> of age; and what sweeps us away only a mortal tide.
> Let there never be a time you wouldn't introduce changes to
>   improve your stock,
> nor times you wouldn't go so far as to supplant them; rather than
>   regret
> your losses later, anticipate them, and each year take your
>   chances on new blood.
>   Horses, too, must be subjected to a course of similar selection.
> On whatever ones you plan to keep for breeding

bestow particular attention from the start.
See at once how well-bred members of the herd as foals in
    fields
step lighter than the others and yet land their feet so daintily.
And one, the first and foremost, will lead the way to brave a river
and the hazards of an unfamiliar bridge.
And he won't tremble at a hollow din. His is a long-tapered neck
and graceful head, his body firm, back broad,
and shoulders showing off their muscle. Roans and chestnuts
are to be preferred, duns and greys to be avoided.
And there's more – at the clang of distant armour
he can't stand still, he's all ears, flanks aquiver,
as he struggles to contain his fiery breath in flaring nostrils.
His mane is thick and settles on his right side when it's shaken.
That horse is in such fine fettle his spine lies in a hollow between
    both sets of loins.
His hooves resound as they eat up the ground and spit it out
    again.[36]

In these lines, the initial portrait of the well-bred, courageous, and alert domesticated horse ('will lead the way to brave a river/ and the hazards of an unfamiliar bridge') modulates into a portrait of a splendid warhorse that 'at the clang of distant armour . . . can't stand still, he's all ears, flanks aquiver, / as he struggles to contain his fiery breath in flaring nostrils'. Fallon's poetic delight in painting such a fine warhorse with assured verbal strokes is brought out in his diction and sonic patterns, such as the repetitions of the short 'a' vowel ('flanks aquiver') and the repeated emphasis on the strong 'f' consonant ('as he struggles to contain his fiery breath in flaring nostrils'; 'in such fine fettle').

Book Three's lessons in equine care proceed with noteworthy advice on the selection and preparation of the stallion and the mare for successful breeding. Virgil writes:

[They] spare no end of trouble to flesh him out and fatten him up,
the stallion they've selected and settled on as kingpin of the line.
They gather fresh greenery and serve his fill of grain and water
so there's no chance that he's not up to the job he seems so keen
    to do,

> no chance the standard of the sire be mirrored in a scrawny foal.
>> On the other hand, they mean to keep the mares lean. . . .
>> This they do so no amount of indolence can curb their field of
>>> fruitfulness
> nor clog and leave its furrows void,
>> but, instead, so that love's seed be grasped and tucked away
> deep where it should come to rest.[37]

The stallion ('kingpin of the line') is readied by a diet that adds to his weight and strength, and Fallon's lines repeat the initial 'f' sound, emphasising the idea of the animal's fullness, in phrases such as 'flesh him out and fatten him up', 'fill of grain and water', and 'fresh greenery'. In fact, the lines describing the breed stallion end with an arresting play on the consonantal 's' sound, and pick up the 'f', hard 'c', and 'k' sounds of the previous lines as well: 'no chance the standard of the sire be mirrored in a scrawny foal'. Fallon's depiction of the mares, on the other hand, uses the auditory repetition of the initial hard 'c' sound in 'curb their field of fruitfulness' and 'nor clog and leave its furrows void' to suggest the potential mischance that can befall the stallion's semen before it inseminates the mare. After suggesting the possibility of this mischance, Fallon ends these lines with two reassuringly strong verbs of possession ('grasped' and 'tucked') and an adverb ('deep') that resonates tellingly with the noun phrase 'love's seed' that he has chosen to burnish the metaphor of sexual union: 'so that love's seed be grasped and tucked away / deep where it should come to rest'.[38]

In Book Four, the reader finds Virgil's well-known didactic treatise on beekeeping, and discovers its salubrious effect on the countryman's achieving genuine peace of mind, marked by internal and external quietude and equilibrium, through the proper care of these industrious and cooperative creatures. However, my imaginative interest in this final book of the *Georgics* is centered in Virgil's portrayal of the story of Orpheus and Eurydice, in particular Orpheus's 'double loss' of his wife. In revisiting the tale of Orpheus and Eurydice, Book Four of the *Georgics* offers several brief yet powerfully rendered passages of classical lamentation. I shall examine Fallon's translation of Virgil's lines, concentrating on the ways in which Fallon successfully evokes the emotions of tragic pathos and of sympathy so familiar to readers of the original Greek version composed by Homer.

Virgil's version of the tale begins as Eurydice, 'in hasty flight' from the pursuit of lustful Aristaeus, fails to see the serpent below her, then dies from its bite.

Fallon, recasting Virgil into a supple and exact vernacular idiom, writes:

> 'Heartsick and sore, Orpheus sought consolation on his lyre,
> a hollowed tortoiseshell. Of you, sweet wife, of you, he sang his
>   sorry song,
> all lonesome on the shore, at dawning of the day, of you, at day's
>   decline, of you.
> He risked even the gorge of Taenarus, the towering portals of
>   the underworld,
> and the abode of spirits where darkness reigns like a dismal fog;
> these he passed through to approach the shades and their
>   scaresome lord,
> those hearts that don't know how to be swayed by human pleas
>   for prayers.[39]

This passage characterises Orpheus as a grieving husband, 'heartsick and sore', and in uniting the image of the sore afflicted singer to his speaking lyre, Fallon pairs that initial descriptor with 'hallowed tortoiseshell' through the alliterative 'h' sound and the 'o' sounds playing through 'sore' and 'tortoiseshell'. There are many other consonantal pairings in these affecting lines, especially 'at dawning of the day, of you, at day's decline'. Furthermore, both the 'o' vowel sounds and the repeated consonants join in making 'the abode of spirits where darkness reigns like a dismal fog', a line that recalls the great mental turmoil suffered by the speaker of Coleridge's 'Dejection: An Ode' and Milton's striking depiction of the burning lake of Hell in *Paradise Lost,* which also evokes an 'abode of spirits' where 'darkness reigns like a dismal fog'.

As Orpheus makes the supreme effort to retrieve his lost Eurydice from captivity in Hades, Virgil narrates Orpheus's apparent success at 'avoid[ing] every pitfall':

> 'And now, on his way home, he had avoided every pitfall,
> and Eurydice, restored to him and trailing close behind (as
>   Proserpina
> had decreed), was emerging into heaven's atmosphere
> when a stroke of madness caught him, who loved her, off his
>   guard–

> a pardonable offence, you'd think, if the Dead knew how to
> pardon.
> He stopped, and for a moment wasn't thinking – no! –
> Eurydice was his again and on the brink of light, and who knows
> what possessed him
> but he turned back to look. Like that, his efforts were undone,
> and the pacts he's entered
> with that tyrant had dissolved. Three peals of thunder clapped
> across that paludal hell.[40]

In this crucial passage describing Orpheus's all-too-human 'stroke of madness', thoughtlessness, and forgetfulness that means that he loses Eurydice a second time, Fallon ensures that we hear the auditory patterns that hold the lines of narrative poetry together: 'when a stroke of madness caught him, who loved her, off his guard— / a pardonable offence, you would think, if the Dead knew how to pardon'. Here he uses the repetition of the 'o' sound, especially in the fraught word 'pardon' and in the phrase 'pardonable offence' to knit these lines together. That repeated and variable 'o' sound becomes all the more significant in the crucial lines that follow, in which errant Orpheus receives no pardon from Hades, makes his calamitous mistake, during which we are told 'who knows / what possessed him', and looks back at her: 'Eurydice was his again and on the brink of light, and who knows / what possessed him / but he turned back to look'. Between 'possessed' and 'look' there is a difference in the pronunciation of the 'o', but more importantly, as the disparate sounds suggest, there is a real irony in meaning as well: Orpheus had hoped to rescue Eurydice and bring her back to the earth's surface to live with him, to possess her in effect, but instead he has been possessed by some unknown spirit and turns and unpardonably, looks at her.

Eurydice's response to this tragic loss of her husband and loss of her freedom to return to the world above is a magnificent lamentation that for full-throated pathos evokes the Homeric (*The Odyssey*) and Ovidian (*The Metamorphoses*) accounts of the separation of Orpheus from Eurydice. Virgil composes her words of deep lamentation, and Fallon renders the lines in supple and idiomatic English, full of well-chosen imagery and metaphor:

> "What" she cried, "what wretched luck has ruined me – and
> you, O Orpheus,

what burning need? Look, cold-hearted fate is calling me
again; sleep draws its curtain on my brimming eyes.
And so, farewell, I'm carried off in night's immense embrace,
and now reach out my hands to you in vain – for I am yours no
    more."
    'So she spoke, and suddenly, like wisps of smoke, she vanished
in thin air. She watched him for the final time, while he,
with so much still to say, attempted to cling on to shadows.
No longer would the ferryman permit him cross
the marshy pool that lay between them.[41]

In this moving scene, the contrast between the 'cold-hearted fate' that now claims
Eurydice and the 'burning need' which motivated Orpheus in his quest to reclaim
her from her captivity in the underworld could not be more sharply drawn.
Eurydice speaks of her 'brimming eyes' full of sorrowful tears but also says that
'sleep draws its curtain' on them, as if to make those tears cease. As she speaks
her farewell to Orpheus, the ensuing lines are marked by images of her bodily
evanescence and wrongful recapture by the underworld: wispy smoke and the
'night's immense embrace'.

It is important to note Fallon's emphasis on the tragic metamorphosis in
Eurydice's final disappearance. Because she tells Orpheus that she is his no more
and is now held in 'night's embrace' instead of his, Orpheus is left with no one to
embrace as Eurydice vanishes: 'So she spoke, and suddenly, like wisps of smoke,
she vanished / in thin air'. Fallon renders this metamorphosis of Eurydice into
wisps of smoke that elude Orpheus's attempts to embrace her with a powerful
image of personified night's carrying her off and embracing her, with the visual
image of evanescent wisps of smoke, and, finally, with Orpheus's utter tactile
deprivation, his desperate clinging 'to shadows'. The two lines that portray their
final separation feature a tragically reduced scope for the life of the senses and
the feelings: 'She watched him for the final time, while he, / with so much still to
say, attempted to cling on to shadows.'[42] This reduced scope for verbal expression
and for heartfelt emotion at the end of Orpheus's pursuit of Eurydice effectively
portrays the manner in which Virgil vocalises lamentation. Whereas Orpheus's
cry to be reunited with Eurydice has been heard in the first lines of this scene,
and her eloquent reply to him lends her womanly voice to the very mode and
manner of what is meant by lamentation, the last lines of this scene achieve true,

classic pathos as the bereft husband 'attempted to cling on to shadows'.

It is my hope that the commentary and interpretation I have presented here will provide readers some insight into the consummate artistry and poetic skill with which Peter Fallon has translated Virgil's *Georgics*, these 'studies in the arts of peace'. My attention has been drawn to select representative passages in the *Georgics'* four Books which invite close scrutiny, either because of their subjects and themes or their pleasing musicality and expert turns of phrase and metaphor, or most often, because of all of these things working together. When I have quoted passages for textual analysis and commentary, I have tried to select passages in which Fallon's handling of both theme and poetic technique is exemplary.

In my view and that of many others, Peter Fallon's translation of the *Georgics* gives the freshest and most satisfying contemporary rendering of Virgil's poem by producing passages of poetry marked by thematically rich, musically distinctive, and memorable lines. In crafting these poetic measures in response to Virgil's original, he has created a poem that is enlivened by his particular gifts for creating vivid imagery and for writing vigorous, idiomatic English. For this distinguished work of translating Virgil's *Georgics*, his readers are most grateful.

REFERENCES

Fallon, P., *Virgil: Georgics* (Oxford: Oxford World's Classics, 2006).

Ferry, D., *The Georgics of Virgil* (New York: Farrar, Straus and Giroux, 2005).

Martz, L., *The Paradise Within: Studies in Vaughan, Traherne, and Milton.* (New Haven: Yale University Press, 1964).

Nussbaum, M., *Poetic Justice: The Literary Imagination and Public Life* (Boston: Beacon Press, 1995).

Perkell, C., *The Poet's Truth: A Study of the Poet in Virgil's Georgics* (Berkeley: University of California Press, 1989).

Putnam, M., *Virgil's Poem of the Earth: Studies in the Georgics* (Princeton: Princeton University Press, 1979).

Twiddy, I., *Pastoral Elegy in Contemporary British and Irish Poetry* (London: Continuum, 2012).

NOTES

1. P. Fallon, *Virgil: Georgics* (Oxford: Oxford World's Classics, 2006).

2. M. Putnam, *Virgil's Poem of the Earth: Studies in the* Georgics (Princeton: Princeton University Press, 1979), p.1.

3. I. Twiddy, *Pastoral Elegy in Contemporary British and Irish Poetry* (London: Continuum, 2012), p.126.

4. Ibid.

5. P. Fallon, *Virgil: Georgics* (Oxford: Oxford World's Classics, 2006), p.xxxvi.

6. I. Twiddy, *Pastoral Elegy in Contemporary British and Irish Poetry*, p.126.

7. C. Perkell, *The Poet's Truth: A Study of the Poet in Virgil's Georgics* (Berkeley: University of California Press, 1989), p.8.

8. M. Nussbaum, *Poetic Justice: The Literary Imagination and Public Life* (Boston: Beacon Press, 1995), p.2.

9. L. Martz, *The Paradise Within: Studies in Vaughan, Traherne, and Milton* (New Haven: Yale University Press, 1964), p.13.

10. Qtd. in Ibid., p.173. P. Fallon, *Virgil: Georgics* II, 42–4, p.28. Subsequent references to Fallon's translation cite by Roman numeral according to the specific 'book' of the poem, line numbers, and page number of the translation.

11. L. Martz, *The Paradise Within*, p.173.

12. P. Fallon, *Georgics*, II: 513, p.45.

13. David Ferry, *The Georgics of Virgil* (New York: Farrar, Straus and Giroux, 2005).

14. I. Twiddy, *Pastoral Elegy in Contemporary British and Irish Poetry*, p.126.

15. P. Fallon, *Georgics*, I, 43–6, p.6.

16. Ibid., I: 51–3, p.7.

17. Ibid., I: 63–78, pp.7–8.

18. Ibid., I: 64–6, p.7.

19. Ibid., I: 71–8, pp.7–8.

20. Ibid., I: 76–8, p.8.

21. Ibid., I: 493–497, p.23; I: 501–514, pp.23–4.

22. Ibid., I: 507–508, pp.23–4.

23. Ibid., I: 511–514, p.24.

24. Ibid., II: 315–326, p.38.

25. Ibid., Note to Book Two, II: 325, p.100.

26. Ibid., II: 323–324, p.38.

27. Ibid., II: 325–327, p.38.

28. Ibid., II: 328–336, pp.38–9.

29. Ibid., II: 336–342, p.39.

30. Ibid., II: 342–345, p.39.

31. Ibid., II: 346–348, p.39.

32. Ibid., II: 420–430, p.42.

33. Ibid., II: 429–430, p.42.

34. Ibid., II: 513–522, pp.45–6.

35. Ibid., II: 516–518, pp.45–6.

36. Ibid., III: 66–88, p.52.

37. Ibid., III: 124–138, p.54.

38. Ibid., III: 127–128, p.54.

39. Ibid., IV: 464–470, pp.90–91.

40. Ibid., IV: 485–493, pp.91–2.

41. Ibid., IV: 494–503, p.92.

42. Ibid., IV: 500–501, p.92.

Part IV

Fallon and America

Notes on Peter Fallon's *The Deerfield Series: Strength of Heart*

JOYCE PESEROFF

The website Quickmuse describes itself as an experiment, 'a series of on-the fly compositions in which some great poets riff away on a randomly picked subject'.¹ Click on one of the archived 'agons' – what Quickmuse calls its fifteen-minute contest to create verse under pressure – and you can watch a poem unfold, over real time, the process of its own making. The site allows readers to look over the writer's shoulder as word choice, line break, point of view, structure and form appear, vanish, and reappear in a series of fluid drafts. It also discloses how a poet relies on certain moves when approaching an arbitrary subject. Some begin with narrative, some with image; others connect a random prompt to personal experience. One poet shapes verse in quatrains from the start. Another gravitates to prose. I find these choices exceptionally revealing of a poet's habit of mind. A poem may take days, weeks, months, or years to develop – give a writer just fifteen minutes and his or her peculiar, individual methods of working into a subject will reveal themselves.

Peter Fallon's *The Deerfield Series: Strength of Heart*, first published by The Deerfield Press in 1997 and comprising a twenty-four-page section in his volume *News of the World: Selected and New Poems*, is an occasional poem commemorating the bicentennial of Deerfield Academy in western Massachusetts, where Fallon taught from 1976–77 and again from 1996–97. The assignment engages Fallon with a subject outside his usual geography, mythology, and history. He must find analogues for the sources of poems rooted in County Meath, as researched history mediated by a compassionate imagination substitute for the hand-knowledge, memory, family, lore, and idiom that inform his Irish poems. I would argue that, like the writers responding to Quickmuse, Fallon reveals his most essential poetic impulses and techniques through his occasional suite.

The Academy Fallon celebrates is situated among sixteen historic houses and buildings that comprise Old Deerfield Village, an interpretive site resembling Colonial Williamsburg and Plimoth Plantation.[2] As poet-in-residence, Fallon was surrounded by a vast collection of physical artifacts, along with docents who acted as flax scutchers, redware potters, tinsmiths, coopers and cooks at open hearths. He could experience total immersion in the eighteenth century while strolling down a twentieth-century lane. The first section of 'Beaver Ridge' replicates the feeling of placing a foot in each of two worlds. The native 'Pocumtuck' and the English 'Beaver' equally locate the direction of sunrise.[3] A series of images from the natural world – sun, mist, valley, rock, water – ends with a meadow, an order of landscape shaped by human presence. This presence evolves from rural to urban: 'still // water as it meanders / at the edge of meadows / near a street . . . '.[4] The poem's final sentence does not quite end, the points of ellipses suggesting an openness that flows, like the water, into the future. In eleven lines, Fallon has telescoped prehistory (the sun rising 'as it has done so often, / so many times'), history (Pocumtuck Range and Beaver Ridge; the replacement of forest by meadow), the present (the street), and the future.[5] In Fallon's worldview, no single moment in time exists without connection to another.

Fallon's instinct is to go wide and deep. In order to understand the essence of an event, he ventures beyond the narrative of the moment into what makes action and history possible. He begins by interrogating and broadening the form itself: 'when is the occasion? Now? The original Charter Day? Or might it include "occasion" as in "happening" or "event"?'[6] he writes in his notes to the sequence. Fallon's Deerfield 'happenings' begin with the land, first overcome by seed and spoor, then by indigenous Indians, then by the English: 'Here was plenty. / Here, after the plants and animals / colonized the continent, the cognoscenti // settled'.[7] Fallon's first response to the tricky subject of colonisation assumes the point of view of the land itself, with everything else a sojourner upon it. He rejects clichés of settler exploitation and native respect for ecology by reminding readers that the English could thrive only 'in their agreement / with the place'.[8] They also 'hunted / and gathered',[9] he notes, while under their hand the soil is 'tickled' into productivity[10]. The natives, meanwhile, 'spent the earth / as if it were / an endless currency',[11] moving their villages whenever 'they looked up / and saw the woods too far away'.[12] By personifying bedrock and soil as a something to be 'colonized', 'tickled' and 'spent'[13], Fallon mediates a third character in the drama between indigenous Indian and colonising English. Land is more than a setting for those who act upon it, and Fallon, alert to its role in developing a community's strength of heart, offers it a voice.

Throughout the series, Fallon advances the point of view of the land and what grows from it. In 'The Buttonball', it is not people, but the Pocumtuck buttonwood sycamore, that Fallon chooses as witness 'on Charter Day'.[14] The tree, which, by its girth, is estimated at over 450 years old[15], is a better metaphor for endurance than the human activity it oversees – the last journey of 'the wheelwright, the smith, / the peltry trader; / the miller, the cartwright, / the ropemaker'[16] – all professions that, in 1997, no longer exist. There is no mention of Samuel Adams, who oversaw the school's original charter. Rather than celebrate a Founding Father who possibly never set foot in Deerfield, Fallon aligns with what has rooted in its soil since 1560: 'Again and again it greened / . . . . / Already its shadow lorded over them, / the sir of sky, on Charter Day'.[17] No civil governor but the *genius loci* – sprouted in wilderness, remaining a piece of it – can preside over the school and settlement.

By establishing landscape as a character in human drama, Fallon adds its perspective to questions of English imperialism that Richard Rankin Russell observes, 'as an Irishman, Fallon would have been acutely aware of'.[18] Poems at the center of the series – 'Backfire', 'Bloody Brook', and '29 February 1704' – relate incidents in which the Pocumtuck tribe massacres or kidnaps Deerfield's colonial settlers. From a European viewpoint, the natives are surrogates in wars between French and English; for Americans, these represent battles for power among various Indian tribes, like the Mohawk and Narragansett, who enlisted the English and French as allies. In 'Backfire', Fallon alludes to the Battle of Mystic Fort, in which Narragansett and English destroyed their common enemy, the Pequots: 'How the natives learned that tactic / introduced at Mystic / and countered with a night attack'.[19] '[T]hat tactic' was total war, instigated by the English against the Pequot villages, in which more than 500 adults and children were killed.[20] Deployed by the Pocumtuck at Deerfield, it would eventually be used against native tribes by the Europeans' American descendants. From the perspective of 'Bloody Brook', both natives and colonials are implicated in staining the land when Indians 'in broken English, mistook, / and blushed, and changed / the name of the Muddy Brook'.[21] The broken bodies of settlers literally ruddy the water, but 'broken English' also alludes to the Indians' mimicry of European brutality at Mystic, and the broken promises ('treachery') of the English 'government'.[22]

It may be counterintuitive to center an occasional poem on the greatest defeats of the town the poem celebrates. But it is not surprising to find that suffering, not triumph, engages Fallon most dearly. In his notes, Fallon writes, 'I have tried in the poem's various parts . . . to comprehend a place and its fate. I wondered, How do we live in a place? Sometimes by suffering, certainly'.[23] In '29 February 1704', the natural world aligns with human grief: widows mourn as 'the sun . . . / squinted', and 'The pitying pines expressed a groan'; the captured had 'frost [that] grew in suppurating wounds'.[24] 'Mehuman Hinsdale' – is the first name a pun? – like an eighteenth-century Job, has 'father, uncles, grandfathers / [who] were killed that noon at Bloody Brook',[25] and his 'own new son' in the Leap Year massacre; Mehuman 'with his wife was captured / and held two years in Canada',[26] and five years later 'was carried off again'.[27] In 'Piecework', Lydia Bascom 'quilted . . . for her trousseau' but 'never married'.[28] In 'A Shiver', landscape becomes a miraculous witness to pain: 'And everywhere / the miracle of trees–' goes on to 'shiver in a human breeze'.[29] Collapsing time, suffering connects

> . . . the quiet boy in his heyday
> cut down by his own hand, the public mystery
> of the smiling boy soaring over Lockerbie,
> and later a boy swept away
>
> from all of us one evening on the Lower Level . . . '.[30]

The luminous product of suffering is 'Strength of Heart', part of the sequence's title as well as its final poem: 'Rejoice / in the prudence of a place as it extols // the election of a spirit to grow / instead of wilt'.[31] Even Hinsdale returns from his forty-month exile to find his horse, cart, and apple-trees intact, 'the horses older, / those apples planted in the ground / and new fruit on their branches'.[32] A pattern scored through Deerfield's history, 'Strength of Heart' might serve as an epigraph to Fallon's work as a whole.

Fallon's music sounds the pattern into coherence. He follows an ear first developed in County Meath to embody the complexities of living in a new world. For each poem in the sequence, the poet finds language that expresses a balance of concord and dissonance. The most frequent pattern employs quatrains with rhyming second and fourth lines, a kind of rough ballad measure without the meter. In other sections, rhymes occur without pattern but with the firmness and clarity of a handful of stones thrown down a well. In the fourth section of 'Beaver Ridge'—'treaties' rhymes with 'prosperity' but also with 'treachery'[33]. The rhyme continues through the second stanza, matching 'currency' with 'far away'[34]. In the final stanza, the end-rhymes vanish, replaced by hard-consonant alliteration – the Pocumtuck 'shed the beaver's blood. / And in return received / the gift of government, / of plagues and poxes'[35] – as harmony devolves to cacophony, one stanza at a time.

The satisfaction of a poem like 'The Street' seems, at first look, all music. Fallon follows what would have been, in 1962, the sequence of perception: first looking overhead ('Something over-') to what shades ('whelms') 'the street:', then identifying it ('elms')[36]. Of course, in 1997 there were no elms; New England's great trees had succumbed to disease. It is a photograph Fallon must be looking at and imagining himself into. The agreeable chime of 'elms' with 'whelms' creates concordance in the body, while the information '1962' creates a dissonance in the mind. The reader strolls in both worlds and time collapses – as in the first section of 'Beaver Ridge', but with sound rather than image provoking a complexity of feeling.

More distressing subjects produce less harmony in sound. 'Mehuman Hinsdale' endures a litany of loss unmediated by any sound or rhythmic pattern. Though each stanza of the poem is fourteen lines, neither is organised in any way that could be construed as a sonnet. Both stanzas begin with the imperative, 'Consider',[37] and both are dated forty years apart, but there are no further structural parallels. Fallon does not employ a rhyme scheme, and the lines vary from two to four beats, with a single five-beat (but not iambic) line devoted to the travail of travel 'to Quebec, and overseas to France and England'.[38] The only end-rhymes occur in the first stanza, with all but one of lines eight through thirteen ending aslant: 'grandfathers', 'slaughtered', 'massacre', 'captured', 'Canada'.[39] One could make a found poem of those words alone; their canny placement conjures a pounding by waves of disaster without break in an otherwise uncontained sea of language.

Fallon language does not shy from humor as a way to enlarge his narratives. There's plenty of wit in *The Deerfield Series*, some of it constructed by sound, as in 'The Street', and some through image, as when the 'broken English' change 'the name of the Muddy Brook'.[40] Fallon enjoys a pun; in 'Piecework', Lydia Bascom 'patterned in a harried / place peace in pieces'.[41] He cracks from the shadows of 'Birches' as they 'cross the road' a joke: 'barcode'.[42] The laconic 'Bicentennial' balances wit and humor: it is, after all, the occasion for Fallon's sequence, and, from the title, a reader might expect some direct reference to the Academy.

Instead, 'A cut stone on a farmhouse / on a corner of Main Street / struggles to convince: // TWO HUNDRED YEARS AGO / NOTHING HAPPENED HERE. / It has been happening ever since.'[43] 'Struggles' because Fallon has spent twenty-one pages musing that what was brewed 'here' four hundred and fifty, three hundred and fifty, two hundred, a hundred and thirty, or thirty years ago still steeps Deerfield's trees, meadows, rivers, ridges, and citizens. Understatement adds dimension to his argument: either nothing, or everything, has been happening since, depending on one's understanding of history. Fallon, as an Irishman, does not have the luxury of ignoring what his American neighbor denies, and mocks his complacency with something close to Yankee humor – that dry, shrewd product of stony acres, unforgiving climate, and ornery society. If this sounds kin to Irish humor, so be it.

As with poets responding to Quickmuse's 'agons', Peter Fallon's signature themes and techniques unfold themselves, prompted by a change of world. One of Fallon's essential questions has always been, 'How do we live in a place?'[44] Deerfield is a village as conscious of its history as any in Ireland, but since Fallon's perspective is bound to differ from his American colleagues', his poems make fresh work of familiar tropes – colonial vs. native, English vs. French, wilderness vs. settlement – in part because his approach to history remains grounded in allegiance to the land and what it produces, whether husbanded or wild, under colonial rule or free government or none at all. Fallon's definition of 'event' remains elastic; tremors from the past pulse through contemporary Deerfield's brooks, meadows, elms, and men, just as radio waves from Earth never completely vanish in space. Because suffering has always been a focus of Fallon's humane vision, the sequence numbers losses, not triumphs; even the Pocumtucks' victory in 'Backfire' and 'Bloody Brook' foreshadows their extermination. Fallon may saturate suffering with meaning – 'the election of a spirit to grow / instead of wilt'[45] – but he never discounts the price of wisdom, even as his particular humor leavens what could otherwise be bitter bread.

All of this is fashioned by a subtle and flexible verbal music that mixes measured, if unmetered, syllables with persuasive end-rhyme. Colloquial enough to include 'cognoscenti'[46] and 'barcode',[47] muscular enough to batter with 'plagues and poxes',[48] lyrical in its elegy for 'the hatter, the housewright / the currier; / the fletcher, the ostler, / the cross-cut sawyer',[49] Fallon's language, minted and refined in County Meath, offers readers a new purchase on Deerfield's history through the rhythm and timbre of its telling. *The Deerfield Series: Strength of Heart* serves as a handbook to Peter Fallon's gifts as a poet, and a primer for those who would study them.

REFERENCES

'Battle of Mystic Fort', http://www.nps.gov/resources/site.htm?id=19052 (accessed 15 November 2012).

Fallon, P., *News of the World: Selected and New Poems* (Loughcrew, Ireland: The Gallery Press, 1998).

'Historic Deerfield: Opening Doorways to the Past', http://www.historic-deerfield.org (accessed 7 October 2012).

Leverett, Robert T., 'Pocumtuck Buttonwood', Native Tree Society BBS, http://www.ents-bbs.org/viewtopic.php?t=1893&p=6965 (accessed 3 August 2012).

'Quickmuse', http://www.quickmuse.com (accessed 21 July 2012).

Russell, R.R., 'Peter Fallon', in Jay Parini (ed.), *British Writers, Supplement XII* (Detroit: Scribner, 2007), pp.112–13.

NOTES

1. 'Quickmuse'. http://www.quickmuse.com (accessed 21 July 2012).

2. 'Historic Deerfield: Opening Doorways to the Past', http://www.historic-deerfield.org (accessed 7 October 2012).

3. P. Fallon, *News of the World: Selected and New Poems* (Loughcrew, Ireland: The Gallery Press, 1998), p.85.

4. Ibid.

5. Ibid.

6. Ibid., p.138.

7. Ibid., p.87.

8. Ibid.

9. Ibid.

10. Ibid.

11. Ibid., p.88.

12. Ibid.

13. Ibid., p.87.

14. Ibid., p.91.

15. Robert T. Leverett, 'Pocumtuck Buttonwood', Native Tree Society BBS, http://www.ents-bbs.org/viewtopic.php?t=1893&p=6965 (accessed 3 August 2012).

16. See P. Fallon, *News of the World*, p.91.

17. Ibid.

18. R.R. Russell, 'Peter Fallon', in Jay Parini (ed.), *British Writers, Supplement XII* (Detroit: Scribner, 2007), pp.112–13.

19. See P. Fallon, *News of the World*, p.92.

20. 'Battle of Mystic Fort', http://www.nps.gov/resources/site.htm?id=19052, accessed 15 November 2012.

21. P. Fallon, *News of the World*, p.93.

22. Ibid., p.88.

23. Ibid., p.138.

24. Ibid., pp.95, 96.

25. Ibid., p.98.

26. Ibid.

27. Ibid.

28. Ibid., p.99.

29. Ibid., pp.104, 105.

30. Ibid., p.108.

31. Ibid.

32. Ibid., p.98.

33. Ibid., p.88.

34. Ibid.

35. Ibid.

36. Ibid., p.100.

37. Ibid., p.98.

38. Ibid.

39. Ibid.

40. Ibid., p.93.

41. Ibid., p.99.

42. Ibid., p.103.

43. Ibid., p.106.

44. Ibid., p.138.

45. Ibid., p.108.

46. Ibid., p.87.

47. Ibid., p.103.

48. Ibid., p.88.

49. Ibid., p.91.

The News of Poetry, or, What Love Does Life Require?

BRYAN GIEMZA

A favourite *New Yorker* cartoon of mine depicts a couple of surly, strapping barbarians going forth on horseback. They are trailed by another rider, a man clad in a tweed jacket who puffs a pipe contentedly. The caption states, 'Two barbarians and a professor of barbarian studies'.

It's an arch comment on the nature of academic enterprise as well as academic careers, in every sense of that word. The subject matters. Certainly there's a professional hazard in having little contact with the actual subjects of one's studies – and perhaps a different kind of hazard from having too much contact. Wordsworth long ago admonished that we murder to dissect. As Wendell Berry pointed out more gently in his National Endowment for the Humanities lecture, nodding to historian John Lukacs, there is no knowledge but human knowledge, and this fact is, or ought to be, an invitation to humility. In the same talk, Berry quotes Keith Critchlow's observation: 'The human mind takes apart with its analytic habits of reasoning but the human heart puts things together because it loves them . . . .'[1]

After delivering a paper at a conference in Chattanooga in which I pronounced confidently on the literary kinship and poetic affinities of Wendell Berry and Peter Fallon, I was approached by a man with a neatly-trimmed moustache and an unassuming, soft-spoken manner. He had something to say about my musings on Peter Fallon. He introduced himself.

He was Peter Fallon.

The poet and a professor of poetics. And the poet was hardly a barbarian, but a gentleman, thank goodness. Suddenly my abstractions about Fallon's aims as a poet and his friendships seemed laughably speculative. It's hard enough to understand one's own friendships, and their mutability or constancy, much less those of another. Besides, why had I not asked the man himself? Mr. Fallon graciously requested a copy of the paper, which I duly promised to mail him. Later, as I reviewed my remarks, I realised that Richard Russell had explored similar territory, albeit more eloquently, in his article 'Loss and Recovery in Peter Fallon's Pastoral Elegies'.[2] First lesson: find the voice that started the conversation. Second lesson: don't tell the poet what he already knows, or at least make certain you've got your story right. I also took stock of some of the things I had turned around in my talk, items which the good poet was too kind to correct. For one thing, I had related a half-remembered anecdote from Tolstoy's *Confession*, something suitably hard-bitten, desperate, and presumably Russian. I had told the tale of a man pursued by a bear, who ends up clinging to the side of a cliff by a branch – a branch that unfortunately suspends a hive of bees as well.

In fact, the tale isn't of Russian origin – Tolstoy calls it 'an old Eastern fable' – and the creature in pursuit isn't a bear but a dragon. And the man leaps not from a cliff but into a well.[3] I had thoroughly Americanised the material. No one could accuse me of letting the facts get in the way of a good story. I had gotten this much right: the cliffhanger, or wellhanger, if you like, ends with the man pausing to lick a few drops of honey from the leaves.

So let the heart put together the things that the mind had sundered. The essential message and spirit of the tale suits the occasion. Suppose that our starting place is entropic, and that the walk on this wormbent road is one of loss. 'Suppose', as Edgar Lee Masters's character Davis Matlock says, 'it is nothing but the hive'.[4] Suppose, as Byron said, that there is no joy the world gives like that it can take away. This is where Berry and Fallon begin. If their shared vision can be reduced to a word such as 'agrarianism', this hardly seems to do justice to a way of being, such that fragments might be shored against ruin, that fragmentation itself might be resisted, that heartbreak might be palliated. In this thought-tormented age, a significant part of the kinship of these two writers consists in finding the sweetness of life in low moments, and in environs that do not, at first glance, seem congenial to grace or indeed life itself. From this epiphany, sweet and simple, comes the common rootstock of their work, and the form that has evolved from their friendship.

In his 2012 Jefferson Lecture, Berry defined imagination in terms that evoke form:

> The term 'imagination' in what I take to be its truest sense refers to a mental faculty that some people have used and thought about with the utmost seriousness . . . . To take it seriously we must give up at once any notion that imagination is disconnected from reality or truth or knowledge. It has nothing to do either with clever imitation of appearances or with 'dreaming up'.[5]

Moreover, Berry suggests that 'imagination thrives on contact, on tangible connection . . . . As imagination enables sympathy, sympathy enables affection. And it is in affection that we find the possibility of a neighbourly, kind, and conserving economy'.[6]

There is an interesting tension between 'clever imitation of appearances' and the truer seeing that Berry says accompanies imagination. In an intertextual sense, form *happens*, it comes into being, when it is made in poetic conversation. Both Fallon and Berry are mindful of how form is itself meaning, but I want to focus not so much on form as a term of poetic art – which Ed Madden does in this volume in his fine analysis of prosody – but on form as the imagination working in affection. Because literary form too 'thrives on contact', and relies on a neighbourly economy, I would like to investigate briefly the relationship between the work of Wendell Berry and his long-time friend, poet, and sometime publisher, Peter Fallon. Theirs is a philosophy prepared to confront more than happy visions of the nurturing pastoral; it is, in fact, much concerned with the incomprehensible tragedies of life.

To that point, beyond the mere inevitability of our ends, surely one of our worst fears must be that a death is wholly unaccountable, or worse, unaccounted for. It seems to me that Peter Fallon's poetry has addressed this topic, across volumes, openly, consistently, and poignantly. When Pat Mullion keels over suddenly in 'Cards', a poem in *The Speaking Stones*, the unprepared players know only to laugh at the unaccountable hand he has been dealt. A profound fear nestles among the relentlessly searching poems collected in *News of the World*: even though the hairs on our heads may be numbered and the sparrows counted, the meting out of life and death eludes our comprehension. In *News of the World*, the abiding hope – and it is a hope, not a certainty – is that the good shepherd minds his flock, even when some are lost.

Or lost before we are ready. In our shopworn formulas for 'death', two kinds immediately come to mind: we have the rare 'noble death', and the more familiar 'senseless death'. 'Senseless death' would make a fine entry in Flann O'Brien's 'Catechism of Cliché'. We don't ever say, 'He died a sensible death', and it's worth asking what such an end would be. If the game is worth what is at hazard, what prize would be sufficient to merit the designation of an orderly or ordained death? Politicians and their ilk merely serve comfort by implying the sensible death in statements such as, 'He died for our freedom'. O'Brien poked at such rhetoric in the 'Catechism of Cliché', where he takes literally the charge that only good be spoken of the dead:

> Of what was any deceased citizen you like to mention typical?
> Of all that is best in Irish life.
> Correct. With what qualities did he endear himself to all who knew him?
> His charm of manner and unfailing kindness.
> Yes. But with what particularly did he impress all those he came in contact with?
> His sterling qualities of mind, loftiness of intellect and unswerving devotion to the national cause.[7]

Naturally. But we would just as soon not examine the senseless life. And we are not as likely to hear voice given to those sensible ends inscribed on our own hearts, the news of the real stories: 'She died for her family', or 'He died from having lost the savour of life'.

Of course, in woolly human understanding, perhaps only poets have full licence to explore the sense in death. *News of the World* deals equally in disappointments and what might be termed mis-appointments: the flourishing of life and death in unexpected places, of cases where souls seem sent to the wrong offices, of the inscrutability of the most fundamental elements of human experience. In short, it looks to the 'breeches' and 'abortions' Fallon earlier described in 'The Positive Season', a poem from *The Speaking Stones*.

> But this is the positive season,
>
> though loss is expected,

a part of the whole,
the breeches, abortions
accepted, it's minor,
the primary pulse is new.[8]

In 'Fostering', Fallon demonstrates how life will out, even when it mis-routed.[9] In the poem, a foster ewe is convinced to accept a lamb only after he is cloaked in his stillborn brother's flesh. The incident is related to Jacob's deception of Isaac, but without patriarchal intent; rather, Fallon concludes, his strange midwifery amounts to 'working kind betrayals in a field blessed for life'.[10] In one of *News of the World*'s central poems he takes on the clichés of Catechism, writing in 'The Herd',

I studied in the hedge school
and learned religions are a cod.
They're all the one.
Ask any fool.
Every lamb's a lamb of God.[11]

Little lamb, who made thee, indeed. The suggestion that religions are a 'cod' brings to mind Guy de Maupassant's recollection that his parochial school 'smelled of prayers the way a fish-market smells of fish'.[12] Before taking this poem to be a token of religious disenchantment, however, a different reading might be suggested. First of all, one might observe that the poems of the collection are literally inscribed by the lambs of God that comprise the 'Herd'. These lambs become the instruments of poetry. Elsewhere Fallon puns on the word 'pen' with the sheep of 'Dipping Day', who 'stand in a pen, dripping'.[13] The poem concludes with another play on 'write' (the verb, to inscribe) and 'right' (as the direction or as in correctness). In 'Caesarean', a scalpel becomes a pen; blood is its 'drib': 'She opened like a bloom / Beneath the red script of the scalpel's nib'.[14]

The stillborn twins that are revealed demonstrate how the poet's pen might penetrate to hidden mysteries of life and death, and indeed open up the partition between them. There are many of these mandorlas that open in *News of the World*, for example, in the words of 'Spring Song':

A new flock flowed
through a breach,
a makeshift gate.
And this is heaven:
sunrise through a copper beech.[15]

This is how Fallon confirms that heaven is under our feet as well as over our heads. Pointedly, 'breach birth' has a different register here. One is put in mind of Mark Spencer's 'Blue Baroque (Hope)', the stunning illustration on the cover of Wendell Berry's *In the Presence of Fear: Three Essays for a Changed World*.[16] The artwork wonderfully illustrates the startling, otherworldly presence of these unanticipated portals, breaches between the worldly and the otherworldly. In Spencer's painting a mandorla forms around the pattern of an egg that is still inchoate, still being revealed. This is the texture of Berry's essay, too; in responding to the violence of 11 September 2001, Berry offers the possibility of being surprised by understanding and forgiveness. Here, too, something might be born. If violence (in a neutral register) in human affairs is merely the manifestation of some form of desire, an announcement of the incipience of change, why may it not be hopeful? Suppose the primary pulse is *new*?

This newness should be news to us, for if evil is banal, every act of love is astonishingly new. As Berry once wrote of Fallon's work, 'This is news that can come to us only by way of poems. It is the news without which, as Dr. [Willam Carlos] Williams saw, "men die miserably every day"'.[17] It does not seem an accident that Wendell Berry's introduction to Fallon's *Airs and Angels* (2007) – not accidentally, also the title of John Donne's poem in which 'Love must not be, but take a body too' – praises Fallon's agility in *News of the World*, his 'turning like a good weather vane to meet the changes and the shifting requirements of the world'.[18] In other words, he is delicately attuned to the signals of change: of weather on the change, of lives on the change. In that sense, Fallon is a news writer who inscribes messages from the natural world and its human remnant. On errands of death, these letters speed paradoxically to life.

And in these very earthy encounters, the poet moves between the vestibule of the worldly and otherworldly, between the mysterious and the mundane. These migrations are far more sacred than profane, notwithstanding a cynical reading of 'The Herd'. Even if every religion purports to be the true religion, and every saviour claims to be uniquely enabled to take away the power of death (like the

Lamb of God), Fallon will repeatedly draw parallels between the confusion of human lives and the lives of sheep. These other sheep too must stumble toward the voice of their shepherd, regardless of stupidity, cupidity, and vice. More than a few will become entangled in bog and wire. With a good shaming, Fallon brings up short the town gossips in 'If Luck Were Corn,' who chatter about the discovery of a baby's body in a lake:

> But if you drained the ponds
> in your back yards
> you'd find more than you bargained for.[19]

And with poignant simplicity Fallon offers these lines in 'Gravities':

> . . . . Thin lines of sheep
> approach a slope, the frantic calls
> resume, the mothers' for lambs,
> the lambs' for milk.
>
> And I've known men
> tell weather by this moment.

In the last lines of the poem, as if compelled by a resurrectionist, 'the lambs – the lambs stood up'.[20] In this way the poem connects gravity (keep this term in mind for I'll return to it) and gravidity and links first steps to last. From the blossom of 'Caesarean', to the plumbing of the dark lake's inkwell in 'If Luck Were Corn', to the breach birth of 'Gravities': this is the way of warm-blooded things, and Fallon suggests, pointedly, that our school is one of hard knocks, ours the uncompromising benches of the hedge school. The hedge schools that sprung up in response to the Penal Laws from one perspective were provisional, unsanctioned, and subversive. Fallon's education is unsanctioned and subversive, too; it takes place along the hedges where sheep are lost and found and lambing. Following Patrick Kavanagh's essay, 'The Parish and the Universe', Fallon affirms in his way that 'A gap in a hedge, a smooth rock surfacing a narrow lane, a view of a wood meadow, the stream at the junction of four small fields – these are as much as a man can fully experience'.[21]

Peter Fallon's poetry, then, means, like Berry, to show us the gaps in our education, to take us to school – the real hedge school, which is to say, an agrarianism that has the hard-won quality of that overburdened word, belief. There are many ways to imagine wholeness, and other forms of husbandry, so in this dispensation, husbandry, too, must take on a new register. And the world must have enough imagination to accept the value of these pursuits. Berry considers that 'the comparative few who still practice that necessary husbandry and wifery [of the world] often are inclined to apologize for doing so, having been carefully taught in our education system that those arts are degrading and unworthy of people's talent'.[22] The scars on the body of Fallon's poetry evince the painful truth of Francis Bacon's statement that 'he who hath a wife and children hath given hostages to fortune'.[23] On news of Fallon's fatherhood, Berry wrote to him, 'I imagine you are surprised somewhat by the intricacy of parenthood. There is, as my father says, no end to it.'[24] Some seven years late he would revisit the subject, writing to Fallon, '[I]t is almost invariably true, I think, that people who have no children are wrong about the difference that children make'.[25]

So here is another sort of lesson in the schooling of a soul, chronicled in the correspondence of poets. Berry's letters to Peter Fallon are now lodged in Emory University's manuscript archives, where they testify, among other things, to the writers' common interest in lambing and calving, an interest that would bring Berry to Ireland and Scotland and eventually into Fallon's home. As early as August 1982 Berry wrote of his desire to visit Yeats's Tower[26]; in subsequent travel to Ireland, Fallon would help to orchestrate Berry's itinerary and the hospitality. Eventually the two did visit the tower and participated in a radio interview. Mindful of his 'great-grandfather's native place' in Cashel, County Tipperary, Berry might have had some hunger for home, and elsewhere he allows that 'it may not be my southerness so much as my Irishness that appeals to you'.[27] As a farmer quite settled in his manner, the American poet would acknowledge, following one trip to Ireland, that it was 'remarkable': 'Here am I, who have always mainly longed to say at home, who hate airplanes, who am so set in my ways as to positively suffer from interruptions of routine, now fairly slobbering at the idea of seeing some more Irish sheep!'[28] Eight years later, he would write to Fallon, 'I am dictating a few letters to Tanya and watching the ewe flock grazing up on the hillside'.[29] Twenty-two years later the ewes, or at least their descendants, are there still.[30]

Berry apparently learned much from the Irish farmers to whom he was introduced by Peter Fallon. He probably profited equally in his writing. The course of their correspondence indicates how the two writers have shared poems over the years, swapped books, and collated their common literary interests and friendships, for example, in their mutual friendship with Seamus Heaney. Heaney's field of gravity exerts its own influence on the poets' conformation, and by his contributions to the imagination working in affection, poetic form is again altered. 'Gravity is grace', Berry writes with proverbial clarity in 'The Gift of Gravity', published by Fallon.[31] If tribute and influence are established poetic traditions, in Berry's definition, they take on their full grandeur via a minute web of relationships, in which the individuality of the writer, impinging on the imaginations of kindred, becomes the butterfly wing that compels the winds. Poets, then, have a special dispensation from the anxiety of influence; in fact, it is more anxious-making *not* to be influenced by bonds of affection, by the person, by his or her word. Indeed, the creative act of one can move the farthest stars in ways that might not be immediately visible. The traditions of Irish poetry resist a chain of attribution, but not the attractive force of what is gracefully said.

So the intimacy of Berry and Fallon's correspondence has its own form in those shifting constellations. The sanctity of it is a gift that only they can reckon fully, but the gifts of its sanctity are on offer in the distinctive form of their work, a dialogue that is part of the continuing dialogue. The contours of that friendship remain, as they must, partially invisible to outside eyes; we have now a one-sided correspondence in the form of Berry's letters in the Emory archive. From those responses one can infer that Fallon writes of signal moments in his life: births, deaths, disappointments, courtship, and joy. There's plenty of humour there as well. Berry writes of an incident in which his grandchild swallowed a penny, resulting in a trip to the doctor. 'But don't you think somebody bigger should swallow that penny next time?' Berry wrote, 'A year-old baby seems a poor place to keep your money'.[32] Berry hams up the part of the wise mentor in a congratulatory note from Berry to Fallon on the occasion of Fallon's marriage. Having saved up good advice for the young Fallon, he confesses that he is 'so much in hopes that you could be as good a husband as I have been: cheerful all the time, always ready to accept blame, no strong opinions, no unseemly displays of stubbornness of self-will, co-operative always, and even willing to "see it from the other person's point of view"'. Without his guidance, Berry can only hope that his young friend is 'blundering along tolerably well on your own'.[33] One sees the subtlety of the exchange, too. There is self-effacing good humour as he telegraphs a gentle warning about marriage's demands in the sublimation of one's own desires, and the difficulty of its vocation. And one begins to see how Fallon might say of Berry that he is 'the most wise and thoughtful man I know'.[34]

Obviously, the act of farming does not a wise man make. Neither writer would say that everyone is fitted to be a farmer, even less a shepherd. But consider the imaginative form that evolves in their exchanges as writers, friends, and poets of mutual influence – both embrace the value of community labour and what Berry terms 'a local economy'. Parochialism, in the positive sense, manifests itself in their poems of emplacement – though that Norman word might be rendered more happily as 'inplacement'. Paradoxically, in 'Northern Lights', Fallon shows how inner place can only be framed in the context of outer Place. The ethereal display of lights dispels the illusion of rooted-ness without negating its importance:

> Morning will show
> us where we are.
> Meanwhile we're incognito.[35]

Emplacement, too, can only happen through the bonds of affection. For example, Fallon takes up community labour in 'Winter Work', and then turns to his individual stance:

> All I approve persists,
> is here, at home. I think it exquisite
> to stand in the yard, my feet on the ground,
> in cowshit and horseshit and sheepshit.[36]

To find this sort of joy, in environs conventionally viewed as less than exquisite, is to understand vocation; it demands a hedge-school education. Seamus Heaney explains that 'Peter Fallon's poetry confirms Keats's notion that an intelligence becomes a soul through being schooled in a world of pain and troubles'.[37] The pastoral lifestyle demands the drudgery of the sweat of the brow, part and parcel of Fallon's presentation of rural life; yes, the hedge school, an education not merely in the gains of bringing forth life but one trenchantly founded in its loss. 'The best teachers teach more than they know,' Wendell Berry wrote in 'Elegy'. 'By their deaths they teach the most.'[38]

This education requires attentiveness not just to place but to time. Fallon marks the seasons carefully in his collections: for instance, there is the poem titled 'Spring Song', and the invocation of Keats's 'To Autumn' in 'Seven Letters Beginning With…'.[39] In 'Winter Work', though, I am reminded of Frost's great interest in that season, and also of Henry Adams's notion that 'Summer was the multiplicity of nature; winter was school'.[40] The positive season of the lambing is not without its lessons in loss, either.

School also implies the learning of the social, most often at the expense of the individual. The careful ambivalence of 'The Herd', with its collective title, must be set alongside the many poems in the collection that draw attention to the individual. This is fitting, for agrarianism affirms respect for individual endowments. Wendell Berry quotes Ananda Coomaraswamy, who writes, 'the principle of justice [in traditional communities] is the same throughout … [it is] that each member of the community should perform the task for which he is fitted by nature'.[41] Enlarging on this notion, Berry lays out an axiom of his vision of agrarianism: 'the two ideas, justice and vocation, are inseparable'.[42]

Fallon's poetry reflects deeply on the importance of vocation in, for example, the confident close of 'The Lost Field' ('I'm out to find that field, to make it mine'), and in the biblically gratifying work of 'The Old Masters' ('That shed's founded on rock / and finished for our time like the work of woodmen . . . ').[43] Likewise, both Wendell Berry and Peter Fallon urge that work gives life value while acknowledging the problem of the life interrupted. For his part, Fallon joins with other poetic voices in exploring the issue. For example, the words are from Adam, but there is also an echo of Edgar Lee Masters in 'If Luck Were Corn' when Fallon writes, 'Flesh of her flesh, / bone of her bone–'.[44] In Edgar Lee Masters's 'Elizabeth Childers' – the epitaph of a child who perished with mother in childbirth – Masters gives,

> Dust of my dust,
> And dust with my dust,
> O, child who died as you entered the world,
> Dead with my death!

Purblind in the darkness of her loss, and speaking from beyond the grave, Childers reaches a cold comfort:

It is well, my child.
For you never travelled
The long, long way that begins with school days,
When little fingers blur under the tears
That fall on the crooked letters.[45]

Yet Elizabeth Childers must be contrasted with Masters's emblematic matriarch of American agrarianism, ninety-six-year-old Lucinda Matlock, who has raised twelve children and lost eight of them before reaching sixty years of age. Matlock knows a life of incessant labour, tempered in measure by 'the dances at Chandlerville', and games of 'snap-out at Winchester'. Matlock says simply of the malcontents of the modern generation, 'Life is too strong for you– / It takes life to love Life'.[46] If agrarian life brings closeness to nature, and sometimes makes stewards of men and women, it also makes one feel acutely all that remains outside of human ken and control. Such vicissitudes hang in delicate balance with appreciation of the fundamental goodness of life, and the mystery that it takes life to love life.
As if to reconcile these views, Fallon writes, in 'A Way of the World:'

Some take life hard,

some take the same life
easy. I'd sooner sing
heartbreak nor cry it.
But a baby's born, the baby
dies. Who knows anything?[47]

This is Keats's negative capability realised. If a great soul is schooled in sorrow, negative capability permits a poet's intelligence to leave sundered those things the mind would attempt to reconcile, and yet to retain its scruples. Fallon's lines again revisit Elizabeth Childers's dilemma concerning how far to trust life. Can God, as the cliché goes, write straight with crooked lines? The meditation of the last poem in Peter Fallon's collection says much of the values of the farm in its title, 'A Human Harvest'. The loss of a child has been remembered, only a page before in 'A Part of Ourselves', with the line, 'He'll die again at Christmas every year', implying, through its disordering of the Christian seasons, that Fallon's faith will not be easily won, if at all.[48]

But here a poem is recorded to the harvest, this time to a daughter: 'We clutch her as a text of faith'.[49] There are indeed worse things than death, as Fallon writes. Similarly, Richard Russell has written about the lines from Wendell Berry's elegy to Owen Flood in the context of Fallon's elegy to his son. In 'Elegy' Berry writes, 'The dead abide, as grief knows. / We are what we have lost'.[50] But in the preceding line, Berry observes, 'So joy contains, survives its cost' – an answer of a kind to Byron's assertion of life's diminishing returns. In one of his letters to Fallon, Berry reminded his friend that broken hearts 'grow either smaller or larger than they were before. And perhaps that is a matter of choice'.[51] It requires a measure of negative capability to believe that nature might draw up the patterns and yet suffer them to be tailored by free will.

Reeling from the loss of a son who had entered young manhood, William Sloane Coffin, Jr., once 'swarm[ed] all over' a would-be comforter who said, 'I just don't understand the will of God'. Coffin fired back at her, 'I'll say you don't, lady!' In this widely-known sermon concerning mourning, he turned to the consolations of poetry, quoting from the poetry of Robert Browning Hamilton, sentimental but apposite, and then from Emily Dickinson's verses: 'By a departing light / We see acuter quite / Than by a wick that stays'.[52] In some of their early correspondence in 1979, Berry sent Fallon a draft of his poem, 'Grief', in which an elderly couple goes about their day in the wake of a loss:

> It is a sharp light that lights the day now. It seems to shine,
> beyond eyesight, also in another day
> where the dead have risen and are walking
> away, their backs forever turned.[53]

As Dickinson has said, after great pain, a formal feeling comes.[54] There are other ways to contend with grief, and one of them is simply to succumb, like Elizabeth Childers, to Job's lament. To do so is to submit to fear. The way advocated by Berry and Fallon, and perhaps the poets of all ages, requires the cultivation of a courage rekindled by the imagination.

Emphasis on local culture, local economy, and ecological restoration as a source of profound healing: these are the hallmarks of agrarian philosophy as Berry and Fallon have known it. But the real affinity goes to the understanding that, in this world of wounds, it does take life to love life. This understanding is perhaps more easily learned than taught, absorbed in the school that would say, the miracle of life isn't so much that it persists – the miracle is that it *is* in the first place. And so we are obligated to honour its contingency.

No prophet is recognised in his own country, though both Berry and Fallon have been appreciated for their auguries. The sort of repossession they advocate is the repossession of form and the power of imagination. Theirs is a remarkably sensible course of action when fear closes in, and when death comes senseless and unaccountable. Learning to love life, to find it in the midst of death, is the lesson, taken close up, in *News of the World*. Its form evolved in friendship, and the news could not be more timely.

The author wishes to express his gratitude
to Richard Rankin Russell and Ed Madden
for their generous insights and contributions to this essay.

REFERENCES

Allen, L. and J. Wilson (eds), *Lafcadio Hearn, Japan's Great Interpreter: A New Anthology of His Writings, 1894–1904* (Folkestone, UK: Japan Library, 1992).

Andrews, R., *The Columbia Dictionary of Quotations* (New York: Columbia University Press, 1993).

Berry, W., Letters to Peter Fallon, Peter Fallon/Gallery Press Archive, Collection number 817, Box 124, Folder 17, Manuscript, Archives, and Rare Book Library, Emory University.

Berry, W., *The Gift of Gravity* (Old Deerfield, Massachusetts: The Deerfield Press/The Gallery Press, 1979).

Berry, W., 'The Irish Journal', in *Home Economics: Fourteen Essays* (New York: North Point Press, 1987), pp.21-48.

Berry, W., *The Selected Poems of Wendell Berry* (Washington, D.C.: Counterpoint, 1998).

Berry, W., *In the Presence of Fear: Three Essays for a Changed World* (Great Barrington, Massachusetts: Orion Society, 2001).

Berry, W., 'In Distrust of Movements', *Citizenship Papers* (Berkeley, California: Counterpoint, 2004), pp.43–52.

Berry, W., Foreword, *Airs and Angels* by Peter Fallon (Carrollton, Ohio: Press on Scroll Road, 2007), pp.ix-xv.

Berry, W., *It All Turns on Affection: The Jefferson Lecture & Other Essays* (Berkeley, California: Counterpoint, 2012).

Berry, W., 'Wendell Berry, Landsman: Interview with Jim Leach', *Humanities*, 33, 3 (May/June, 2012). http://www.neh.gov/humanities/2012/mayjune/conversation/wendell-berry-landsman (accessed 2 December 2012).

Coffin Jr., W.S., *The Collected Sermons of William Sloane Coffin: The Riverside Years*, Vol. 2 (Louisville, Kentucky: Westminster John Knox Press, 2008).

Critchlow, K., *The Hidden Geometry of Flowers: Living Rhythms, Form and Number* (Edinburgh: Floris Books, 2011).

Fallon, P., *The Speaking Stones* (Dublin: Gallery Press, 1978).

Fallon, P. and D. Mahon (eds), 'Introduction' to *The Penguin Book of Contemporary Irish Poetry* (London: Penguin, 1990), pp.xvi–xxii.

Fallon, P., *News of the World: Selected and New Poems* (Loughcrew, Ireland: The Gallery Books, 1998).

Fallon, P., *The Georgics of Virgil* (Loughcrew, Ireland: The Gallery Press, 2004).

Heaney, S., 'Tributes to Peter Fallon: 25 Years of Gallery Press', *Irish Literary Supplement*, 14, 2 (Fall 1995), p.6.

Masters, E.L., *Spoon River Anthology* (New York: Touchstone, 2004).

Nadel, I. (ed.), *The Education of Henry Adams* (Oxford: Oxford University Press, 1999).

O'Brien, F., *The Best of Myles* (Normal, Illinois: Dalkey Archive Press, 1999).

Redpath, T. (ed.), *The Songs and Sonnets of John Donne* (Cambridge, Massachusetts: Harvard University Press, 2009).

Russell, R.R., 'Loss and Recovery in Peter Fallon's Pastoral Elegies', *Colby Quarterly*, 37, 4 (Dec. 2001), pp.343–356.

Tolstoy, L., *Confession*, trans. D. Patterson. (New York: Norton, 1996).

NOTES

1. K. Critchlow, *The Hidden Geometry of Flowers* (Edinburgh: Floris Books, 2011), p.39.

2. R.R. Russell, 'Loss and Recovery in Peter Fallon's Pastoral Elegies', *Colby Quarterly*, 37, 4 (December 2001), pp.343–356.

3. L. Tolstoy, *Confession*, trans. D. Patterson (New York: Norton, 1996), p.30.

4. E.L. Masters, *Spoon River Anthology* (New York: Touchstone, 2004), p.215.

5. W. Berry, *It All Turns on Affection: The Jefferson Lecture & Other Essays* (Berkeley, California: Counterpoint, 2012), p.14.

6. Ibid.

7. F. O'Brien, *The Best of Myles* (Normal, Illinois: Dalkey Archive Press, 1999), p.203.

8. P. Fallon, *The Speaking Stones* (Dublin: Gallery Press, 1978), p.46.

9. P. Fallon, *News of the World: Selected and New Poems* (Loughcrew, Ireland: Gallery Books, 1998), p.41.

10. For more on gender inversion, in this poem and in others, see Madden in the present volume.

11. P. Fallon, *News of the World*, p.43.

12. See 'Une Surprise', quoted in L. Allen and J. Wilson (eds), *Lafcadio Hearn, Japan's Great Interpreter: A New Anthology of His Writings, 1894–1904* (Kent, UK: Japan Library, 1992), p.3.

13. P. Fallon, *News of the World*, p.42.

14. Ibid., p.38.

15. Ibid., p.19.

16. W. Berry, *In the Presence of Fear: Three Essays for a Changed World* (Great Barrington, Massachusetts: Orion Society, 2001).

17. W. Berry, Foreword, *Airs and Angels* by Peter Fallon (Carrollton, Ohio: Press on Scroll Road, 2007), p.xii.

18. T. Redpath (ed.), *The Songs and Sonnets of John Donne* (Cambridge, Massachusetts: Harvard University Press, 2009), p.198; W. Berry, Foreword, *Airs and Angels*, p.ix.

19. P. Fallon, *News of the World*, p.55.

20. Ibid., p.37.

21. Fallon, P. and D. Mahon (eds), 'Introduction' to *The Penguin Book of Contemporary Irish Poetry* (London: Penguin Books, 1990), pp.xvi–xxii, xvii.

22. W. Berry, 'In Distrust of Movements', *Citizenship Papers* (Berkeley, California: Counterpoint, 2004), p.47.

23. In context of the complete quotation, Bacon cautions that the carefree days of the bachelor will be stopped short by such responsibilities. Husbands and fathers might feel the sense of it in a different fashion. Qtd. in R. Andrews, *The Columbia Dictionary of Quotations* (New York: Columbia University Press, 1993), p.313.

24. 'W. Berry Letter to P. Fallon', 23 December 1987, Peter Fallon/Gallery Press Archive, Collection number 817, Box 124, Folder 17, Manuscript, Archives, and Rare Book Library, Emory University. The author is grateful for the generous permission of Wendell Berry and Peter Fallon in reprinting these quotations.

25. 'W. Berry Letter to P. Fallon', 6 February 1994, Peter Fallon/Gallery Press Archive, Collection number 817, Box 124, Folder 17, Manuscript, Archives, and Rare Book Library, Emory University.

26. For an account of Berry's Irish travels, see W. Berry, 'The Irish Journal', *Home Economics* (New York: North Point Press, 1987), pp. 21–48.

27. Ibid; 'W. Berry Letter to P. Fallon', 4 November 1978, Peter Fallon/Gallery Press Archive, Collection number 817, Box 124, Folder 17, Manuscript, Archives, and Rare Book Library, Emory University.

28. 'W. Berry Letter to P. Fallon', 9 September 1982, Peter Fallon/Gallery Press Archive, Collection number 817, Box 124, Folder 17, Manuscript, Archives, and Rare Book Library, Emory University.

29. 'W. Berry Letter to P. Fallon', 23 May 1982, Peter Fallon/Gallery Press Archive, Collection number 817, Box 124, Folder 17, Manuscript, Archives, and Rare Book Library, Emory University.

30. Berry, W. 'Wendell Berry, Landsman: Interview with Jim Leach', *Humanities*, 33, 3 (May/June 2012). http://www.neh.gov/humanities/2012/mayjune/conversation/wendell-berry-landsman (accessed 2 December 2012).

31. W. Berry, *The Gift of Gravity* (Old Deerfield, Massachusetts: The Deerfield Press/The Gallery Press, 1979), n.p.

32. 'W. Berry Letter to P. Fallon', 10 February 1986, Peter Fallon/Gallery Press Archive, Collection number 817, Box 124, Folder 17, Manuscript, Archives, and Rare Book Library, Emory University.

33. Ibid.

34. P. Fallon, ' An Afterwords', *The Georgics of Virgil*, trans. P. Fallon (Loughcrew, Ireland: The Gallery Press, 2004), p.124.

35. P. Fallon, *News of the World*, p.126.

36. Ibid., p.55.

37. Jacket blurb, *News of the World*. See also S. Heaney, 'Tributes to Peter Fallon: 25 Years of Gallery Press', *Irish Literary Supplement*, 14, 2 (Fall 1995), p.6.

38. W. Berry, *The Selected Poems of Wendell Berry* (Washington, D.C.: Counterpoint, 1998), p.134.

39. P. Fallon, *News of the World*, pp.18, 56–7.

40. I. Nadel (ed.), *The Education of Henry Adams* (Oxford: Oxford University Press, 1999), p.14.

41. W. Berry, *In the Presence of Fear: Three Essays for a Changed World* (Great Barrington, Massachusetts: Orion Society, 2001), p.27.

42. Ibid.

43. P. Fallon, *News of the World*, pp.16, 20.

44. Ibid., p.55.

45. E.L. Masters, *Spoon River Anthology* (New York: Touchstone, 2004), p.185.

46. Ibid., p.214.

47. P. Fallon, *News of the World*, p.72.

48. Ibid., p.77.

49. Ibid., p.78.

50. W. Berry, *The Selected Poems*, p.135.

51. 'W. Berry Letter to P. Fallon', 9 July 1992, Peter Fallon/Gallery Press Archive, Collection number 817, Box 124, Folder 17, Manuscript, Archives, and Rare Book Library, Emory University.

52. W. S. Coffin, Jr., *The Collected Sermons of William Sloane Coffin: The Riverside Years*, Vol. 2 (Louisville, Kentucky: Westminster John Knox Press, 2008), pp.3–6.

53. Qtd. in 'W. Berry Letter to P. Fallon', undated, but included among correspondence of spring 1979. Peter Fallon Archive, Collection number 817, Box 124, Folder 17, Manuscript, Archives, and Rare Book Library, Emory University. The poem was eventually published in W. Berry, *The Gift of Gravity*, and reprinted in *The Selected Poems*, pp.139–41.

54. Ed Madden traces the maternity of 'fellow feeling' in Fallon's 'A Part of Ourselves' in his essay in the present volume.

Foreword to *Airs and Angels* by Peter Fallon

WENDELL BERRY

In his earlier work Peter Fallon committed himself to the news of the world, gladdening himself by the implied mischief of bringing the dislocated curiosity of the aerial media down to his home ground. The principal 'world' of his poems was, as it still is, the farms and gathering places in the neighborhood of Oldcastle, County Meath, Ireland. To be committed to the news of so local and personal world is to be committed to change, and by 1998, the year of the publication of *News of the World: Selected and New Poems*, Mr. Fallon had proved himself a poet quick and alert, turning like a good weather vane to meet the changes and the shifting requirements of the world as it presented itself to him and as he found it.

In these poems he writes with an acute particularity of eye and ear, recording ordinary events made extraordinary by the amplitude of his care and the precision of his notice. The poems of the 1998 volume are poems of observation and experience, sometimes emotionally intense, but presented as reports, declarative and forthright. They are written in a strong and flexible prose syntax, usually in stanzas of a set number of unmetered lines, often rhyming strictly at, say, lines two and four or two and five. The rhymes, and the poet's sustained attentiveness to sound make a music that seems to suggest itself into the air around the poems and around us as we read. The technique is insistent but not intrusive; it involves a kind of propriety, a kind of modesty, by which the subject is granted a precedence over the poet. Here is the beginning of 'The Woman of the House', in which the woman speaks for herself:

It's not that I minded at first.
God knows the warm word
was welcome.
Such thoughts – and me my age.
Soft talk and silly sayings slurred

into rough touch.
He'd push and forage
and him back from the town
and not within an ass's roar of himself.
Was this his notion of a marriage?

When metaphor came into those poems it came as a help to presentation, as in these lines about a ewe flock at lambing time: 'They were clouds come down to ground to yean, / clouds from which clouds of breathing 'broke'. ['Caesarean'] And there can be a hint or an ambiance of myth, as in this opening stanza of 'The Late Country':

Come again and we'll go back
to the late country. On the long way in
we'll hone an appetite
for drinks and stories. A knock. A silent
password. A 'Come in'. We're home and dry.
We'll see things there in a different light.

But the mythification here, which reminds me of Edwin Muir or of Frost's 'Directive', leads to no myth, strictly speaking, but rather to the strangeness of the daily world late at night and the epical funniness of conversation in a pub illegally open after closing time. And yet this daily place is given a metaphorical reach: it is a haven, and it is a little bit heavenly.

I once travelled a few days with this poet in the place most of his poems come from, and I take, therefore, a personal pleasure in the news of it that he broadcasts in his poems. In its present tense, so to speak, Mr. Fallon's homeland is as insistently and materially real as any other. The countryside is in pasture mainly, green and sloping, and it is very beautiful. The human present, as one would expect, involves much local knowledge, practical and otherwise, and also much local humor of the kind in 'The Late Country'. But also insistently present, because the building has been mostly of stone, is the past – both the remembered past of Christian ruins and the unremembered past of prehistoric graves. It is not a place that can be in a simple sense contemporary. Present and past light it in a single shimmer. The news there cannot have the newness of a collision on an expressway, but incorporates its history like the shell of a living snail. It is a place where one's sense of time, to be true, has to be somewhat wobbly:

> We mind the apparition
> of an osprey and egret . . .
>
> where we live now, in a future past.
> We don't regret. We treasure all that's bred
> to pass away, like fingerprints
> on water. The worn thread
> was woven honestly and served its while.
> The hearth was warm once in the broken stead . . . .

Moreover, and by an implied insistence, this is news that can come to us only by way of poems. It is the news without which, as Dr. [William Carlos] Williams saw, 'men die miserably every day'. And so, from the beginning of Mr. Fallon's work we are being led away from the conventional realism of the news media. We are asked to grant to metaphor an unusual seriousness. By it we are moved or carried beyond the singular appearance that is merely present into the conviviality of likeness, which is timeless.

In 'Gate', the metaphor assumes the force of metanoia, and perhaps hints at the concern with transformation in these new poems of *Airs and Angels*. The gate is a sort of relic, unsurprising in the ancient pastures of County Meath. It is no longer a gate in a fence; it hangs anomalously alone between two stone posts in the midst of a field once, but no longer, divided in two. It is 'a gate that stops nothing'. However:

> Say for a moment
> The field is your
> life and you come

to a gate at the centre
of it. What then?
Then you pause. And open it. And enter.

Outwardly, in their prosodic manner, the new poems presented here are much like Mr. Fallon's earlier work. Inwardly, however, they register a remarkable change of vision. Metaphor has now come to the fore, no longer as a function of description but as a clue to metamorphosis. It is not by happenstance that among these poems are two written 'after Ovid'. The metaphor no longer moves only in one direction. The interest of the poet has shifted to the equation, to the likeness itself. Now the perception that sheep are cloud-like would involve directly the perception that clouds are sheep-like.

In the first of these poems, an ivy leaf is seen as a 'geography' –

above, a ridge,
below, a valley,

streams and rivers
worthy
of attention

– which incites the unspoken perception that such a landscape is leaf-like, because it belongs to a system of reversible likenesses; the leaf is further likened to the skeletons of flying terns. In the fourth poem, a flock of sparrows flies like leaves – and like angels – from a woodland's edge. The likeness is central. It is the subject, denoting a barely graspable delicacy, for the system of likenesses is always tending toward flight. Lives of the grossest substantiality become angelic as they lift into the air. The crane is a 'hunched heap', a 'sack of shite', but

Pressing downward on the bed

of air
he transforms his slack
machinery
to flight . . . .

230

The operation of metaphor, the perception of likeness, grants the dimension of myth to everyday 'reality'. These poems, by their likening of things, compose a mythology of the daily world that makes it unworldly, more than we expected, better than we would have bargained for if we had been given a chance to bargain:

> I'd begun to think
> the like of this
> might never strike
> again,
> the dance of days
> in their rightful place.
>
> And when we wanted
> music
> there it was–
> the rain.

Thus the world speaks to us, presents a 'verdict', which it does not translate, but from which we may learn to live considerately in it. I don't know what the literary world will think of these poems' bold flirtation with the 'pathetic fallacy' – 'the vine dithers and wings say hush' – but without waiting to hear I gladly allow it. It is one of our ways of staying in touch and even in harmony with the everyday world. Stay tuned.

RICHARD WILBUR

Horsetail

It grows anywhere.
This jointed stalk, with branches
Like green floating hair,

Thrives in ditches and
Trackside gravel, and even
In oil-spattered sand.

Careless of all that,
Its foot-high grace enhances
Any habitat.

Like a proud exile,
It will not boast that elsewhere
It lived in high style;

And who, after all,
Would credit what its vague head
Must in dreams recall–

How it long looked down
On the backs of dinosaurs
Shadowed by its crown?

Sugar Maples, January

What years of weather did to branch and bough
No canopy of shadow covers now,

And these great trunks, when the wind's rough and bleak,
Though little shaken, can be heard to creak.

It is not time, as yet, for rising sap
And hammered spiles. There's nothing there to tap.

For now, the long blue shadows of these trees
Stretch out upon the snow, and are at ease.

Part V:

Poems in Honour
of Peter Fallon

On Cutting One's Finger While Reaching for Jasmine

MEDBH MCGUCKIAN

She talked about the aboutness of life, the eternal
False illumination of the leftover nights, her lavender-
Skirted self who paced around the tousled
Bedroom, the otherwise good you.

She incessantly made 0s, 0s of all sizes,
0s inside one another, always drawn backwards
In lilac ink by her beckoning finger,
On fine paper, gilded and musked.

Ramrod straight in her harp-backed
Horse-grey chair, she beheld the most beauteous
Scrawl of the same love as never
Floated to the house as if rain water

Captured in the water-whipped square
From thundering icequakes and the smaller
Curves of a river missing its valley
Were the one place a flying creature could feel safe.

The Dark Room

BERNARD O'DONOGHUE

In Praise of Peter Fallon

From all corners of the land they came
to the Poetic Seminary, seldom
from any but the most remote parts,
after the drudgery of crops and cattle
in the cold season of the year.
Assigned their subject, they were locked all night
in a dark room to compose their verse.

In the morning lights they were brought so they could
commit their lines to writing. Whereupon
with the publisher's blessing they could go home
to the grace and favour of '*the gentlemen
and rich farmers of the countryside,
by whom they were richly entertained
and made much of*. That is what Bergin says.

I have seen such places even today:
the roadside milk-stand at Gullane, not far
from the stone circle whose radius points
to the sun rising east of Caherbarnagh;
or the Damhscoil at Coolea behind the mountain
where Ó Riada's bees, intent in their darkness,
generate the honey that will bring them praise.

Colmcille on Exile

PAUL MULDOON

It would be such a blast, O Son of God,
to be able to scud
across the heavy seas
to Ireland, to go back to the exquisite

Plain of Eolarg, back to Benevanagh,
to go back across the Foyle
and listen to the swans
singing at full

tilt as my boat, the Dew-Red,
puts in to port,
with the very seagulls coming out
for a ticker tape parade.

I sigh constantly to be in Ireland,
where I still had some authority,
rather than living among foreigners,
dejected, dog-tired.

A pity, O King of Mysteries,
I was ever forced off my home turf,
a pity I ever got caught up
in the Battle of Cul Dreimhne.

Isn't it well for Cormac of Durrow
to be back there in his cell
listening to the self-same sounds
that once lifted up my soul,

the wind in the elm-tree
getting us into the swing,
the blackbird's droll lamentation
as it claps its wings,

the early morning belling
of a herd of big bucks,
the music of summer edging through woodland
from the cuckoos' beaks . . .

The three things I left behind
I liked best on earth
were Durrow, Derry of the heavenly choirs,
and Gartan, my place of birth.

I so loved being in Ireland
and still rail against being displaced.
To hang with Comgall in Bangor, Canice in Kilkenny,
it would be such a blast.

Revision

CONOR O'CALLAGHAN

For Peter Fallon

The Street acquires a name while you are gone.
Sunset, Queen, or maybe the intersection
between them you couldn't picture first time round
and sidle through one evening lately

while a Latina paints her shingle plum. See?
There is always time. Even those times
when there are no lights on inside and the key jams
and every drafty room has been repossessed.

Then the best revision is starting over,
much as a fall of unblemished snow
from that system the weather channel's satellite
billows all day towards you across the state.

Only, snow doesn't know, you know,
its symbolism has long been ground to dust.
You just have to take it with a pinch
of the salt they are gritting on the roads

while you mark your place and I talk on.
See, again. The back yard is black at first.
The white stray mewls for a fistful of 9Lives
somewhere past your landlord's midden.

If this is immortality, let it slide.
The chicken coop fades up, the boundary fence.
There is still hope, even now,
and for all those light years shining overhead.

An Chaor Aduaidh / The Northern Lights

NUALA NÍ DHOMHNAILL

(Translation by Caoimhin Mac Giolla Léith)

An chaor aduaidh:–
olagón bog bin na cruinne
ag casadh ar a fearsaid;
sioscadh na gaoithe grianda
os cionn folús an duibheagáin:
dán mascalach an domhain, a phaidir gheal
ag soilsiú an mhaighanéadasféir.

Titeann bréithre na teangan domhanda seo
chun talaimh ceann ar cheann
ina néalta bána is uatihne
ar nós cuirtíni

The northern lights:–
The soft, sweet lamentation of the world
spinning on its axis;
the whisper of the solar wind
above the black abyss;
the planet's strenuous poem, its shining prayer
illuminating the magnetosphere.

The words of this planetary tongue
fall to earth one by one
in clouds of white and green
like a curtainfall.

The Dapple-Grey Mare

(Translated from the Italian of Giovanni Pascoli, 1855–1912)

SEAMUS HEANEY

For Peter Fallon, with his hands on the reins

I

At La Torre farm silence reigned already.
By Rio Salto the poplars gave a sigh.
Big workhorses stabled in the farmyard
Nosed their feed and munched it, milled and hard.

In the farthest stall a wild one stood, a mare
Born among pine trees on a salty shore.
Sting of spray in her nostrils she remembers
And roaring of the sea in her pricked-up ears.

Beside her there, one elbow on the hay-rack,
My mother stood and very softly spoke:
'O little dapple-grey, my little mare,
You brought the one back who comes back no more,

You understood his words and horseman's ways.
He left a son, the first of my family's
Boys and girls, the eldest of the eight,
Who has never touched a bridle or a bit.

You who live exposed to the hurricane,
Be obedient to his small hand on the rein,
You with the salt-stung strand inside your heart,
Be obedient to this child, his horseman's word'.

II

The mare then turned her slender listening head
To my sad mother who still more sadly said,
'O little dapple-grey, my little mare,
Who brought the one back who comes back no more,

I know you loved and bore him on his path,
Out on your own there with him and his death.
And you, sprung from the wild woods, wind and wave,
You quelled the terror in your breast, stayed brave.

Between your cheeks you felt the bit go loose.
You took care to slow down and mind your pace
As you drew him gently on, to give him ease
In his agony, and let the end be peace'.

The slender long head with its pricked-up ears
Bent to my mother then. She spoke through tears:
'O little dapple-grey, my little mare,
You brought the one back who comes back no more.

Two words at least he must have, O, cried out
Words that you understand but can't repeat,
You with your legs looped in the dangling reins,
And in your eyes the muzzle-flash reflections.

With the echoing of gunshot in your ears
You kept on going beneath tall poplar trees.
You brought him back as the sun blazed on its pyre
That he might speak his words and we might hear'.

The mare's long proud head was all attention.
My mother clasped her arms around her mane:
'O little dapple-grey, my little mare,
You carried back the one who comes no more,

The one who won't return to me again.
You were good, but cannot speak – not now or then.
Poor thing, you cannot; others do not dare.
But you must tell the one thing I must hear'.

III

'You saw the man, you saw the murderer.
His features linger on behind your stare.
Who is it? Who is he? When I say a name,
With God's help, give a sign if he's to blame'.

The horses now no longer munched their feed.
They slept and dreamt the whiteness of the road.
They didn't stomp the straw with heavy hooves.
They slept and dreamt of turning wheels in grooves.

In that deep silence my mother raised a finger.
She spoke a name . . . A great neigh rang in answer.

The Given Light

MICHAEL COADY

For Peter and Jean Fallon
in appreciation of the vision and the work

The moon hangs there as though that setting
and that space between the trees
had always been intended to receive it–
those two trees I planted years ago
on a day that I remember for the urgent
press of spring informing earth and air,
my daughter playing beside me on the grass,
the ache of limbs after digging and planting–

such a day of seeded consequence . . .
never imagining that on this particular
night of my own future I'll step out
from my house into the dark and there
be ambushed by the moon this moment ripe
between the silhouetted birch and ash,
each tree just as I positioned it that day,
but now grown many times my stature.

Unearthly radiance here reveals to me
all things as one but individual: roots
embracing and embraced by clay, communing
vitally with leaf and branch and dreaming bird,
beneath the moon in its cold orbit framed,
held for a moment in the lucent space
presented there between live plantings.

How perfectly the parts seem to fit
as though designed for this, along with
all else implicit and complicit in the frame,
such as this older self rooted in surprise
here now on moonstruck Earth, breathing my share
of its slim envelope of air while heart
beats out its little time under this light
where others I have known are gone ahead
into a radiance or dark that's absolute.

Before What Will Come After

ALAN GILLIS

Morning, when it comes, might ease the burden,
the way McCandless, when I flipped him the bird in
1986 and he went buck mad altogether,
hunting me down like spleen-clouded weather
through the estate, up the winding hill-lanes
into Killynether, hounding me till we came

to thorn scrub where I got tangled,
snagged and haw-stained in the bramble,
and he viced me in a headlock, towed
me through green wood to an ash by the road–
the bracken in my ear an itching noise–
rubbed moss in my face, then eased off my corduroys.

Morning, when it comes, might well stuff a thumb
in this seep of night-tremors, for what will come
could surely not outweigh the heavy night's
burden of waiting for it. Thinking back on it,
bar the cuts and bruises, it was a geg
the way McCandless hung my breeks, as if with pegs

on a line, on one of the ash branches
hung over the road, then fell on his haunches
and broke his hole laughing. Not that it felt
funny right then, I suppose: nettle welts,
aching arms, tree spleets poking at my thighs,
snatters streaming from nose and eyes.

Morning, when it comes, might snigger
the way Shonagh O'Dowd raised her finger
to McCandless, then near split her smackers
at the sight of me in my undercrackers
dangled over the road, clinging to the tree,
as she drove past in her Ma's red Audi.

I can still feel my raw hands lose grip
on the shaking branch, the wind-trembled tips
of the leaves. I'm still trying to grapple
with the wood, my spinning head unable
to take in the slopes of overripe whin,
deep fields, blue lough, curved roads, all in a spin,

Shonagh O'Dowd a big-bellied teenage bride,
McCandless inside, then outside, then inside,
then scot-free altogether, to do harm
here and there, guns in McGilligan's farm
somewhere, wrapped deep in the turnip fields,
her leaf-green eyes, spinning like a flywheel.

My body aches, my ears abuzz with furze, stunk
by the night, sinking through the ash's trunk:
her lying back in the ferns and harebells,
him teaching me to smoke by the quarry's walls,
laughter like bird noise, through the screeching leaves,
laughter in the night, in the pillow sleeves.

Morning, when it comes, will be welcome
as McCandless when he helped me down from
the ash, grabbed my slacks and called me a tit,
as I hoicked them back up on me by the pockets,
hiding my shaking hands, my ears still huzzed,
as we talked mushrooms, home games, the fuzz,

the apple-flesh of Shonagh O'Dowd's thighs,
and I came alive in the sharpness of his eyes,
darting, ready to target what they could,
making our way back through that green wood
in lines straight as the woodcock's flight.
Morning may come, but this will be a long night.

Shed

JOHN MCAULIFFE

For Peter Fallon

I bought the shed, for a song, off a neighbour
who'd stopped using it after he paved the garden.
He'd inherited it or got it somewhere he couldn't remember,
not that I gave a second thought to its origin.

It was heavier than it looked so he helped take the roof to pieces;
after an hour prying out each crooked nail and tack
we'd levered off the roof's grey-green sandpaper stiffness
and rested it, on the drive, like a book stranded on its back.

The neighbour, looking at his watch, said, 'Let's push',
and the four walls and floor moved – a little.
We got it in front of the garage, sweating, feeling each
ounce of the previous night, seeing too late

it was too big to go through. We counted the nails but couldn't,
they were like stars, more the more we looked; 'Heave it over,'
over the garage and through the back yard, down, he joked
the garden path to its resting place under the magnolia.

No joke: we made a ramp of the ladder and slowly inched
this half-tonne crate of pine up out of the road.
The scraped-flat garage roof pitched
under our careful feet. Two euphoric beers later, after we'd lowered

it into its corner, we agreed on twenty quid. Now, every so often
he still calls in: today he's selling the house and getting out.
He asks about the shed. I say it's fine, so half hidden
by the April gusts of leaf and petal you wouldn't know it's there.

But work makes work: paving it, he volunteers, makes more sense.
I'm on the point of offering him a cup of tea
when, before he can collect himself, he starts to resent
the twenty quid and leaving the shed behind: 'It was', he says,
'almost free'

as we look, out the window, at its unlocked door
behind which, we'll take it, the lawnmower edges grass with rust,
a garden fork's sunk to its handle in the compost
and a can of petrol evaporates into the cooped-up air.

EAMON GRENNAN

Minute

and it's how birds are awake to that single minute in the life of
the world
 that keeps going by that keeps him keeping a peeled eye on
them in their
infinitely minute changes of colour their speedy heartbeats
hammering
 their brisk rivets of breath onto air he's staring through at
them while
Breathe in now says Cezanne as he eyeballs another brilliant
square
 inch of the perpetually unsettling here and now gone world
and hold it

Out and About

and high up in a white pine where crows raise a cracked racket is
the spot
 a redtail's finding it hard to settle on with his electric blood
and brain
unsettled by corvine clamour that harries him till he rises and
goes and
 spreads broad mantle-wings to brood on this where-you-live
abyss
in which morning's quick-eyed kingfisher is well away before you
can
 catch anything beyond the white flash of his torc and gorget

251

as he lifts on a loop of hackle-cries and arrows across the waterfall along

    a network of wet willow branches to land far down the marly bankside

where try as you might to follow his full-throated cry he is lost to you

Leaving

and emplaned and cutting all connections you move at speed through the wet

    greens of Shannon up into the blank stage-curtain of mist to a blind

nothing that grows lighter every second until blue happens and that's it —

    the whole island a vanished thing where yesterday you saw you heard

a flock of airborne mourners (curlews and plovers) winging into their own

    vanishing – the wind a steady slapping at your shoulders and neck and

whipping the sea to a rock-dousing cosmos of foam from which a tern

    two gulls three shrieking oystercatchers twist away so wind takes them

as air now takes you into the blue with the sun behind you the way

    yesterday you caught it catching one jackdaw on a fencepost and lighting it to a brilliant polish and turning it for a minute

    of stillness to an ebony icon of the place you were leaving before the bird (remembering birdness) opened its wings and slowly

    rose and stayed spread-winged for a moment and only then shook off

the place it had been and drifted first then flapped hastily away the way you've had to having bolted doors and windows and left the chaffinches quarrelling among the crumbs and the cat licking last milk off its whiskers

and the bees tirelessly trawling the fuchsia as it shall be forever for nectar

DAVID WHEATLEY

The Blue Pencil

ꝰ /cut

    But how about. . .?

ꝰ /cut

    Yes, but suppose we. . .?

        ꝰ

          /cut!

Mm? Keep?? ꝰ

    /cut!!!

        Keep . . . ???

          Stet.

A Bee-Hive

Sitting under the crook of the eaves
in my black and yellow jumper
I turn ultraviolet blue
in the gaze of a honeybee
I watch enter the roof.

Like a postman's round, the sex
drags on all morning, its fine
filigree residue dispatched
journey by journey to our
asylum of honeycombed dark.

All round me masterpieces
of morbid secretions find their
invisible form, perfection raised
to the level of self-devouring,
a stomach digesting its body.

The bounty of innumerable
foxglove lips parted
slaveringly has brought us to this:
a jelly pleasure sea
I float on, hapless acolyte

of a queen I nourish and dread.
Am I so much as noticed, I wonder,
I and my furious labours? I feel
the jelly throb with her need for me, me
and those billions of others, my kind.

Ancestral Roads

GERARD SMYTH

Her medicine box was full of stuff –
cures and remedies and panaceas,
but all she wanted was something to kill
the pains of ageing and blow the years

all the way back to the time she thought
she heard a banshee's wail,
when she was a girl – on an errand maybe
or returning from a céilí,

blue with the cold on her ancestral roads
that Cromwell's army set ablaze
between Laracor and Dún ná Rí

before she was born, before she knew
the kindness and cruelties of neighbours,
the colours that tell that summer is fading.

Monet's Palette, Musée Marmottan

VONA GROARKE

For Peter Fallon

The wood of the palette is
a notional pond, paint
suggesting petals, leaves,
blossoms, even, and

the play of weather. The rim
of the palette is the edge of
the pond, his thumb arching
as the green bridge does

a clasp of shadow
by a willow tree
in the real world's
first impression.

In the dining room
with yellow walls
someone is saying one thing
and the garden says another.

But the room with no wall
is clear of words and facts
akin to names of paints
so colour makes one kind of sense

and texture makes another.
Between them, thumb and forefinger,
they draw the world on

to a skim of wood
as a pond held
in an outstretched palm
acquires depth and lustre,
rising to the light of day

to the moment when
paint applied to a palette
imagines itself a painting
and coheres.

Nothing goes to waste.
Sunset colour will do as well
for rainfall lacquering a summer pond
or cloud, perhaps, in a second draft,

midnight over rooftops,
an establishing city glow.
Faith. Finesse and carefulness.
Daylight edits its high hour,

learns to begin all over again,
only steadier this time,
if it's lucky: able to trust
the need for change,

the will to make good
on the promise, anew,
that one thought would
always call on the next,

one sensation pin a rhyme
onto another. It happens rightly
when it does, the way colour
and the shape of colour

come lightly through
so the canvas recalls the palette
as a stone in a Japanese garden does
mountains unknown to it.

And the paint remembers
the wooden palette as mist over
an inland field has something
of the ocean in it still,

the difference being one and the same
as oils make to grain and ridge,
everything worked out from there
in russet and violet; hidden and lit;

winter songs and summer songs,
the pond as stillness over time
from which is whittled a slip
of morning to ripen, even so.

Blackberries

CIARAN CARSON

For Peter Fallon, after Francis Ponge

From the typographic thickets which
the poem composes on its route that neither goes
beyond the pith nor to the gist

of things, sprout these particular fruits:
conglomerate globules, each swelled
by a droplet of ink.

❀

Blacks and pinks and khakis mingle in the bunch,
generations in a dynasty of such prickly caviar
you'd be loath to single any out:

slim pickings even for the birds,
given the ratio of pip to pulp, each gulp
from beak to bum becoming skitter.

❀

But the poet, on his daily ramble, rightly takes
a leaf – I mean a seed – from the book of blackberry:
'Look', he tells himself, 'with what patient efforts

this frail flower works its way through a tangle
of rebarbative bramble, till it burgeons
exuberantly into fruit.

For all its problematic, pale beginnings, the blackberry
does what it says when ripe, just like this poem,
the words at last becoming right'.

Index

Endnotes are only cited if they give substantive information on a particular literary work, figure, or movement.